Nelson's Sailors

The beginning of the Battle of Trafalgar

Nelson's Sailors
The Exploits of Officers & Men
of the Royal Navy

Edward Fraser

Nelson's Sailors
The Exploits of Officers & Men of the Royal Navy
by Edward Fraser

First published under the title
The Sailors Who Nelson Led

Leonaur is an imprint of Oakpast Ltd
Copyright in this form © 2012 Oakpast Ltd

ISBN: 978-0-85706-868-2 (hardcover)
ISBN: 978-0-85706-869-9 (softcover)

http://www.leonaur.com

Publisher's Notes

The views expressed in this book are not necessarily those of the publisher.

Contents

Preface	9
"We Are Few, But the Right Sort"—Captain Nelson's "Agamemnons"	11
At the Nile	79
At Copenhagen	144
At Trafalgar	183
The Man Who Hoisted Nelson's Signal at Trafalgar	279
The Avenger of Nelson	284
How England Heard the News of Nelson's Death	290

Dedicated By Permission To
Admiral Lord Charles Beresford,
G.C.B., G.C.V.O.

He leads, we hear our Seaman call.
In the roll of battles won;
For he is England's Admiral,
To the setting of her sun.

George Meredith

Preface

My aim here has been, as far as possible throughout, to describe how Nelson's sailors won their battles, using the words of officers and men who fought on board ship, and were actual eyewitnesses of what took place under fire. In regard to that, I think I may venture to claim for this book a place on its own account, as taking a line of its own that is original and new. Nelson himself and some of his officers and men, for example, relate in their own language the doings before the enemy of the ever-famous *Agamemnon*, which Nelson commanded as captain. The "Band of Brothers" tell of things that occurred within their own knowledge and before their own eyes at the Battle of the Nile. The Copenhagen captains and others in that battle contribute narratives of personal experiences in like manner, and a number of those who fought at Trafalgar, captains and lieutenants, midshipmen, seamen, and marines, answer between them for events on that triumphant final day. In this manner, and by these means, I have attempted to call up a series of living pictures, as it were, which I trust will have an interest of their own, and prove alike instructive and attractive.

E. F.

THE BLIND-EYE SIGNAL OF COPENHAGEN AND NELSON'S ANSWER

THE BULLET WHICH KILLED NELSON

Drawing made immediately after extraction by Sergeant Beatty of the "Victory," in December, 1805.

1

"We Are Few, But the Right Sort"— Captain Nelson's "Agamemnons"

"We are few, but the right sort." French bombshells were bursting in the neighbourhood when Nelson wrote that sentence in a letter home, one April afternoon of the year 1794, from the trenches before Bastia. A reminder of that time, and of Nelson and his Agamemnons in particular, is to be seen in London now, in the form of five faded French flags, which hang in the historic banqueting-hall of the old-time palace of Whitehall, the present home of the Royal United Service Institution. The five are military flags of the period of the French Revolution, and the men who had the lion's share in making them British trophies were those splendid hard fighters who ever had a foremost place in Nelson's affectionate regard as his "Old Agamemnons," the fine fellows who manned the first ship of the line which Nelson commanded.

East Anglians, lads of the old Norse breed, formed a fair proportion of them: 24 *per cent*, or so of the total crew—120 sturdy fellows from Nelson's own county of Norfolk and from Suffolk, got together mainly by Nelson's own exertions, on first learning of his appointment, in sending officers round the coast towns and villages of the two counties to beat up capable hands. A number came from Burnham Thorpe and the other Burnham villages round about Nelson's birthplace, also from Wells, and King's Lynn, and Cromer, and Sheringham, who had volunteered to ship with Captain Nelson, that month of February, 1793, when, one fair and mild winter's morning—a Thursday, by the way—the most famous commissioning pennant that British man-of-war ever flew was hoisted on the stumpy main-mast of a yellow-sided two-decker, then lying a hulk in Ordinary, among the ships in reserve, at moorings in the Medway off Chatham Dockyard.

His Norfolk men were first favourites with Nelson at all times. "I always reckon one of them as good as two others," said he to a brother captain one day during their first cruise. A score and more of tough Yorkshire lads from Hull and Bridlington, and as far north as Robin Hood Bay and Whitby, were among the Old Agamemnons as well; and nearly as many good hands from Lincolnshire, from Grimsby and the Humber estuary—coaster-seamen and fisher-lads mostly, picked up by some of Nelson's friends to whom he had written when he first knew he was to be appointed to a ship, asking them to get together for him as many likely fellows as they could.

The men so obtained came in slowly at first, but fairly steadily. By the end of the first week, 74 men had joined; by the end of February, 143; by the middle of March there were 190 names on the *Agamemnon's* muster-books; by the first week in April, 266; and 396 by the eighteenth of the month, when the *Agamemnon* weighed anchor from the Nore to join the fleet at Portsmouth.

Half a hundred promising fellows—fifty-two exactly, according to the ship's books—came in from Kent and Essex while the *Agamemnon* was fitting out at Chatham. In that manner, and with volunteers from Thames merchantmen, about half Nelson's crew was made up. The other half was mostly sent on board by means of the press-gangs and tenders belonging to the guard-ship at the Nore. Thanks to the ready aid of his former-time captain and devoted friend ever since those never-forgotten West Indian days, old Commodore Locker, just then in command at the Nore, together with an additional draft received when at Spithead, Nelson was able to sail from England in the first week of May with on board a total ship's company of 433 officers and men; just 58 short of the regulation complement of a sixty-four-gun ship.

Content in the main with the stamp of men who were to form his Agamemnons, Nelson from the outset was no less pleased with his officers: "All good in their respective stations and known to me," as he wrote.

Lieutenant Martin Hinton, the first-lieutenant of the *Agamemnon*, a smart and energetic officer, and described as "a first-class seaman," had been Nelson's second-lieutenant in the *Albemarle* ten years before, when he showed something of his quality in the boat attack on Turk's Island in the West Indies. Lieutenant Hinton breakfasted with Nelson at the Mitre at Chatham (the bedroom that Nelson occupied during the two months his ship was in dockyard hands is one of the "sights" of the modernized hotel) on the morning that the *Agamemnon* was commissioned, and came off with him to the ship, and was beside him at the hoisting of the pennant. The second-lieutenant of the *Agamemnon*, Joseph Bullen, an older man, and a remarkably fine officer, had been Nelson's Fourth-Lieutenant in the first ship that Nelson commanded as a post-captain—the *Hinchinbroke*.

In that capacity he had served with Nelson in the pestilential Nicaraguan Expedition during the American War, in which, out of a ship's company of 200 officers and men belonging to the *Hinchinbroke*, only 10 survived—among them Bullen, whose tough constitution brought him through, and Nelson himself, invalided to Jamaica and thence to England just in time to save his life. Captain Polson, of the then 60th Regiment, the military officer in command of the expeditionary force, gives in a private letter, by the way, perhaps the earliest glimpse that we have of what Nelson looked like in his young days: "A light-haired boy came to me in a little frigate," he relates, "of whom I first made little account. In two or three days he displayed himself, and afterwards he directed all the operations."

Lieutenant George Andrews, the *Agamemnon's* third-lieutenant, was the brother of the young lady, an English clergyman's daughter, to whom Nelson proposed, while at St. Omer during his visit to France to learn the language after the American War, and was rejected from motives of prudence—he having nothing beyond his pay, and she nothing at all. The lady seems to have been of an attractive and winning personality. Had the two been able to marry, would the Capuan witchery of Lady Hamilton have had power to prevail over Nelson—in his inmost nature a true-hearted and faithful mate? If only the Viscountess Nelson had been of a less cold and formal type, she might well have saved the situation—of the danger of which she had timely warning during those months of temptation at Naples—and no shadow of any kind would have rested over Nelson's memory. George Andrews after that was taken by Nelson as a midshipman into the *Albemarle*, where two other midshipmen, as principal and second, forced a duel with one of them on the boy, in which young Andrews was seriously wounded, to Nelson's extreme grief.

He put both the two aggressors in irons for their conduct, and turned them out of the ship. "They will," he wrote, "stand a good chance of hanging if the youth should unfortunately die." Of Nelson's previous acquaintance with his fourth and fifth lieutenants, Wenman

Allison and Thomas Edmonds, little is known. The master of the *Agamemnon*, Mr. John Wilson, had been with Nelson as master at the time of his first independent command of all, as master of the *Badger* brig, to which Lieutenant Nelson was promoted commander.

Another old acquaintance, whose services Nelson took special steps to obtain for the *Agamemnon* was a naturalized foreigner—a Portuguese—his former boatswain in the *Boreas*, Mr. Joseph King. Mr. King, at the time, was serving as Commodore Locker's boatswain in the *Sandwich*, the guardship at the Nore. Nelson specially wrote to the Duke of Clarence, who also knew Mr. King well, having had to do with him in the West Indies, and through the duke got the Admiralty to grant leave for the commodore to transfer King to the *Agamemnon*. A very exceptional man was Boatswain King, at all times in high favour with Nelson.

Among the *Agamemnon's* midshipmen was a distant relation of Nelson's, Maurice Suckling, who also had been with him in the *Boreas*, and was before long promoted a lieutenant of the *Agamemnon*, for good service; his stepson, Josiah Nisbet, now going to sea for the first time, and several Norfolk boys, the sons of friends. William Bolton was one (afterwards Sir William and a distinguished captain); William Hoste was another, destined by reason of his many noble qualities to be Nelson's special pet and great favourite, and later in the war to prove himself as brilliant a frigate leader as the British Navy has ever known. Both these were the sons of near neighbours at home. Other Norfolk lads with Nelson in the *Agamemnon* were Thomas Withers, from North Walsham, a Christ's Hospital "mathemat"; and the two sons of a Norfolk clergyman, named Weatherhead, one of whom was killed by Nelson's side at Teneriffe.

On the day that he left the Nore to join Lord Hood's fleet at Spithead, April 18, Nelson wrote this to his father:

> I not only like the ship, but think I am well appointed in officers, and we are manned exceedingly well; therefore have no fear but we shall acquit ourselves well should the French give us a meeting.

"We are all well," he wrote to his wife on getting to Spithead; "indeed, nobody could be ill with my ship's company; they are so fine a set."

Midshipman Hoste tells the story of the *Agamemnon's* first fight in one of his letters home, as also does Nelson himself; the midshipman's account, however, will serve for our purpose. It was after Lord Hood and the main fleet had taken possession of the French fleet and arsenal of Toulon in the autumn of that year. So far, during that opening phase of the Mediterranean campaign, cruising by themselves, with no luck at all coming their way, had been the lot of the Agamemnons. "Here," said Nelson, "there is no prize-money; all we get is honour and salt beef."

They had their first fight while on their way to join a detached squadron, sent off by Hood at Toulon to Tunis, in charge of Commodore Linzee, in order to put pressure on the Bey of Tunis, and, if possible, induce him to close his ports to the French, who were using them as havens of shelter and sources of supply. Young Hoste relates:

> On October 22, running down the Isle of Sardinia, we saw five sail of ships, about two o'clock in the morning, standing to the north-west, when, on seeing us, they tacked and stood to the east. Captain Nelson, suspecting them to be a French convoy, immediately stood after them.
> About four o'clock we got to within gun-shot of the hindermost, and hailed her in French. On her returning no answer, we fired a gun ahead, for her to bring-to and shorten sail. We observed her making signals with sky-rockets to her consorts, who were some distance to windward. After we had repeatedly hailed to no purpose, we fired one of our eighteen-pounders at her, to oblige her to shorten sail; at the same time opened our lower-deck ports, which frightened her, as she immediately made more sail to get away; by that it appears she took us for a frigate. It was daylight before we got up with her again, as she had the start of us.
> About five a.m. we were within half gun-shot, and found her to be a fine forty-gun frigate. She hoisted National colours, and favoured us with a broadside. We returned the compliment, though our situation was rather unfavourable, as our shot did not at all times hit her, while the frigate, owing to her superiority of sailing, kept her position and pointed her guns to advantage, firing in an angular direction, which did more execution. She bravely engaged us in this way for three hours, both sailing at the rate of six knots an hour, till, by our constant firing, it fell calm. The other frigates were coming after us with a fresh breeze, consequently we expected to have some warm work;

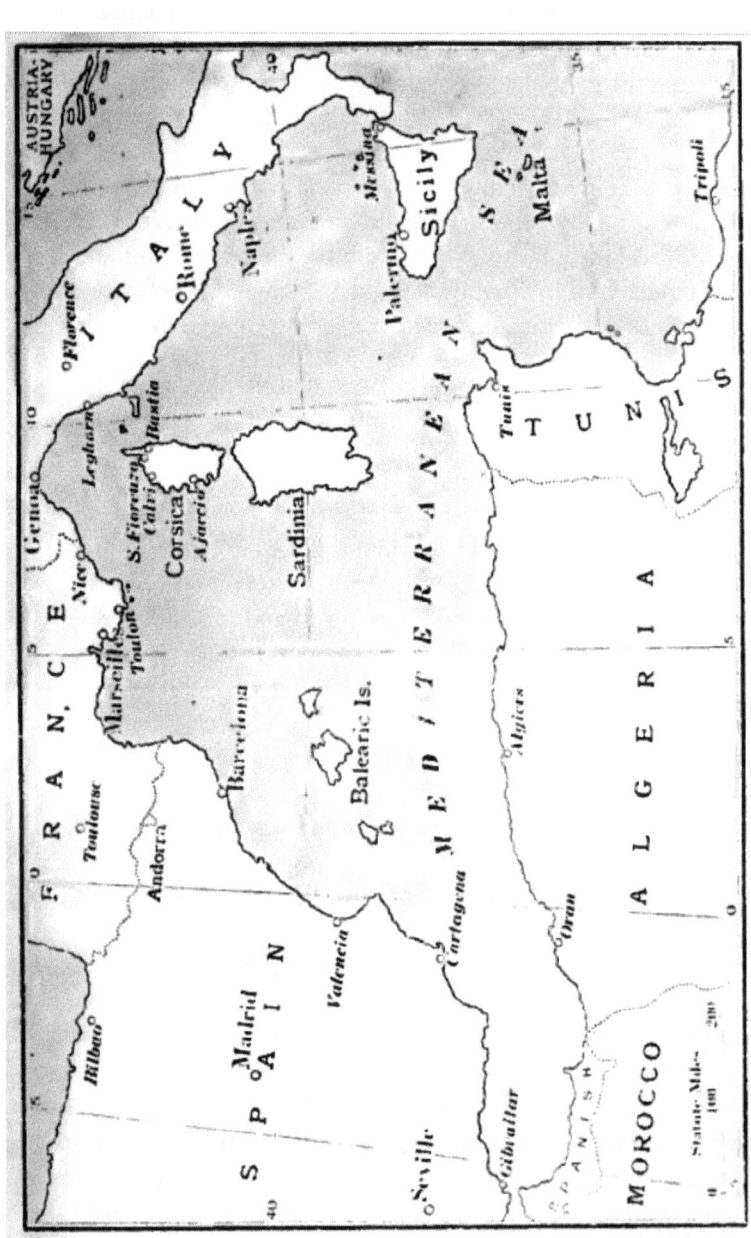

Chart of the Western Mediterranean: where Captain Nelson of the "Agamemnon" served.

therefore were anxious to despatch this gentleman before the others came up.

About eight o'clock, by a change of wind, the frigate got out of range of our guns. Our last broadside did her infinite damage; nor was ours inconsiderable, as our rigging was shot away and our main-top-mast sprung, which prevented us from going after her. We had one man killed and two wounded.

By this time the other ships were within a league of us (the nearest one appeared of the same force as ourselves), and were coming down with all sail set. We expected nothing less than that they would engage us, and were prepared for their reception; but their courage failed them, as we had given their friend so complete a drubbing. She made signals of distress; all of them went to her assistance, and hoisted their boats out. We pursued our journey to Cagliari, being satisfied with offering them battle. Had the breeze continued, we should have preserved our distance from the other frigates, and our antagonist must have either struck or sunk; though, if she had struck, we could not have taken possession of her in sight of a force so superior. The *Agamemnon* had only three hundred and fifty men at quarters, consequently she was no better than a fifty-gun ship.

None of the five frigates, it may be added, ever saw Toulon Harbour again. In the course of the next twelve months they were all taken or destroyed in the Corsican ports to which they fled for refuge.

The Agamemnons were at the time on their way to join Commodore Linzee at Tunis. Nelson went on there after the fight, and found his consorts at their destination. Some of them had, for their part, been balked of a fight in another way.

One of *Berwick's* officers, whose ship had had the adventure, relates the story; which further, incidentally, helps to nail down a small modern lie about a certain naval detail.

During the cruise before we put into Cagliari and joined the commodore, we fell in with six sail of the line, who, not answering the private signal, were taken for a French squadron. It being late in the evening, we made all sail and stood from them; they gave chase the whole of the night, but only two could come up with us, and they took good care not to come alongside, and well for them they did not; all our guns were loaded with round and double-headed shot, and our sixty-eight-pounders (carronades) on the forecastle were crammed with grape and canister, and our fellows (two-thirds of them Irish) were determined to give them a lesson that would never be forgotten. This they seemed to anticipate, as they kept hankering on the quarter until morning, when they hoisted Spanish colours; one of them sent a boat on board of us.

The officer seemed so astonished when he saw our men at quarters, their black silk handkerchiefs tied round their heads, their shirt-sleeves tucked up, the crows and handspikes in their hands, and the boarders all ready with their cutlasses and tomahawks, that he told Sir John Collins they put him in mind of so many devils.

This statement knocks on the head the persistently told story that the black silk neckerchiefs our bluejackets wear nowadays were introduced into the navy "as a mark of mourning for Nelson." Equally a cock-and-bull yarn is the other modern popular tale, to the effect that the three stripes of white tape worn on our sailors' collars were placed there by the Admiralty to commemorate Nelson's three great victories of the Nile, Copenhagen, and Trafalgar.

Nelson's Agamemnons had their forbearance tested while they were at Tunis. A French seventy-four, the *Duquesne* was at anchor in the bay with a convoy of fifty sail of laden merchantmen, sheltering under the protection of Tunisian neutrality. Commodore Linzee made a display of what he would like to do, but he lacked the moral courage to take on himself the responsibility of doing it, of making short work of the French man-of-war and the convoy—suffering the man-of-war, indeed, to make mock of the British squadron. The *Berwick's* officer, says:

> The *Agamemnon* and *Lowestoft* were sent to watch the convoy, and the three seventy-fours anchored, one abreast, another on the bow, and one on the quarter of the *Duquesne*, ready to bring her to action, and there were six sail of the line (Spanish) to assist in this great undertaking. But all this mighty preparation came to nothing. The cargoes were safely landed from the convoy, and the *Duquesne*, after laughing at us for several weeks, and singing the *Marseillaise* hymn morning and evening, with the English jack spread over her round-house, got under way and arrived safe at Toulon, which had been evacuated by the fleet and army; and all this because Tunis was a neutral port. Now

everybody knew that before the squadron sailed, and also that Tunis was nothing less than a nest of thieves; besides, we were out of gunshot of their forts, and might have taken the whole with the greatest ease imaginable."

Nelson said as to that, in a letter written while on his way back to rejoin Hood:

> I am just returned from Tunis, where I have been, under Commodore Linzee, to negotiate for a French convoy from the Levant. You will believe the English seldom get much by negotiation, except the being laughed at, which we have been, and I don't like it. Had we taken, which in my opinion we ought to have done, the men-of-war and the convoy, worth at least £3,000,000, how much better we should have negotiated—given the *bey* £50,000, he would have been glad to have put up with the insult offered to his dignity. . . . Thank God, Lord Hood, whom Linzee sent to for orders how to act, after having negotiated, ordered me from under his command.

The Bey of Tunis, indeed, scored off Nelson at a conference the captain of the *Agamemnon* had with him, when Nelson, expostulating with the *bey* for dealing with the French Government, described the French as, in terms of Lord Hood's instructions, "murderers and assassins, who have recently beheaded their queen in a manner that would disgrace the most barbarous savages."

Retorted the *bey* to Nelson in a dry tone: "Nothing could be more heinous than the murder of their sovereign; and yet, sir, if your historians tell the truth, your own countrymen once did the same!"

How did Nelson answer? We are not told.

The sailors of the squadron, for their part, liked the tame role that their commodore's political timidity compelled them to play at Tunis little better than did their officers. Once, indeed, they very nearly brought about a fight with the French on their own account. How that happened the *Berwick's* officer also tells us:

> We had a rugged-headed, squint-eyed boatswain's mate, who early one morning passed the word for all those who were quartered on the main deck to come below and fight the lower-deck guns. He was instantly obeyed, and the people, of their own accord, were absolutely going to bring the French seventy-four to action, and the above boatswain's mate, as the

head of the party, was in the act of setting the example, when the second-lieutenant snatched the match out of his hand just as he was going to fire. Lord Nelson, who commanded the *Agamemnon*, happened to come on board soon after, and when this was told him he seemed quite pleased. 'For then,' says he, 'we must have taken them.' If he had commanded we certainly should have taken them, and not have stayed wasting our time for months in the bay doing nothing.

The scene now shifts elsewhere—with work of a very different sort going forward, and with Nelson and his Agamemnons in the forefront.

The five French flags now at Whitehall were captured on shore at Bastia and Calvi, in Corsica, where the Agamemnons made their first real mark, and Nelson made his name as the most brilliant captain in the British Fleet.

It was just under a twelvemonth from the day when Nelson first hoisted his flag in the *Agamemnon* in the Medway, that he and his men set foot on shore on the north coast of Corsica. What the Agamemnons did is told best of all in the words of their captain, set down from day to day by Nelson's own hand in his Journal, or written in private letters and in official communications to his commander-in-chief in the Mediterranean, Admiral Lord Hood.

The campaign of the Agamemnons in Corsica opens with this entry by Nelson in his journal, in the first month of 1794:

> *January 21st.*—Landed sixty troops and sixty seamen within a very short distance of Fiorenzo with some opposition. The soldiers (the detachment of the 69th Regiment doing duty in the *Agamemnon* as marines) stood guard, and the seamen destroyed a large store of flour for the garrison, and set the mill on fire. The enemy sent 1,000 men, but our activity had done the job before their arrival, and they only got a few scattering shot at us. I was not on shore, but may say it was amazingly well conducted. My merit, if that is any, was seizing the happy moment. The enemy lost many men; we had not a man hurt.

A very severe storm blew the *Agamemnon* off the coast after that for many days. "The hardest gale almost ever remembered here. The *Agamemnon* did well, but lost every sail in her. . . . The *Victory* was very near lost," records Nelson of the storm. No time was wasted in getting to work again as soon as the weather moderated, and they were before long able to get back to their station off Corsica.

This is how the Agamemnons promptly announced their return to the enemy:

> *February 5th.*—Landed the troops, and anchored two frigates off the port of Centuri. After a very trifling opposition, took possession of the town and harbour. It being low water, was obliged to burn six sail, four of them loaded with wine for the garrison of Fiorenzo. Only one man, belonging to a frigate, was killed. Received the thanks of the inhabitants for sparing the town.

Next day the Agamemnons were sent off to blockade Bastia. They began their work with a sharp affair to prevent supplies being conveyed to the garrison, which Nelson records thus:

> *February 8th.*—At eight o'clock anchored with the *Tartar* off the town of Maginaggio; sent a flag of truce on shore to demand an immediate surrender. Having received a very insolent answer—*viz.*, 'We are Republicans; that is sufficient. Go to St. Fiorenzo, to Bastia, or Calvi. There you will get such an answer as you desire; the troops which I command, and which are ready to give you a meeting, are true French soldiers'—I immediately landed, when this famous commander and his troops ran away, and I had the satisfaction of striking the National flag with my own hand. We found the town full of provisions for Bastia, which we destroyed, and ten sail of vessels. . . . Our time could be but short. In a few hours ten times our number could be got together to oppose us; therefore we could carry nothing away.

Four days after that Nelson's Agamemnons had another skirmish with the enemy. Says Nelson, reporting to the admiral on February 13:

> I had occasion yesterday to send my barge to the gunboat at the farther end of the island. Passing a small cove, where a boat was lying, she was fired on, and one of the men severely wounded. This was too much for me to suffer. I took the boats, troops, and *Fox* cutter, and went to the cove, where a number of people were posted behind rocks (where we could not land), who fired on us. It was a point of honour to take her, and after attempting to dislodge the people, I boarded the boat and brought her out—I am sorry to say with the loss of six men wounded.

She was a French courier-boat from Bastia to Antibes; an officer with a National cockade in his hat was killed, with several people.

A week later one of the outposts of Bastia learned that Nelson had arrived in that neighbourhood.

February 19th.—Went on shore with sixty troops five miles to the north of Bastia; marched to within two and a half miles of Bastia, where we took the village and tower of Moim, the French running away. These successes induced all the Corsicans in this part of Corsica to declare for us, and they are now acting against the French. At night saw over the hills the frigates on fire at Fiorenzo.

The main garrison of Bastia had not long to wait after that for their first experience of how the Agamemnons could fight their guns. That came on February 23. Says Nelson:

Wishing to reconnoitre Bastia, and to southward of it close, I passed a battery of six guns, which began on us, the ships proceeding as named, *Agamemnon, Romulus, Tartar.* At the third shot we got the distance so exact, that we very soon drove the French out of the battery, and totally destroyed it, getting within shot of the town. They began on us with shot and shells, and from the works over the town. I backed our main-topsail and passed slowly along the town. The cannonading lasted one hour and three-quarters. We did them great damage, as we see, and by a Dane, who immediately came out, we hear they lost a number of men. We supposed they fired on us with twenty-seven guns and four mortars, besides those on the outworks; and although each ship was struck in the hull, not a man was killed or wounded.

Nelson, a few days afterwards, heard something of what his guns had done in Bastia, as he relates:

We now know, from three Ragusa ships and one Dane, that our cannonade on Sunday, February 23, threw the town into the greatest consternation; that it almost produced an insurrection; that La Combe St. Michel, the commissioner from the convention, was obliged to hide himself, for had he been found and massacred, to a certainty the town would have been surrendered to me. But St. Michel, having declared that he would blow up the citadel, with himself, was the only thing which prevented a boat coming off to us with offers. A magazine blew up, and the people believe we fired nothing but hot shot. The French shot were all hot.

Two days later, on the 25th, there was another sharp fight with the batteries of Bastia. The enemy had things their own way at first, the *Agamemnon* having drifted within range of their guns while becalmed.

At half-past noon, we being within shot of the town, they fired on us with hot shot and shells: did not return a single gun. Many went over us, and all round us, but not one struck the ship. The bursting of one shell shook the ship very much.

The Agamemnons, however, were soon to get their turn.

In the afternoon, at four o'clock, bore down to the enemy's new work (just to the southward of the town), and began to cannonade it; but it falling calm, could not perceive we did the enemy much harm: hauled off. Being within shot of the town, they fired on us with both shot and shells; returned the fire, and did good service.

The skipper of one of the Ragusan merchantmen gave Nelson a description of that afternoon in Bastia. "Many people were killed and wounded, and the master of the Ragusan, who has been on board me," says Nelson, "had a piece shot out of his leg, and the man next him killed. I lament that several women were killed, and a most beautiful girl of seventeen. Such are the horrors of war!"

Nelson adds this about his Agamemnons:

My ship's company behaved most amazingly well. They begin to look upon themselves as invincible, almost invulnerable; believe they would fight a good battle with any ship of two decks out of France.

It fell to Nelson, immediately after this, to take personal charge of the siege operations against Bastia. General Dundas, the officer in command of the British troops landed by Lord Hood for the conquest of Corsica, refused to co-operate in any attack on Bastia, unless a reinforcement of 2,000 men were provided him from the Gibraltar garrison. "I consider the siege of Bastia with our present means of

Nelson as a Post-Captain

force to be a most visionary and rash attempt, such as no officer would be justified in undertaking." So Dundas protested to the admiral in command.

Lord Hood, happily for the honour of England, thought otherwise. "Nothing," answered Hood to Dundas, "would be more gratifying to my feelings than to have the whole responsibility upon me, and I am now ready and willing to undertake the reduction of Bastia at my own risk with the force and means at present here, being strongly impressed with the necessity of it." Nelson was of the same mind as his chief. Said he, indeed: "A thousand men would to a certainty take Bastia; with five hundred and *Agamemnon* I would attempt it."

The five hundred soldiers were forthcoming by drafting on shore those doing duty temporarily as marines on board the ships of Hood's fleet. Thereupon the attack of the most formidable French stronghold in Corsica was taken in hand forthwith. Nelson being appointed, in association with Colonel Villettes of the 69th, to carry out the operations. "My seamen," he wrote of his Agamemnons at this time, "are now what British seamen ought to be . . . almost invincible. They really mind shot no more than peas."

Meanwhile, before the land bombardment opened, the Agamemnons were undergoing hardships little less trying, practically, than those of the enemy they were facing. "We are really," reports Nelson to the admiral on March 16, "without firing, wine, beef, pork, flour, and almost without water; not a rope, canvas, twine, or nail in the ship. The ship is so light she cannot hold her side to the wind. . . . We are certainly in a bad plight at present; not a man has slept dry for many months."

After landing and examining the fortifications on the land side. Nelson went off to St. Fiorenzo to report to the admiral.

> *March 19th.*—At 8 a.m. got into Fiorenzo. Gave Lord Hood my free opinion that 800 troops, with 400 seamen, would take Bastia, and that not attacking it I could not but consider as a national disgrace.

Nelson wrote to his brother:

> I feel for the honour of my country, and had rather be beat than not make the attack. If we do not try, we never can be successful. I own I have no fears for the final issue; it will be conquest; certain we will deserve it. . . . My reputation depends on the

opinion I have given.

In another letter to the father of one of his midshipmen (young Hoste), Nelson adds this characteristic touch:

> Success, I trust—indeed, have little doubt—will crown our well-meant and zealous endeavours. If not, our country will, I believe, sooner forgive an officer for attacking his enemy than for letting it alone.

In that spirit it was that Nelson led his Agamemnons into action against Bastia. He describes the place as:

> ... a large town, walled in, with a battery to the north and south of it, a citadel in the middle, defended by thirty pieces of cannon and eight mortars, four stone redoubts on the nearest hills, and three other posts above them.

He speaks elsewhere of the garrison as numbering 1,000 Regulars, with 1,500 National Guards and Corsican troops, bringing up the total to between 4,000 and 5,000 men.

The small besieging force of soldier-marines (drafts from the 11th, 25th, 30th, and 69th Regiments), with a handful of artillerymen, two companies of Royal marines, some Corsican volunteer levies, and the seamen landed from the *Agamemnon* and three or four other ships, made up from 1,200 to 1,300 men in all. They were landed close to Bastia on April 4.

This, as Nelson's journal tells the story, was how they began their work:

> From April 4th to the 10th all the seamen were employed in making batteries and roads, and in getting up guns, mortars, platforms, and ammunition; works of great labour for so small a number of men, but which was performed with an activity and zeal seldom exceeded.
>
> On the 9th, about eleven o'clock at night, the enemy opened a very heavy fire upon our camp from their mortars and guns. The alarm was beat, and Captain Nelson fully expected an attack. This firing lasted until daylight, and yet, what was extraordinary, not a single man was hurt. The tents were much damaged; but from the troops being under arms they escaped.
>
> Lord Hood sent in a flag of truce on the 11th at seven o'clock in the morning in one of the *Victory's* boats. The officer on

his landing was grossly abused until the arrival of La Combe St. Michel, the commissioner from the convention, when the mob became quiet. Having offered his letters to St. Michel, our officer was informed by the commissioner that he could not receive Lord Hood's summons. 'I have hot shot,' he exclaimed, 'for your ships, and bayonets for your men. When two-thirds of our troops are killed I will then trust to the generosity of the English!' On the officer's return with this message, Lord Hood hoisted a red flag at the maintop-gallant-masthead of the *Victory*, when our batteries opened on the town, citadel, and redoubt of Camponella, English colours having been hoisted on the rock over my tent, and every man giving three cheers.

In our batteries were two 13 and 10-inch mortars, one 8-inch howitzer, five 24-pounders, two 18-pounders, carronades, three 12-pounders, one 4-pounder field-piece; distant from the redoubt of Camponella 800 yards, from the town battery 1,800 yards, and from the centre of the citadel 2,300 yards.

The garrison on their side met the attack with a fierce resistance. They were successful at the outset in destroying an ex-French frigate, a prize brought from Toulon, which was being used as a floating battery. The Corsican shot cut through her cables, she drifted round, facing her unprotected side, on which no guns were mounted, to the enemy, stuck fast aground close under the French guns and then took fire.

> The enemy returned a heavy fire during the whole day. The *Proselyte* frigate anchored off the Tower of Torga, about 1,200 yards from the town battery. Captain Serocold informed me that she took fire from red-hot shot, and that as he found the impossibility of getting the ship off the shore, he thought it right to set her on fire in several places, and she burnt to the water's edge.

The opening bombardment lasted twenty-four hours. At the end of that time Nelson pushed forward his siege works nearer to the enemy—a week's hard labour for the sailors.

"It is very hard service for my poor seamen, dragging their guns up such heights as are scarcely credible," describes Nelson in a letter. "The loss of the enemy, we know," he goes on, "has been very great. Reports state it as much as five hundred killed and wounded; ours is not more than twenty. The *Agamemnon* has to number five amongst them; they are not the men to keep out of the way."

"We are few, but the right sort," wrote Nelson on April 16.

The second attack, at closer quarters, began as soon as the guns could be advanced to their new positions. These are Nelson's notes of its progress:

> The Torga battery opened on the 21st of April at daylight on the town battery and Camponella, and apparently with good effect. The enemy kept up a most heavy fire on us the whole day, with shells and shot from the citadel, town, Stafforella, Camponella, a square tower, and the two batteries newly raised under Stafforella.
>
> The next day, the 22nd of April, the enemy were hard at work on the heights, strengthening all their posts. . . . A constant firing is kept up night and day. We are informed by several deserters that our batteries have done great damage, and killed and wounded many of the enemy. Our guns have twice totally demolished the town battery, and very much damaged Camponella; but from our not having a sufficient number of men to take advantage of this, the enemy are enabled to repair them, and indeed make them stronger than ever.

Something then came out that told its own tale in regard to the enemy in Bastia. Records Nelson;

> On the night of the 25th of February (? April) La Combe St. Michel quitted the town, and embarked in a *felucca* for Cabrera, and got in, although chased by the lugger; with him also went M. Rochon, the commander-in-chief of the troops, and some of our deserters.

Nelson, two days after that, again pushed in nearer. He now posted a new battery on a ridge, 900 yards from the citadel, and only 700 yards from the town. "The labour of getting up guns to this battery," he wrote in his journal, "was a work of the greatest difficulty, and which never, in my opinion, would have been accomplished by any other than British seamen." It was put in the special charge of Lieutenant Andrews, of the *Agamemnon*, with forty-five seamen to man the guns. Their position was so exposed that the detachment of the 11th Devonshires, with a number of Corsican *chasseurs*, was specially told off for the protection of the post.

Nelson wrote to his wife on the day the new battery opened fire,

May 1:

> I will tell you as a secret, Bastia will be ours between the 20th and 24th of this month if succours do not get in. Our ships are moored across the harbour's mouth, and three boats from each row guard every night.
>
> In speaking of the casualties among his Agamemnons so far. Nelson remarks: "I have had my escapes."

The third and final phase of the attack began in that first week of May, with the making of another and heavier battery, yet closer to the enemy.

> On the 3rd of May we began a battery for one 24-pounder and a 9-inch howitzer, which was finished by the 7th at night.
>
> To prevent the surprise of so advanced a post, the seamen, who as usual manned it, "always slept on the battery with their pikes and cutlasses."
>
> The enemy were again summoned to surrender, but they remained as defiant as before.
>
> Lord Hood, on the 8th, sent in another flag of truce, at eight o'clock, which was refused, the mayor telling the officer 'that they would return bomb for bomb, and shot for shot.'
>
> Opened the 24-pounder and howitzer with the greatest good effect; nor could all the efforts of the enemy knock down our works. A continued and increasing fire was kept up on the outworks.
>
> Four days afterwards, an accidental circumstance disclosed the exact state of things among the enemy, and incited the besiegers to more strenuous efforts still.
>
> In the night of the 12th a large boat came out of Bastia; she was closely pursued by our guard-boats, and taken; in her were three deserters, the captain of *La Fortunée* frigate, twelve seamen, eight Corsicans, and thirty wounded soldiers, going to Capraja. Her dispatches were thrown overboard; but in the morning of the 13th, Lieutenant Suckling, of the *St. Croix* schooner, saw the packet floating on the water, which he took up, and brought to me. Probably in the hurry of throwing them overboard, the weight that had been tied to them had slipped out of the string; they were all letters from Gentili, the commander-

in-chief at Bastia, saying how much they had been annoyed by our fire which had been opened on them near forty days, and that if succours did not arrive by the 29th of the month, they must look upon the town as lost to the Republic.

On the 14th, as Nelson notes, "our batteries kept up an incessant fire."

A vessel trying to run the blockade into Bastia with powder on board was cut off and taken by the guard-boats during the night of the 15th, and two more were intercepted on the following day. A fourth vessel, however, managed to evade the boats and get in, aided by a strong north wind. The enemy were still full of fight, "although our batteries kept up an incessant fire." On the 16th they got up a 13-inch mortar, and for three days "fired night and day more than usual. We had also," adds Nelson, "often five shells in the air all at once, going to Bastia." As Nelson describes:

The end came in sight suddenly. On May 19 a message reached Lord Hood "that if he would condescend to send a boat with a flag, a negotiation would be entered into for the surrender of the town and its dependencies.

In consequence at four o'clock that evening, May 19th, a flag of truce was hoisted on board the *Victory*, and a boat went from her to the town, and one from the town to the *Victory*. The enemy from Camponella met us without arms, and our officers advancing, they shook hands, and were good friends; they said that it was all over, and that Bastia was ours.

The formal surrender took place from within three days from then. Here is Nelson's description of what happened:

On the 22nd of May, our troops at six in the evening marched from their posts, the band playing 'God Save the King'; at seven the French colours were struck upon Camponella, Stafforella, Croix de Capuchin, Monseratto Rock, Fort St. Mary's, and all the other outposts, and the British colours were hoisted under three cheers from every seaman and soldier. The French troops all retired to the town and citadel.

May 23rd.—This morning the British grenadiers took possession of the town-gate and the gate of the citadel: and on the 24th at daylight, the most glorious sight that an Englishman can experience, and which, I believe, none but an Englishman could bring about, was exhibited;—4,500 men laying down their arms to less than 1,000 British soldiers who were serving as marines.

He wrote also:

I am all astonished, when I reflect on what we have achieved. . I was always of opinion, and have ever acted up to it, that one Englishman is equal to three Frenchmen.

Proceeds Nelson in his journal:

Our loss of men in taking Bastia was smaller than could be expected. Seamen killed, and who died of their wounds, 12; wounded, 14: Soldiers killed and who died of their wounds, 7; wounded, 23: Total killed, 19; wounded, 37. . . . By the most accurate account we can get of the enemy's killed and wounded, they had killed 203, wounded 540, most of whom are dead. We consumed 1,058 barrels of powder, and fired 11,923 shot and 7,373 shells.

As a further result of their success, Nelson records this:

Seventy-seven pieces of ordnance, with an incredible quantity of stores are taken. The *Fortunée* was destroyed at Fiorenzo, the *Minerva* taken. *La Flèche* here: therefore three out of four of my antagonists (the frigates the *Agamemnon* had the fight with off Sardinia in the previous October) are gone. The *Melpomene* is at Calvi, and will, I hope, fall into our hands, with *Mignonne*, a small frigate. Thus I shall have the satisfaction of seeing this squadron taken, which could not have happened had they not fallen in with me. They were bound to Nice, but *Melpomene* being so much damaged they were obliged to put into Corsica.

Nelson found time in the midst of all his activities to do one of those kindly acts which so endeared him to all who served under his command: to write a letter, specially expressing his sympathy, to the father of one of his seamen, a Welsh lad from Swansea, named Davis, who had been killed in action. As Nelson put it in his letter:

From the nature of our profession we hold life by a more precarious tenure than many others, but when we fall, we trust it is to benefit our country. So fell your son by a cannon-ball under my immediate command at the Siege of Bastia. I had taken him on shore with me, from his abilities and attention to his duty.

It is more than probable that Nelson wrote similar letters to parents of some of his Agamemnons who fell, but only the Swansea letter appears to have been preserved.

Within a week of the fall of Bastia the Agamemnons were getting ready for another land siege: this time against the second strongest French place of arms in Corsica, Calvi, "which, although very strongly situated, will soon fall," as Nelson wrote to his old friend and captain, Commodore Locker.

Before they could start, however, the Agamemnons were called off elsewhere. News reached the admiral, Lord Hood, that the French had refitted their partially destroyed fleet at Toulon and had put to sea to try and save Corsica.

Nelson wrote in a letter to his wife in the first week in June:

> We are just got to sea after the French fleet, which we hear is out of Toulon.
> Our squadron is after them, steering for Calvi where I fear they will get, in spite of Admiral Hotham's endeavours. The enemy are nine Sail of the Line, Admiral Hotham seven; two will join from St. Fiorenzo and Lord Hood goes with six of us. If we have but the good fortune to catch them at sea, we shall, I am sure, give a good account of them. Lord Hood only got the account of them last night at eleven o'clock, and by seven this morning we were all under sail. The *Agamemnon* had two hundred tons of ordnance to get out, and Lord Hood had given me orders to follow him as fast as possible: I was enabled to sail in half an hour after him, and we are now alongside the *Victory*, I pray God we may meet this fleet.

Nelson, expecting a battle, added this:

> If any accident should happen to me, I am sure my conduct will be such as will entitle you to the Royal favour: not that I have the least idea but I shall return to you, and full of honour; if not, the Lord's will be done. My name shall never be a disgrace to those who may belong to me.

The hoped-for battle, though, did not take place. The French fleet, on sighting Lord Hood, turned back, and ran for shelter under the coast batteries in Golfe Jouan—or Gourjean Bay, as naval men then called it. It proved impracticable to attack them there, and the Agamemnons were forthwith ordered back to Corsica. "His Lordship wished to attack them; a council of flag-officers prevented him," wrote Nelson home, much disappointed.

They were off Calvi on the night of June 17, with, under their charge, a convoy of transports carrying soldiers. Anchors were let go at ten at night at a short distance from Calvi, and between three and four next morning Nelson went on shore with the new commander of the British troops in Corsica, General the Hon. Charles Stewart, a very different stamp of man from the military officers hitherto in authority, as active and determined an officer as Nelson himself.

> *June 18th.*—In the morning I went on shore with General Stewart to examine the coast, with the hopes of finding a better landing-place; but we both agreed that it could only be at the inlet called Porto Agno, though by no means a convenient place for landing guns or stores, as sunken rocks lie twenty feet from the shore, with deep water between them, and with a common sea-breeze such a swell sets in as to prevent boats from landing. This inlet is three and a half miles from the town of Calvi. Examined the enemy's outposts, and found them as follows: Monachesco, about 2,200 yards from the town, on the south-west side of it; the Mozelle Fort, west from the town about 900 yards; and the Fountain Battery on a shoulder of the hill, between Mozelle and San Francesco; which last stands on a rock on the north side of the peninsula, and is washed by the sea. The town is apparently well fortified, but without any ditch.

Nelson continues in his diary:

> *June 19th.*—The troops were disembarked on the morning of the 19th under the direction of Captain E. Cooke, with six field-pieces, which the seamen dragged up the hills. I landed in the afternoon with 250 seamen, and encamped on the beach, getting on shore baggage for the Army.... During the whole of the 20th and 21st it blew so strong, with a heavy sea and rain, and with such thunder and lightning, as precluded all intercourse with the shipping, most of which put to sea. The seamen were employed in making roads for their guns and in getting up three 24-pounders to the Madona, about two miles and a half from the landing-place, ready to act against Monachesco. The road for the first three-quarters of a mile led up a steep

mountain, and the other part was not very easy.

Telling Lord Hood the difficulties of the siege preliminaries, Nelson describes "the mountain we have to drag the guns up" as being:

> .... so long and so steep that the whole of yesterday we were only able to get one gun up, and then we have at least one mile and a half to drag them.... We shall have more than forty pieces of ordnance to drag over these mountains; my numbers are 200, barely sufficient to move a 24-pounder.

Rough weather interfered greatly with the earlier operations. Reported Nelson to Lord Hood two days later, on June 23:

> No more guns have been able to be landed, the swell has been so great; therefore the battery against Monachesco cannot be opened till another battery of four 24-pounders is erected to draw off the enemy's fire. Twelve guns are judged necessary for the first parallel.

Nelson notes in his journal:

> On the 27th of June, we got up two 10-inch howitzers, and were employed all day in carrying the heavy guns and carriages about three-quarters of a mile forward, during the constant rain. Throughout the whole time a gale of wind cut off all intercourse with the ships.

Nelson wrote to Hood:

> The seamen are in want of tents, except the *Agamemnon's* ten; all the others (*Victory's*, who came yesterday, excepted) are lodged in sail-tents, which are wanted for the artillery stores, commissaries, and hospitals..... I had not shoes more than sufficient for the transport's people, and mine are barefooted.

One and all, though, bore up against their difficulties without flinching, and by the first week of July they had begun to beat back the enemy from their outlying posts.

On July 3 Nelson was able to report to the admiral:

> All our guns are within 300 yards of the intended battery against Mozelle; the battery against Monachesco was made last night.... We have nine 26-pounders, two 24-pounders, two 18-pounders, three 12-inch mortars, two 10-inch howitzers, one 8-inch howitzer, six field-pieces, all in their proper places.

On the night of the 7th they had their first serious fight with the garrison of Calvi, and scored the opening success—the destruction and capture of the Monachesco position.

Nelson relates in his journal:

> At half-past nine o'clock, as a feint of an attack was carried on against Monachesco, which succeeded amazingly well. Not a shot was fired at us, for the enemy turned their whole fire during the night towards the post which they imagined was attacked. By excessive labour, and the greatest silence in every department, the battery was completed for six guns within 750 yards of the Mozelle, and without the smallest annoyance, before daylight on the 7th, and the guns brought close to it; but from unavoidable circumstances, the guns could not be mounted on the platforms until two hours afterwards. The enemy did not fire at us until the fifth gun was getting into the battery, probably never thinking of looking so near themselves for a battery, when they opened a heavy fire of grape-shot on us; but the seamen did their duty.
>
> Considering our very exposed situation, our loss was small in numbers: yet amongst those who fell was Captain Walter Serocole of the Navy, who was killed by a grapeshot passing through his head as he cheered the people who were dragging the gun. In him the service lost a gallant officer and a most able seaman. Three soldiers were also killed, one of the *Agamemnon's* seamen, and Mr. Thomas Corney, mate of the *Grand Bay* transport, who was one of the volunteers.
>
> A little before six o'clock we got two English 24-pounders and four 26-pounders mounted on their platforms, in defiance of all opposition. At ten o'clock opened our fire from this battery on the Mozelle and Fountain Battery; not a gun from the town can bear upon us, being so much covered by the Mozelle. We also opened our hill-battery of two 26-pounders and a 12-inch mortar 1,500 yards from the Mozelle, with the Royal Louis Battery of three 36-pounders and two 12-inch mortars in rear, and to the left of our advanced battery; all of which kept up during the whole day a constant fire on the enemy. At three o'clock in the afternoon the enemy set fire to the fascines in Monachesco, and abandoned the spot.

Two days of hot work in the batteries on both sides followed, as

Nelson describes:

> Throughout the whole of the 8th, both sides had kept up constant and heavy fire. They totally destroyed two of our 24-pounders, greatly damaged a 26-pounder, and shook our works very much. One of their shells burst in the centre of our battery, amongst the general, myself, and at least one hundred persons, and blew up our battery magazine, but, wonderful to say, not a man was much hurt. We, on our part, did considerable damage to the Mozelle and Fountain Battery; but when any of their guns were disabled, they had others to supply their place. At night we repaired our works, and got two of the *Agamemnon's* 10-pounders to replace the 24-pounders. During this day we had three seamen killed, and two soldiers wounded.
>
> By ten o'clock on the 9th of July, we had evidently the superiority of fire, and, before night, had dismounted every gun in the Fountain Battery and Mozelle which bore upon us; but the guns in Saint Francesco annoyed us considerably, being so much on our left flank, and at so great a distance, that we could not get our guns to bear on it with any effect. In the night, we mounted the howitzer of 10-inches, 150 yards in the rear, and a little to the left of our battery, both of which fired on the enemy every three minutes during the night to prevent their working. Hallowell and myself each take twenty-four hours at the advanced battery. During this day one soldier was killed, and one soldier and two seamen were wounded.

The attack made more progress still on the next day, and, as before, with surprisingly few casualties.

> On the 10th at daylight, we opened our fire on the Mozelle, and occasionally a gun on the Fountain Battery, and found that the enemy had not done any work in that battery during the night, everything being exactly in the same state. At the Mozelle that place had great numbers of sand-bags, to prevent our shot from striking under the arches of the bomb-proof of the *cavaliere*, which we did yesterday by beating down the *merlins* of the lower work. By seven o'clock in the morning the sand-bags were mostly beat down, and our fire went on without any opposition. By the evening, the Mozelle was much shaken, and I am sure a breach may be made practicable, whenever the general thinks it right to turn his attention to it. To the honour of

General Stewart he is not sparing of himself on any occasion: he every night sleeps with us in the advanced battery.

Nelson adds:

> At ten o'clock on the same day, saw the enemy carry off their field-pieces and howitzer, and totally abandon the Fountain Battery; which was no sooner done than they opened a fire from the bastions of the town over their old battery and the Mozelle; and although they could not see our battery, yet great numbers of their shot struck it. By the evening a very large breach was made in the lower work of the Mozelle; and during the night Lieutenant Moutray joined, with twenty-five seamen: at ten o'clock they got up two 36-pounders and one 26-pounder. We had this day one soldier killed.

The attack was again vigorously pressed on the 12th. It was during this day's bombardment that Nelson received the injury which cost him the sight of his right eye. This is what he says about it in his journal:

> At daylight on the 12th the enemy opened a heavy fire from the town, and San Francesco, which, in an extraordinary manner, seldom missed our battery; and at seven o'clock, I was much bruised in the face and eyes by sand from the works struck by shot.

That was all that Nelson said about the injury at the time. His journal continues:

> The Mozelle was by this time much breached. At night replaced the guns destroyed, and fired a gun and mortar every three minutes. At half past twelve the town was on fire, and burnt for three hours. We had three seamen and two soldiers wounded.

Nelson, of course, had to report his injury to the admiral; but he merely made a brief mention of it at the end of his daily letter to Hood on the progress of the siege, only calling it "a little hurt." He referred to it at the end of his letter in his next report by simply saying:

> My eye is better, and I hope not entirely to lose the sight. I shall be able to attend to my duty this evening if a new battery is to be erected.

Nelson's journal records:

> During the whole of the 13th, a constant fire was kept up from the town, which struck our battery very often, and dismounted another 26-pounder. This is the fifth gun which has been disabled since the 7th, when our battery opened; and having only six guns in it, it is quite wonderful. At night we landed four 18-pounders, with a quantity of shot and shells, in Port Vaccaja, and were employed in getting them up to the rear of our work. By computation to this night we may be supposed to have dragged one 26-pounder, with its ammunition, and every requisite for making a battery, upwards of eighty miles, seventeen of which were up a very steep mountain.

They were by now drawing near into the town of Calvi.

> If it is practicable, the general wishes to get Mozelle without erecting another battery, and then our efforts will all be against the town-wall.

Writing home on the 14th, Nelson said: "A fortnight will, I have no doubt, give us Calvi." In his letter to the admiral on the 15th, he noted this significant detail:

> I made yesterday thirteen scaling-ladders on board *Agamemnon* and landed them this morning.

The ladders were used on the night of the 18th, when Fort Mozelle was stormed by the soldiers, the garrison of the post offering an unexpectedly weak resistance.

Nelson says:

> The Royal Irish were to attack the Fountain Battery and tower, and then to fire their two field-pieces at San Francesco. Colonel Wemyss certainly performed his part in an officer-like manner: then the two field-pieces, under Colonel Moore, began to fire into the breach of the Mozelle, and the new battery opened at the same time. Carpenters went forward and cut down the *pallisadoes*; the Light Infantry went to the right of the Mozelle to cut off the retreat of the enemy; but before our troops could get to the bottom of the breach all fled, except half a dozen, who threw over two 13-inch shells. The grenadiers only found two men in the place, who were killed; and the Light Infantry got a few shots at the fugitives, and took two prisoners, who

say they are told succours will certainly soon be sent them. I could have wished to have had a little part in the storm, if it was only to have placed the ladders and pulled away the *pallisadoes*. However, we did the part allotted for us.

The garrison of the town of Calvi were formally summoned on the next day.

On the 19th of July, General Stuart sent in to ask if they had any terms to propose to him. Their answer was the motto of the town: '*Civitas Calvis semper fidelis.*' We were then only 650 yards from the centre of the citadel.

The final advance of the besiegers began immediately after that, involving yet more severe exertions for Nelson's seamen, who had to drag forward the great guns and mortars for the breaching attack by main force during four days and nights, over rough and steep heights and through deep mud. "Except *Agamemnon's* boats' crews and the Maltese," said Nelson, speaking of his own ship's company, "every man is landed."

Nelson wrote to Hood:

> We will fag ourselves to death before any blame shall lie at our doors; and I trust, my dear lord, it will not be forgotten that twenty-five pieces of heavy ordnance have been dragged to the different batteries and mounted, and all but three at the Royal Louis battery have been fought by seamen, except one artilleryman to point the guns, and, at first, an additional gunner to stop the vent; but, as I did not choose to trust a seaman's arms to any but seamen, he was withdrawn. All the mortars have also been worked by seamen: every man landed is actually half barefooted.

Nelson adds also:

> Our seamen from noon yesterday, until nine o'clock, were employed carrying shot from the beach to the battery, mounting the guns on the seven-gun battery, and mortars on theirs. This morning have been making a road to remove the Royal Louis battery, which is to be done with a party of seamen tonight. The others are now at work carrying shot.
>
> Our seamen dragging and mounting the guns under a heavy fire of grape-shot.

Sixty seamen were with the field-pieces, and as exposed as any of the troops the morning of the storm.

I shall not forget this fact, that every gun is dragged and fought by seamen.

Such are some of the references to the way his men did their duty in Nelson's reports to Lord Hood.

The last act of the drama then opened. Nelson's description of it, as given in a letter to the Duke of Clarence (afterwards William IV.), will suffice:

> On the 28th, in the morning, our batteries, 560 yards from the citadel wall, were ready to open, their force consisting of twenty-one cannon, five mortars, and four howitzers. The general sent in to say that he should not fire on the black flags (hospitals). This note produced a negotiation, by which the enemy wanted to obtain a truce for twenty-five days, when, if no succours arrived, they agreed to surrender the town, frigates, etc. Lord Hood and the general agreed to give them six days; but, while this was going on, four small vessels got in, which gave them hope, I suppose, of more effectual relief; for on the 30th of July they rejected our offer, and our fire opened with all the effect we could expect.
>
> On the 1st of August, at eleven o'clock, when much of the parapet was beat down, and the houses of the citadel were either in ruins or in flames, the enemy hung out a white flag, and requested a suspension of hostilities for a few hours to prepare terms. In twenty-four hours everything was settled:—That on the 10th of August we were to be put in full possession, and the garrison, and such of the inhabitants as chose, were to be transported to Toulon, without being prisoners of war; provided no effectual succours were thrown in by the French.

None were thrown in, and the end came about in due course, as Nelson records in his journal.

> August 10th, at nine o'clock, about 300 troops, a party of seamen, some Royal Louis, and some Corsicans, were drawn up opposite the great gate to receive the garrison of Calvi, who, at ten o'clock, marched out with two pieces of cannon and the Honours of War; amounting in the whole to 300 troops and 247 armed Corsicans. I immediately sent Lieutenant Moutray

and a party of seamen, to take possession of the frigates, gunboats, and merchant vessels in the harbour, and I also ordered six transports to come in; and was employed all the day embarking the garrison, the sick, and such inhabitants as chose to return to France. Out of their armed men, the enemy had three hundred and thirteen sick in their hospital. We have had six killed, six wounded, and two are missing. We expended 11,275 shot and 2,751 shells.

The French flags taken at Bastia and Calvi—five in number—are, as has been said, trophies in London now, displayed in the Royal United Service Museum. Four of the five were surrendered at Bastia. One is the flag of the 1st Battalion of the French 52nd of the Line—a white flag with a blue and white and red tricolour in the upper canton, and having at each of the other corners a tricolour border of blue, white, and red. The second Bastia trophy is the standard of the Corsica Volunteers, of which at that time Napoleon Bonaparte was colonel—a blue, white, and red tricolour flag, with, on one side, a wreath and the inscription, "*Viver Liber o Morir*" (*sic*), and on the other side the legend, "*Republica Francese.*"

The third flag is that of the 2nd Battalion of the Departmental Regiment of the "*Bouches du Rhône,*" a tricolour flag, bordered alternately blue, white, and red, and bearing, inscribed in letters of gold, on one side the name of the corps, and on the other, "*Égalité, Liberté.—2me Bn.*" The fourth flag from Bastia is that of the 1st Battalion of the Departmental Regiment of Aveyron—a tricolour with a white stripe across it, inscribed on one side, "*Subordination, Obéissance a la Loi.*" On the other side are the words, similarly lettered in gold, "*1er Bataillon d'Aveyron—République Française.*"

The flag surrendered at Calvi is the standard of the 26th Regiment of the Line, apparently the former standard of the regiment under the Monarchy altered in a rough-and-ready manner into the Republican form. It is a white Bourbon flag, with the number of the corps lettered in gold, surrounded by a green wreath, and bearing tricolour "*lozenges*" of blue, white, and red, sewn on over the Royal *Fleur-de-Lys* which the flag originally bore.

There is also preserved in London, at the Royal United Services Institution, the sword which Nelson wore while on board the *Agamemnon* and in the trenches before Bastia and Calvi—Nelson's "Fighting Sword" is what it is styled. He wore it also when he boarded the two Spanish first-rates at the Battle of Cape St. Vincent. The sword had been an heirloom in the family of Nelson's mother, and had been given to him by his uncle. Captain Maurice Suckling, on board whose ship Nelson first entered the navy as a boy. It was originally the sword of Nelson's great-uncle, a distinguished naval captain of the time of George I.—Galfridus Walpole of the *Lion*, who had that sword in his hand when his right arm was shot off in battle. Nelson himself had it in his hand when he lost his right arm at Teneriffe. It is a curved broadsword, of a pattern that was out of use in Nelson's day; but he always wore it as a matter of sentiment whenever he was going to be in action.

The fifty-five days of hardship, privation, and exposure on shore at Calvi, at the most unhealthy season of the year, in Corsica, took heavy toll among Nelson's sailors. Within eight days of the surrender no fewer than 130 of the gallant Agamemnons were down with fever—"black fever" the men themselves called it—on the sick-list, or, in Nelson's words, "in their beds." Notes the log of the *Agamemnon* on September 9, at Leghorn, three weeks and three days from leaving Calvi;

> The physician of the fleet came on board and surveyed the ship's company; found them unfit to serve, being in a very weak state.

Within a month of leaving Calvi no fewer than fifty of the men had died, and there were still seventy sick and unable to do duty at the end of October.

In spite of everything, the spirit of the Agamemnons as a crew remained unshaken and invincible. During October two of their boats did a smart little piece of cutting-out work, carrying off a French brig from under the guns of a fort near Cap Martin. "We are few, but the right sort," Nelson had said of them while before Bastia, as we have seen, and he knew his Agamemnons. In less than three months after they left Calvi he wrote this:

> My ship and ship's company, though not in half the strength as when I left Spithead—several of my guns that were landed at Corsica having been destroyed—yet, I am sure, feel themselves equal to go alongside any seventy-four out of France.

The Agamemnons did certainly not waste their time as convalescents while pulling themselves together at sea. They kept Guy Fawkes'

Day, November 5, 1794, inside Toulon Harbour, in carrying out, by themselves, a daring reconnaissance of the French fleet, all lying there at the time. So far up the harbour, indeed, did Nelson and his men venture, that, as Nelson put it, "a most diabolical report" got about to the effect that the *Agamemnon* had been cut off within the batteries of the land-locked entrance and captured. The bare idea of such a thing made Nelson furious. "Rest assured," said he, writing home at the first chance to reassure his wife in case the tale had got into the London papers—"rest assured that the *Agamemnon* is not to be taken easily; no two-decked ship in the world, we flatter ourselves, is able to do it."

How dangerous the adventure was may be judged from the experiences undergone a short time earlier, when only half the French fleet were in port, on board another of our men-of-war; which, moreover, did not push in nearly as far as the *Agamemnon* did. Our Tunis Bey acquaintance, Midshipman Gardner of the *Berwick*, whose ship was the man-of-war concerned, gives this vivid account of that affair:

> Having stood in with a fine breeze the enemy never fired a shot until we hove in stays. At this time it fell on a sudden a dead calm, and we were within gunshot. They then began to blaze away from all their forts, the red-hot shot flying in every direction. I was looking out of the gun-room port, when a shot came right under our counter, which made the water hiss and nearly struck the rudder. At this time things looked queer. All the boats were hoisted out and began to tow; but still we drifted in, the shot flying full half a mile beyond us, when, luckily, a breeze came off the land and saved the *Berwick* from being sunk or blown up.

Nelson calmly carried out his reconnaissance in spite of the harbour batteries and fifteen French ships of the line with two frigates, several of them lying ready for sea in the outer roadstead with sails bent. Returning as he came, he proceeded to San Fiorenzo Bay, where the British fleet was then at anchor, bringing an exact report of the state of the enemy's preparations for putting out.

Lord Hood had gone home to England some three weeks before this, on short leave, to recruit his health at Bath—he was a man in his seventieth year. The second in command, Admiral Hotham, was in charge during Hood's absence—an officer unfortunately of a very different stamp, trustworthy and capable as a second in command, but nervous of responsibility, unenterprising and inefficient as a leader. It was during Hotham's tenure of the command, as it befell also that the only opportunities occurred for bringing the French Toulon fleet to action in the open, at sea. Nelson's Agamemnons, though, did their best, and managed, in spite of everything, to win distinction for themselves.

The Agamemnons had the principal part in capturing two French men-of-war, the *Ça Ira*, an eighty-gun ship, and *Le Censeur*, a seventy-four—the *Agamemnon* was a sixty-four-gun ship—in Hotham's first action with the Toulon fleet ("our brush with the French fleet—a battle it cannot be called," was Nelson's description of the affair), off Genoa in the following March. Says Nelson in one of his letters:

> Fortune favoured us in a most extraordinary manner by giving me an opportunity, which seldom offers, of being the only line-of-battle ship who got singly into action, when I had the honour of engaging the *Ça Ira*, absolutely large enough to take *Agamemnon* in her hold. I never saw such a ship before.

It was on the first of the two days over which the encounter lasted that the Agamemnons had the fight with the *Ça Ira*. The French eighty-gun ship had lost her fore- and top-masts in a collision with one of her own consorts, and, while in tow of a frigate, had dropped to leeward within reach of the British.

First, one of Hotham's frigates—the *Inconstant* (Captain Fremantle)—pluckily ran close in and opened fire on the *Ça Ira*; but the huge French man-of-war was of too heavy metal for the *Inconstant*, and the frigate had to draw off just as the *Agamemnon* was coming up. Pressing ahead. Nelson stood in to the frigate's assistance, and then proceeded forthwith to fight his own battle with the enemy. A big three-decker, the *Sans Culottes*—destined to be met by Nelson again under another name, as *L'Orient*, the ill-fated French flagship at the Nile—together with a seventy-four, the *Jean Bart*, stood towards the *Ça Ira*, as if to support her against Nelson's attack; but, all the same, the *Agamemnon* unhesitatingly advanced. "We could have fetched the *Sans Culottes*," said Nelson, "by passing the *Ça Ira* to windward; but, on looking round, I saw no ship of the line within several miles to support me."

Nelson himself again, in his journal, best tells the story of how he delivered his attack:

> As we drew up with the enemy, so true did she fire her stern guns that not a shot missed some part of the ship, and latterly

the masts were struck every shot, which obliged me to open our fire a few minutes sooner than I intended; for it was my intention to have touched his stern before a shot was fired. But seeing plainly, from the situation of the two fleets, the impossibility of being supported, and, in case any accident happened to our masts, the certainty of being cut up, I resolved to fire so soon as I thought we had a certainty of hitting.

At a quarter before eleven, a.m., being within one hundred yards of the *Ça Ira's* stern, I ordered the helm to be put a-starboard and the driver and after-sails to be braced up and shivered, and as the ship fell off, gave her our whole broadside, each gun double-shotted. Scarcely a shot appeared to miss. The instant all were fired, braced up our after-yards, put the helm a-port, and stood after her again.

This manoeuvre we practised till one p.m., never allowing the *Ça Ira* to get a gun from either side to fire on us. They attempted some of their after-guns, but all went far ahead of us. At this time the *Ça Ira* was a perfect wreck, her sails hanging in tatters, mizzen-topmast, mizzen-top-sail, and cross-jack yards shot away. At one p.m. the frigate hove in stays, and got the *Ça Ira* round. As the frigate first, and then the *Ça Ira*, got their guns to bear, each opened her fire, and we passed within half pistol-shot. As soon as our after-guns ceased to bear, the ship was hove in stays, keeping, as she came round, a constant fire, and the ship was worked with as much exactness as if she had been turning into Spithead.

On getting round, I saw the *Sans Culottes*, who had before wore with many of the enemy's ships, under our lee bow, and standing to pass to leeward of us under top-gallant sails. At half-past one p.m., the admiral made the signal for the van ships to join him. I instantly bore away, and prepared to set all our sails; but the enemy, having saved their ship, hauled close to the wind and opened their fire, but so distant as to do us no harm, not a shot, I believe, hitting. Our sails and rigging were very much cut, and many shot in our hull and between wind and water; but, wonderful, only seven men were wounded.

Nelson remarks also, in a note:

> I observed the guns of the *Ça Ira* to be much elevated, doubtless laid for our rigging and distant shots; and when she opened

her fire in passing, the elevation not being altered, almost every shot passed over us, very few striking our hull. The captain of the *Ça Ira* told Admiral Goodall and myself that we had killed and wounded no men, and so cut his rigging to pieces that it was impossible for him to get up other top-masts. *Agamemnon* had only 344 at quarters, myself included.

He said this in a letter to his brother:

> I cannot account for what I saw; whole broadsides within half pistol-shot missing my little ship, while ours was in the fullest effect.... Our sails were ribands, and all our ropes were ends. Had our good Admiral followed the blow, we should probably have done more, but the risk was thought too great.

When the fighting ended on the second day, Lieutenant George Andrews, now the *Agamemnon's* first-lieutenant (Lieutenants Martin Hinton and Joseph Bullen had been promoted commanders for good service in the Corsican campaign, and appointed to ships of their own), went on board the two surrendered ships, and hoisted British colours on each; then carrying off the two French captains in the *Agamemnon's* boat to the nearest British flagship, as a point of etiquette, for the formal ceremony of giving up their swords to the senior officer in command of the squadron to which the *Agamemnon* belonged.

Midshipman Hoste, carrying on the story of the two days, says this:

> We were at quarters all that night, hoping to have another brush with them in the morning.

Next day, however, the unenterprising British admiral in command once more let his chance of forcing on a battle slip. Nelson outlines in his journal what happened on the occasion when again the Agamemnons were in the middle of what fighting there was:

> At eight a.m. the enemy's fleet began to pass our line to windward, and the *Ça Ira* and *Le Censeur* were on our lee side; therefore the *Illustrious, Courageux, Princess Royal*, and *Agamemnon*, were obliged to fight on both sides of the ship. The enemy's fleet kept the southerly wind, which enabled them to keep their distance, which was very great. From eight to ten, engaging on both sides. About three-quarters past eight the *Illustrious* lost her main and mizzen masts. At a quarter past nine the *Cour-*

ageux lost her main and mizzen masts. At twenty-five minutes past nine the *Ça Ira* lost all her masts, and fired very little. At ten, *Le Censeur* lost her main-mast. At five minutes past ten they both struck. Sent Lieutenant George Andrews to board them, who hoisted English colours, and carried the captains, by order of Admiral Hotham, on board of the *Princess Royal* to Admiral Goodall. By computation the *Ça Ira* is supposed to have had about 350 killed and wounded on both days, and *Le Censeur* about 250 killed and wounded.

Beyond some long-range firing after that, until about half-past one, when the enemy sailed off westward, there was no further fighting.

What Nelson thought of his admiral's behaviour on that day is on record. He wrote to his wife:

> Sure I am, had I commanded our fleet on the 14th, that either the whole French fleet would have graced my triumph, or I should have been in a confounded scrape. I went on board Admiral Hotham as soon as our firing grew slack in the van, and the *Ça Ira* and *Censeur* had struck, to propose to him leaving our two crippled ships, the two prizes, and four frigates, to themselves, and to pursue the enemy; but he, much cooler than myself, said, 'We must be contented; we have done very well.' Now, had we taken ten sail, and had allowed the eleventh to escape, when it had been possible to have got at her, I could never have called it well done. Goodall backed me. I got him to write to the admiral, but it would not do; we should have had such a day as I believe the annals of England never produced.

Timidity on the leader's part only it was that spoiled the opportunity. The captains and men were ready to do their part. Added Nelson in his letter:

> I verily think if the admiral can get hold of them once more, and he does but get us close enough, that we shall have the whole fleet. Nothing can stop the courage of English seamen.

The French, on their side, had come out for the recapture of Corsica, believing the British fleet to be near Minorca, in which neighbourhood it had last been heard of. A large force of troops was on board, together with the Republican commissioner of Corsica, and a crowd of civil officials, including the mayor of Bastia. Napoleon himself, indeed (then "General Bonaparte"), was to have been in the fleet as leader of the expedition. But his appointment had been cancelled by an order from Paris, and he had been recalled, after having been a month at Toulon waiting to sail.

The brilliant display that Nelson and his Agamemnons made in the action would appear, it is a somewhat curious fact, to have been the subject of eulogy among the enemy. Nelson wrote to his wife:

> I may venture to tell you, but as a secret, that I have a mistress given to me, no less a personage than the Goddess Bellona, so say the French verses made on me, and in them I am so covered with laurels that you would hardly find my sallow face. At one period I am 'the dear Nelson,' 'the amiable Nelson,' 'the fiery Nelson.' However nonsensical these expressions are, they are better than censure, and we are all subject and open to flattery.

Nelson said this to his brother, in a letter summarizing what he and his men had gone through and done up to that time:

> Certain it is *Agamemnon* has given experience to her crew; five times my ship has been engaged, three at sea, two against Bastia, three actions in boats, and two sieges, ought to make us stand fire; but we are too far from home to be noticed.

Speaking of himself, in another letter, he says:

> I have to boast, what no officer can this war, or any other that I know of, being, in fifteen months, 110 days in action at sea and on shore.

He wrote that just a fortnight before starting on his first cruise at the head of a frigate squadron for special service off the Genoese Riviera, to assist the Austrian army in its efforts to beat back Kellerman's "Army of Italy" in its advance along the coast. So far the Austrians had kept the enemy at bay, but the reinforced French troops were beginning to press them back, and co-operation had been asked for from the British Mediterranean Fleet.

Nelson set off from Hotham's fleet on July 4, with the *Agamemnon*; two frigates, the *Meleager* and the *Ariadne*; a sloop, the *Mozelle*; and the cutter *Mutine*. Three days later the little squadron came hastening back to the fleet at its anchorage in St. Fiorenzo Bay, with the French Toulon Fleet in hot pursuit.

They had stumbled on the French fleet at sea in full force off Cape Delle Melle, and had to run for it, in great danger of being captured, until off St. Fiorenzo, where, at the sight of Hotham's ships lying in the bay, the French turned back and drew off. With his usual remissness, Admiral Hotham was unprepared to follow them at once. He was unaware of their having put to sea from Toulon, having taken no steps to keep the port under efficient observation, and his fleet was lying out of order, the ships being occupied in refitting and taking in stores.

It had been an adventurous race back for the Agamemnons and their fellows. Indeed, the escape of Nelson's squadron had looked at one moment like a very near thing, and one of his ships was all but cut off. Nelson, however, had no intention of leaving any of them in the lurch. One of the officers of the sloop *Mozelle*, which vessel had the narrowest escape of all, tells this about the chase and their getting away:

> The enemy were at first discovered, under Spanish colours, late on the evening of the 6th of July, and at daylight next morning it was found that they had gained considerably on the British detachment, which consisted of the *Agamemnon* (sixty-four), *Meleager* and *Ariadne* frigates. *La Mozelle*, and *Mutine* cutter. *La Mozelle*, then commanded by Captain Charles Brisbane, had lost her main-gallant-topmast in the night, which obliged the heroic Nelson to shorten sail repeatedly to support her; and the enemy were so intimidated by his daring behaviour that they did not open their fire till the British were close in with Cape Corse, which the *Agamemnon* very fortunately weathered by about half a mile.

> Her captain's daring and clever seamanship got the *Mozelle* off when, as it seemed, cornered hopelessly.

> The *Meleager*, *Ariadne*, and *Mutine* were well to windward; *La Mozelle*, however, the dullest sailer, being to leeward of it, had no alternative but to surrender, run on shore, or attempt the almost impracticable passage between the rocks near the Cape and a little islet at a short distance from it. Captain Brisbane, with his usual intrepidity, having decided upon trying the passage, *La Mozelle* bore up, and the Frenchmen, knowing it was impossible to follow, opened their fire in succession to sink her. All the spare sails had previously been spread between decks, with a quantity of tar and everything else inflammable; Captain Brisbane being determined to destroy his sloop rather than she should be captured.

They just scraped through and managed to rejoin their consorts, practically unharmed by the French fire.

But almost to the last the situation was one of peril for Nelson. Describes Midshipman Hoste, continuing the story, in a letter from the *Agamemnon:*

> Just as we got near to St. Fiorenzo it fell almost calm, and what little wind there was, blew right out of the bay, the Frenchmen coming up fast and nearly within gunshot. You may guess our situation was not very comfortable; the first time I thought I should have the pleasure of seeing a French prison. However, we cleared ship for action and got our stern chases out, determined to fight to the last extremity. About twelve, a breeze luckily springing up, enabled us to reach the bay. The French, seeing this, tacked and stood to the westward, and we saw no more of them.

Nelson made for St. Fiorenzo, firing alarm guns to call up help from Admiral Hotham; but no help came, the whole fleet, as has been said, having been caught unprepared to put to sea. Nelson himself describes, writing on July 8:

> The chase lasted twenty-four hours, and, owing to the fickleness of the winds in those seas, at times was hard pressed; but they, being neither seamen nor officers, gave us many advantages. Our fleet had the mortification to see me seven hours almost in their possession; the shore was our great friend.

The French fleet disappeared, and were not followed until next day. It took Admiral Hotham nearly a week after that to find them; and then came Hotham's second affair, which Nelson called "our miserable action of the 13th."

The Agamemnons again did all that it was within their power to attempt.

> I had every expectation of getting *Agamemnon* close alongside an eighty-gun ship, with a flag or broad pennant, but the west wind first died away, then came east, which gave them the wind, and enabled them to reach their own coast, from which they were not more than eight or nine miles distant. Rowley (Captain Bartholomew Samuel Rowley of the *Cumberland,* a seventy-four) and myself were just getting into close action, when the admiral made our signals to call us off. The scram-

bling distant fire was a farce.

Was Nelson's contemptuous criticism of the way the fighting was dragged through. Nelson also wrote:

To say how much we wanted Lord Hood on the 13th of July is to ask, 'Will you have all the French fleet or no battle?'

A twelvemonth, on and off, of hard work on flying squadron service followed for the Agamemnons off the Genoese Riviera, where, in two campaigns, Nelson did his utmost to assist the Austrians against the French invading columns. It was a service which involved at times the cannonading of coast forts and batteries, and cutting-out expeditions by the boats to bring off or destroy French ammunition and store vessels. That was the most that in the circumstances Nelson could effect. In his first coast campaign, in the autumn of 1795, the proposed co-operation with the Austrian troops on shore, in the shape originally intended, fell through in spite of Nelson's endeavours.

On arriving at Vado Bay, some eighteen or twenty miles along the coast to the west of Genoa, and the headquarters of the Austrian army, in the third week of July, Nelson took the Austrian generals in the *Agamemnon's* cutter to reconnoitre the French outposts towards Nice; but the plan of campaign put forward by General de Vins, the Austrian commander, did not accord with Admiral Hotham's views. De Vins proposed to land 10,000 men as a detached corps in rear of the French, beyond Nice, the expedition to be covered by Hotham's main fleet. The project was rejected by the British admiral as a "wild scheme," although Nelson supported it, and went off to urge it personally on Hotham. Asked next to meet the Austrian General at Vado and discuss a plan, Admiral Hotham declined to do so.

Although passing with his fleet close off Vado Bay one day, to take in provisions at Leghorn, Hotham refused to bring-to, even for a few hours. "The general," wrote Nelson, commenting on that, "was much hurt." In the result, De Vins and his troops did nothing. The Austrians stood fast where they were, with their advanced posts pushed out beyond Loano, until, in November, the French army, heavily reinforced by masses of fresh troops brought up from the Spanish frontier, suddenly attacked them, and, breaking through their defences at all points, drove them with the loss of all their artillery in headlong rout beyond the Apennines.

To the last, until after the final catastrophe to the Austrians, Nelson and his squadron did all they could to prevent war-supplies reaching the French posts along the coast to the west of Vado—a very difficult task, as most of the vessels employed in the traffic sailed under neutral colours which Nelson had stringent orders to respect. The French vessels sailed mostly at night, keeping at anchor by day, close under the shelter of the coast batteries. Whatever was possible, however, was attempted.

On August 12 the boats of the *Agamemnon* and her frigate consorts cut out seven French vessels in Alassio Bay; but in the end, after a sharp fight, being attacked by the forts and French gunboats, they had to abandon six of their prizes. On August 26, again at Alassio, the boats, backed up by the cannon of the squadron, cut out and carried off a French fourteen-gun *corvette*, an eight-gun vessel, two French galleys, and five transports, laden with shells, powder and provisions, besides destroying three other transports.

Nelson manned the two captured galleys with fifty-four men, mostly Agamemnons, and sent them off three days later, in charge of two of the *Agamemnon's* lieutenants—First-Lieutenant Andrews and a newly-joined officer, Peter Spicer—to cut out a French storeship at Oneglia, of which Nelson had had word. On the way, at night, they fell in with three large ships, which, on their refusal to declare their nationality when challenged, were attacked. One of the three was boarded and taken. The three ships closed in side by side and lashed themselves together, making it impossible for the Agamemnons, being too few in number, to board the second and third, which were crammed with men. Said Nelson:

> The attack on these two was renewed with the greatest spirit, but the number of men in the vessels was too great, united with the height of the vessels, for our force; and my gallant officers and men, after a long contest, were obliged to retreat.
> The spirited and officer-like conduct of Lieutenants Andrews and Spicer, I cannot sufficiently applaud; and every praise is due to each individual for their exceeding bravery and good conduct.

Seventeen men were wounded, practically a third of the attacking party, and some of them mortally, was the cost of the sharp affair to the British.

A week after that the Agamemnons exchanged shot with Oneglia Fort and a French gunboat, and on the following day, off San Remo, their boats cut out and carried off two more French vessels.

So things took their course with the Flying Squadron during September and October, Nelson and his captains never missing a chance of getting in a blow at the enemy. One of the *Agamemnon's* men, a boatswain's mate, John Wilkinson by name, used to say, when a Greenwich Hospital pensioner, speaking of Nelson:

> We could always tell of a morning, when he came on deck, whether we should have anything to do. When he came up with his *iron-bound hat* on and his *roast-beef coat*, we knew he was up to something, and it used to be a sort of warning to us to get ready!

The admiral, meanwhile, did not make Nelson's task easier. Once again, in October, Nelson tried to get Hotham to help forward the Austrian general's scheme of raiding the French posts in rear with a division of 10,000 men. Nelson asked to have two seventy-fours placed temporarily under his orders, to act as a covering force, and permission to employ a number of transports then lying idle in Leghorn Harbour. Hotham, however, anxious about another possible sortie by the Toulon Fleet, once more refused flatly. More than that, indeed, he withdrew two of Nelson's frigates, thus weakening Nelson's little squadron materially.

The Agamemnons, though, still managed to harass the French along the coast. On November 3 they stopped one large convoy and chased it into Alassio. Additional batteries and heavily-gunned works had, however, been recently erected nearby, which prevented Nelson from bringing away more than one transport, boarded and taken by the *Agamemnon's* cutter. "Not less than three sail of the line could attempt to take or destroy them," said Nelson, speaking of the situation of the convoy as it lay under the batteries.

After that came a hasty recall of the *Agamemnon* to Genoa, to block in a large French frigate, the *Brune*, which had put in there, taking advantage of Genoese neutrality. The French man-of-war's presence threatened to cause a dangerous outbreak among the numerous partisans of France in the city. On Nelson's arrival the *Brune* landed her powder and disarmed, but the *Agamemnon* had to remain at Genoa and keep guard over her.

All through Nelson had loyally co-operated with the Austrians on shore. He had kept one of his frigates opposite the Austrian advanced posts "until," in Nelson's words:

> .... .the season was such as to render that measure no longer

possible; for it was persevered in until two of His Majesty's ships were nearly lost. When this defence was taken away, in the first week in November, I stationed the *Flora* and *Speedy* brig off Cape Noli, within six miles of Pietra (General de Vin's headquarter camp).

The *Agamemnon* at that time lay at single anchor in Vado Bay, with two Neapolitan galleys:

> . ... ready to proceed by the first gun being fired by the enemy; and so anxious was I to render every assistance to our Allies, that I requested General de Vins to establish a signal by guns from Pietra to Vado, that I might be with him, if the wind was fair, long before any messenger could have reached Vado. On the 9th of November, General de Vins sent me word that he believed the French thought his position too strong to be attacked, and that, as he was coming from Savona in a few days, we would talk over the subject of signals.

The opportunity, however, never came. Nelson received his urgent summons to Genoa. Within a week, De Vins and his army were badly beaten fugitives.

Before Nelson could get away from Genoa, the Battle of Loano had been fought, and the Austrian army driven back and routed all along the line, leaving thousands of prisoners and eighty guns in the hands of the French. Six of Napoleon's future marshals led General Schérer's victorious columns: Masséna, chief of the staff; Augereau and Lannes on one flank; Marmont, Suchet, and Victor on the other.

Yet the Agamemnons were able to do something to assist the cause.

Anchoring his ship broadside on across the entrance to the inner harbour of Genoa, with guns run out. Nelson overawed and cowed the French adherents in the city, enabling the only pass by which the left wing of the routed Austrian army could escape to be kept open. The *Brune*, the French frigate in Genoa Harbour, getting her powder back on board surreptitiously, was to have sailed, together with a number of small craft, carrying an armed expedition secretly organized in Genoa, to seize the pass on the first news of fighting near Loano being received. According to a report in the city also, four French ships of the line had escaped from Toulon, taking advantage of the British fleet being, as usual, in St. Fiorenzo Bay, and were coming round to attack the *Agamemnon* and help the *Brune* out.

Nelson stood fast, and his barring of the harbour enabled nearly half the Austrian army to escape. "I have the consolation," he wrote, reporting his doings to the new British commander-in-chief, Sir John Jervis, who was expected to arrive at St. Fiorenzo at the end of the month, "that to the *Agamemnon's* staying at Genoa so many thousands owe their safety, owing to the pass of the Bochetta being kept open; and amongst others General de Vins himself."

Three of the *Agamemnon's* officers—Lieutenant James Noble, the fifth-lieutenant, who had not long joined the ship, with Midshipman Thomas Withers and another midshipman—fell into the hands of the enemy through the disaster to the Austrian army at Loano. "I had a lieutenant, two midshipmen, and sixteen men taken at Vado," wrote Nelson home. They had been sent off in one of the ship's boats, with orders to land Lieutenant Noble in Vado Bay, whence the Lieutenant was to take an important dispatch from Nelson to the acting Austrian commander-in-chief at Savona, Count von Wallis, who had relieved General de Vins, recently incapacitated through illness. The two midshipmen and the boat's crew were ambushed on proceeding to Vado town to wait off there for the lieutenant's return and to bring back the *Agamemnon's* purser, who had been left behind there by Nelson on business.

The purser escaped, and making his way along the coast, rejoined Nelson at Genoa. "The purser of the ship, who was there," wrote Nelson, "ran with the Austrians eighteen miles without stopping; the men without any arms whatever, the officers without soldiers." Lieutenant Noble, who tried to get through with his dispatch, was intercepted and taken, outside Vado, by some French hussars. The British prisoners were marched off forthwith to Perpignan. They were released, in a special exchange of prisoners, after three months' captivity, as a return, it was said, for Nelson's courtesy in returning some private property belonging to General Schérer, the French commander-in-chief at Loano, which one of the *Agamemnon's* boats had taken on board a prize. Nelson, writing some time before they were released, makes this remark in one of his letters:

> My officers and people who are prisoners in France are exceedingly well treated, particularly so by the naval officers; and, as they say, because they belong to the *Agamemnon*, whose character is well known throughout the Republic.

It was some time during that autumn, apparently, that this very curious incident took place. Here is the story, as related in a document in the handwriting of the second Countess Nelson, now preserved among the Nelson archives at Trafalgar House, near Salisbury. It speaks of generous aid having been rendered by Nelson, while in the *Agamemnon*, to Cardinal York, brother of the Young Pretender, and the last prince of the Royal House of Stuart, during a time of very great distress. The manuscript reads as follows:

> The *Agamemnon* was cruising near the coast under the orders of Captain Nelson, and he learnt the deplorable situation of the cardinal. Forgetting all those antipathies called up by the name of Stuart, and the cardinal being an heir-presumptive to the British crown. Nelson determined to assist the last of the Stuarts. He went on shore himself, and invited him on board his ship, and found the illustrious unfortunate in rags. The cardinal hesitated not to throw himself on his generosity. He was accommodated with a part of the captain's cabin, and proper apparel suitable to his dignity was furnished him. He remained on board seven weeks, during which period the ship was engaged three times in action. The cardinal walked the deck with Captain Nelson, quite undismayed, amidst a scene of carnage to which he had been a perfect stranger. As soon as convenient, Captain Nelson landed him on the Austrian territories, forcing upon him £100 to defray his expenses to Vienna. The old man shed tears when he left his benefactor, and was regretted by all on board, to whom he was endeared by his mild and unassuming manners. Nelson frequently spoke of him with admiration, and said: "That man's example would almost make me a convert to the Catholic faith."

> A short while afterwards, we are told, the cardinal had a pension assigned him by the Austrian emperor, and within six months he was again on board the *Agamemnon* at Genoa, whither he had come especially to see Nelson.

> In the fullness of his gratitude he embraced all the officers, and ran about the ship shaking hands with all the crew. He repaid his pecuniary obligation to the admiral, and would have trebled the sum, but Nelson refused to allow it. When leaving the ship, he presented the admiral with a sword, or dirk, which is still preserved at Trafalgar House.

What the three occasions were of Nelson's being under fire while Cardinal York was on board the *Agamemnon* it is hard to say. There is no mention of the cardinal's presence in the ship in any of Nelson's letters, or any reference in the ship's log to his being on board. Nor is it clear where or when the three actions took place during the cardinal's stay afloat. No doubt the *Agamemnon* was under fire from the enemy, at one point or another along the coast, in various affairs that Nelson's extant letters do not record; one, for instance, the affair in Larma Bay, where the ship got aground under fire at close range from a French battery, and Captain Cockburn, of the *Meleager*, coming on board to offer assistance in towing the *Agamemnon* off, found Nelson calmly seated in his cabin writing letters until his own boats should be able to get the ship afloat again.

In the same generous spirit in which he acted towards Cardinal York it was that Nelson, in December, 1796, some six months after he left the *Agamemnon*, dealt with another member of the former Royal House of England. That was Don Jacobo Stuart, then serving in the Spanish Navy, the captain of the frigate *Sabina*, who was taken, after a ship-to-ship fight, by the *Minerve*, on board which frigate Nelson was temporarily flying his commodore's pennant.

> A descendant from the Duke of Berwick, son of James II., was my brave opponent; for which I have returned him his sword, and sent him with a flag of truce to Spain. I felt it consonant to the dignity of my country, and I always act as I feel right, without regard to custom.

So Nelson wrote in one of his letters home. He added this in another letter, going into details in his chivalrous record of the brilliant fight his gallant antagonist made:

> When I hailed the *don*, and told him 'This is an English frigate,' and demanded his surrender or I would fire into him, his answer was noble, and such as became the illustrious family from which he is descended: 'This is a Spanish frigate, and you may begin as soon as you please!' I have no idea of a closer or sharper battle; the force to a gun the same, and nearly the same number of men, we having 250. I asked him several times to surrender during the action, but his answer was: 'No, sir; not whilst I have the means of fighting left.' When only himself of all the officers were left alive, he hailed, and said he could fight no more, and begged I would stop firing.

The autumn campaign on the Riviera ended after the Battle of Loano. Over, too, very nearly were the *Agamemnon's* capabilities for active service during that commission. Nelson, though, with the exertions of his indefatigable Portuguese boatswain, Mr. Joseph King, managed to make the worn-out ship last for yet one more cruise.

Going into dock at Leghorn during December, for a refit that took five weeks' hard work to get through, it was found possible to patch up the *Agamemnon*, and make her strained and battered timbers hold together for a few months more at sea. Once already since she left England her shot-scarred and bullet-pitted masts and spars had had to be replaced by fresh masts and spars. Now again the *Agamemnon* had to be rerigged entirely, and in addition the ship's body had to be frapped tightly with cables passed under the keel and strapped round the hull, so as to make the strained frame-timbers hold together. When, at length, in the following August, Nelson's much-battered man-of-war arrived at Chatham Dockyard, the officers of the yard, we are told, were all astonishment at her state:

> There was not a mast, yard, sail, nor any part of the rigging, but was obliged to be repaired owing to the shot she had received.

Work at sea began again for the Agamemnons in the third week of the new year.

First came their introduction to their newly-arrived commander-in-chief, Sir John Jervis, the "Man of the Hour" for the British Navy.

Great leader as was Hood, Jervis was a greater leader. There was an end now for the Mediterranean fleet of *rois fainéant* such as Hotham had been and Hyde Parker—Nelson's future titular chief at Copenhagen—who for a few weeks was in charge as Hotham's successor until Jervis came out.

Already, indeed, the main fleet had learned something of the quality of their new overlord. Sir John Jervis took over the command in St. Fiorenzo Bay, where the fleet was lying at anchor. "Before the smoke of the salute to the commander-in-chief had blown off, the signal to unmoor flew," as an eyewitness describes, who was looking on when the frigate *Lively*, with Jervis on board, rounded-to at the head of the starboard line. Before nightfall the whole fleet was on its way to take up the close blockade of Toulon, and established a watch on the harbour that never ceased for eight months on end.

Jervis's appearance in force off Toulon, it may be added, totally unexpected by the enemy as it was, paralysed their activities for the time, and stopped a bold move that the French had in view. Believing Hotham to be still in command, a great French military expedition had been preparing for the conquest of the Papal States, and was about to sail across to Civita Vecchia, escorted by the Toulon ships. The sudden appearance of the British fleet off Toulon put an end to the project once and for all; the men-of-war were dismantled for the winter, and the soldiers sent back to rejoin the army on the Riviera.

Nelson met his new chief for the first time at Leghorn, when Jervis and part of the fleet came there, escorting a large convoy of merchantmen and store-ships just arrived from England. That was on January 17, the day before the *Agamemnon* sailed. At the first interview the men understood one another.

Nelson was confirmed in his independent command, and, with his squadron reinforced to efficient strength, was detached to carry on his work of harassing the French coast between Toulon and Vado Bay, preventing the transport of supplies by sea to the French army, then halted in its winter camps along the Riviera.

Within ten days the flying squadron was at its work of cutting out store-ships and exchanging shots with the shore batteries. Then, one day in February, Nelson took his Agamemnons for the second time into Toulon, sailing into the harbour under fire and counting the ships at their moorings; examining with his own eyes their readiness for sea. "Two batteries from the shore," said he, "opened their fire upon us; many shot went over, but none struck us." He repeated the enterprise in March, reporting to the admiral the enemy's exact numbers as seventeen sail of the line, and that most of the French ships appeared now so far advanced that they would be able to put to sea in a fortnight. On the previous occasion he had reported them as not likely to be out of port under a month.

On getting Nelson's second report, Jervis tightened his grip on Toulon, and set on foot a close blockade, with the fleet cruising within sight of the harbour, which he never relaxed by day or night until the end of the following autumn, keeping his ships at sea all the time. Water and provisions were taken on board every few days from commissariat-transports, sent regularly to the fleet from St. Fiorenzo, the transports as they arrived being made fast close astern of each man-of-war in turn, which supplied herself and then passed on the vessel to the next ship on the list, and so from one to another until the transport's hold had been cleared bare. In that way the fleet was kept supplied while they cruised.

Nor, apparently, was it such a hard time for some people on board some of the ships. Says a young officer of Jervis's flagship, the *Victory*, in a letter, describing their life:

> We live very happily. We had a dance last night in the gunroom (where we mess). We began at eight, and left off at ten. We all stripped off our coats and waistcoats and shirts, and kept on only our trousers ... We have hot rolls for breakfast, and eggs, and fresh beef for dinner. Our grub and water are brought off by the transports from Corsica every fortnight. We go so near the land that the French fire at us, and have killed some few of the *Britannia's* and *Goliath's* men. They wounded the *Zealous'* bowsprit, but did no damage to signify.

Sir John Jervis, reporting to the Admiralty in February on the services of the captain of the *Agamemnon*, used these words:

> Captain Nelson, whose zeal, activity, and enterprise cannot be surpassed.... I have only to lament the want of means to give him the command of a squadron equal to his merit.

As soon as the Austrian army advanced again to the Riviera, said Jervis in an interview with Nelson, he would co-operate with it actively. Nelson conveyed the message to the Austrian headquarters through the British Minister at Turin. He had it direct from the Admiral, he wrote, that:

> ....nothing would be wanting on his part towards an effective co-operation, and that Sir John would come to Vado for the concerting of plans with the Austrians. Vado should be taken at once, before the French advance in force.

Nelson wrote also on his own account that, as soon as the Austrian army reached the Riviera, it would find his squadron there ready to help them by night and day.

> At whatever part of the coast the army comes, whether the anchorage is good or bad, I am determined to risk every ship rather than the army should be annoyed by a single gunboat.

There was more than a new admiral in command of the British fleet.

De Vins was dead, and a new general of great reputation was at the head of the Austrian army now—the Freiherr von Beaulieu, Grand

Cross of the Order of Maria Teresa, a veteran of the Seven Years' War, in which, as a colonel on the staff of Frederick the Great's celebrated antagonist, Marshal Daun, he had won distinction at Kolin, Hochkirch, and Maxen.

But, on the other hand, a new general had also been appointed as the head of the French "Army of Italy"—Napoleon Bonaparte, or "General Bonaparte," as he was then styled, now about to open his career with perhaps one of the most brilliant of all his great campaigns. Napoleon's generalship, as things turned out, was to make all the difference to Nelson,

The Agamemnons had not long to wait before they learned how events were to shape in the new campaign.

Bonaparte arrived at Savona, the French headquarters, on April 9, direct from Paris. General Beaulieu, who had reached the Riviera with an Austrian army, nearly 40,000 strong, some ten days earlier, made his first move on the 10th, advancing on Savona and the passes of the Maritime Alps to the north.

He proposed at the outset to surprise the French advance-guard at Voltri at daybreak on the morning of the 11th, arranging for the *Agamemnon* to assist by bombarding the French out of the town during the battle, while Nelson's frigates took post, ranged at intervals beyond, close inshore, so as to sweep with their guns the only road along which the enemy's troops at Voltri could retreat. Nelson duly carried out his part of the programme. He waited in Genoa Harbour, quietly at anchor, until after dark. Then he sailed secretly, and before ten o'clock was at his post. He brought-to the *Agamemnon*, with only her kedge anchor down and the sails clewed up ready for an early move forward at the appointed hour, within a mile of the Austrian camp fires, which were plainly seen from the ship. Reported Nelson:

> My movements I kept secret, and after the shutting of the gates weighed the squadron from Genoa; and at half-past nine I anchored within half gun-shot of the Austrian army, sending the *Diadem* and *Blanche* to anchor between Voltri and Savona.
> But the French were aware of their perilous situation and passed our ships in the night.... Had the Austrians kept back, very few of the French could have escaped.

Austrian blundering spoiled the carefully laid plan, and enabled the French in that neighbourhood to escape out of the trap. A rashly opened skirmish with a French outpost on the previous afternoon had given the French general warning of Beaulieu's proximity, after which the enemy, a division of 6,000 men, hastily retreated under cover of darkness and joined their main army.

No second opportunity was given to the Austrians.

Within twenty-four hours Bonaparte struck back. Blow after blow fell on the Austrians with lightning rapidity and overwhelming effect. It was on Sunday night that Nelson took post in sight of Voltri with 10,000 Austrians encamped close to him on shore. By the Saturday following, all that was left of Beaulieu's whole army of 40,000 men, cut in two and beaten in the centre and on either flank on three successive days—in the three great battles of Montenotte, Dego, and Millesimo—with its camps and cannon captured, and leaving thousands of prisoners in the hands of the French, was hustling in a disorderly, panic-stricken mob through the passes of the Apennines; its Generals hoping against hope to be able to rally and make a stand near Milan.

A terrible week of anxiety and excitement was that on board the *Agamemnon*. Nelson, who had returned to Genoa on the 15th, could get no reliable news of what was happening. The Austrian troops near the coast had fallen back into the mountains at the outset, during the previous Monday night and Tuesday, to support their comrades already threatened at Montenotte. All sorts of wild rumours were current in Genoa. First came one story; two hours later its contradiction. The Austrians had defeated the French. Then they had been repulsed. Then they had won at some points, but had been driven back elsewhere. The French agents in Genoa spread the most alarming reports, which the Austrian minister to the *doge's* court, in reply to Nelson's inquiries, would neither affirm nor deny. In the end the French version proved to be only too well founded. On the 19th, Nelson knew the worst for certain. "I am full of sorrow and amazement at what has passed," he wrote. "It seems by land the French are invincible."

To render what aid he could to the Austrian army, Admiral Jervis had, during the week, come close in off Vado with a squadron of ships from off Toulon; only to find French troops with artillery in full possession, and see a large French ammunition convoy steal along the coast and get round into the bay, to windward of him, and so near the rocky shore that it was impossible to get at them without serious risk to his ships.

One of Nelson's captains, whose frigate had been off Vado on the day the French seized the place, had a narrow escape of being taken prisoner. He had gone on shore early to see what could be done to defend the town; only to find the last Austrians of the garrison hurrying away. The captain, as Nelson wrote, "was very near being taken by a party of French cavalry."

At least though, even after the catastrophe to the Austrian army, something might be done towards impeding the enemy in their general advance into Piedmont and Lombardy, by harassing their line of communications along the coast road. So Jervis thought, and to that Nelson next turned his energies. The Agamemnons did their best, assisted by their consorts in the squadron; but the duty was an almost impossible one to perform, owing to the coasting vessels, as before, sailing mostly under neutral flags, which Nelson was prohibited from interfering with.

Nearly every vessel that was chased hoisted Genoese colours, to pass as harmless traders carrying local merchandise. Wrote Nelson impatiently one day:

> The French have no occasion to send provisions from France. The coasts are covered with Genoese vessels with corn, wine, hay, etc., for places on the coast, and they know I have no power to stop the trade with the towns. I this day saw no less than 45 Genoese vessels, all laden, passing along the coast. What can I do?

The nature of the shore, further, was all in favour of small vessels creeping along out of reach of the men-of-war. As Admiral Jervis himself put it, in a report to the Admiralty embodying Nelson's complaints:

> With respect to the enemy's convoys of ammunition and stores, they may be impeded a little on their passage, but not prevented from getting to Vado, even if the line-of-battle ships were placed from headland to headland.

Day after day in that last week of April, and throughout May, the boats of the squadron—their men armed with cutlasses, pistols, and muskets—were actively employed in chasing suspected vessels, or in fights with French gunboats and shore batteries; the chases but too often, unfortunately, resulting in the overhauled vessels at the last moment producing Genoese or other neutral papers, and having in consequence to be liberated. In one affair with the batteries, one of Nelson's frigates was set on fire by a red-hot shot. The Genoese shore batteries, for the most part built in front of the coast towns, gave Nelson continual trouble. The greater number of them were in French hands, and their fire had to be returned; but Nelson tried to spare the houses from damage as much as he could. Wrote Nelson:

> I never have nor ever will, fire the first shot; but if shot are fired I will do my utmost to destroy the battery firing at the English flag.

The weather throughout the time made the service unusually trying; "extraordinary weather," Nelson called it, "fogs, heavy swells, and calms." The Agamemnons in their boats had also brushes now and again with French soldiers along the coast—once with a French cavalry regiment. They "harassed the enemy's troops very much. Field-pieces, etc., are drawn out on our standing inshore."

Three boat affairs with French convoys were specially reported by Nelson. In speaking of them, he said this:

> The boats' conduct and gallantry could not on any occasion have been exceeded, and I wish fully to express the sense I entertain of the gallantry of every officer and man engaged.

The first affair took place on April 25, in front of the batteries the French had just completed near Loano. "Our little business at Loano," Nelson called it. He had heard that a convoy of twenty-two sail, carrying military stores, had just put in at Loano, and hastened to the place, having with him, in addition to the *Agamemnon*, the *Diadem*, a sixty-four-gun ship Jervis had placed under his orders, and the *Meleager* and *Petrel* sloop. To Nelson's disappointment only four French vessels were there, but he attacked at once, first cannonading and mastering the fire from the shore batteries. Then five boats were sent in at the French transports: three from the *Agamemnon*, under Lieutenants Suckling, Noble, and Compton, and one each from the *Meleager* (Lieutenant Culverhouse) and *Diadem* (Lieutenant Ryder). After a sharp musketry fight with French soldiers, who fired from close to the water's edge—all four vessels were lying aground a few yards from the shore—the transports were boarded and brought off.

One of them was a bombard, with eight heavy guns and twelve swivels mounted. On board the others were found chests of muskets and barrels of powder and army provisions; also a number of cannon, intended for the armament of a coast battery elsewhere. Among the *Agamemnon's* casualties was Lieutenant Noble, "a most gallant and worthy officer," Nelson calls him, who had recently returned from his captivity in France. He received a dangerous bullet wound in the throat, which was believed for some time to be mortal. But, happily, after lying between life and death for some days, Lieutenant Noble recovered; to be again wounded in the fight with Don Jacobo Stuart—for the fourth or fifth time since coming under Nelson's command.

On the night of May 8, the boats, manned and armed, rowed in silently and boarded and carried off five vessels from under the fort of Finale, with which some of the squadron had exchanged shots that afternoon, and where the French gunners set the *Blanche* on fire with a red-hot shot. The French commandant, apparently, was slack in his guard that night, for not a shot was fired until the boats had carried off the prizes. To the general disappointment, they proved to be under the protection of the Genoese flag, and had to be liberated next day.

The third affair was the sharpest of all, and produced a valuable haul, besides having useful after-results. It took place on the afternoon of May 31. The *Agamemnon* and squadron were cruising along the coast, on the lookout for a large French ammunition convoy reported to be on its way from Toulon, when six ships flying French colours were sighted running in under all sail for the town of Oneglia, to shelter under the guns of a fort which displayed the Genoese flag. The squadron was standing in to intercept the vessels, when the fort opened fire on the *Agamemnon*. "The Tower of L'Arena, which had Genoese colours hoisted, fired on His Majesty's colours"—so Nelson reported to the British minister at Genoa in justification of the action that followed. Nelson goes on to say:

> I instantly directed the squadron to anchor in L'Arena and take the French vessels. In running in, a gun went off from the *Agamemnon* by accident, but did not, I believe, go near the shore—certainly not near the tower. The French vessels of war and the squadron exchanged a few guns, when our boats boarded the enemy resolutely and took them.

Describing the affair in his report to Sir John Jervis, Nelson said this:

> At two p.m. yesterday, seeing some vessels running along shore which I believed to be French, and knowing the great consequence of intercepting the cannon and ordnance stores, which I had information were expected from Toulon to be landed at

St. Pierre d'Arena for the siege of Mantua, I made the signal for a general chase, when the vessels got close under a battery and anchored. Three o'clock, the *Meleager* and *Agamemnon* anchored, as, soon afterwards, did the *Petrel* and *Speedy*. After a short resistance from the battery and vessels, we took possession of them. It is impossible I can do justice to the alacrity and gallantry ever conspicuous in my little squadron. Our boats boarded the National ketch in the fire of three 18-pounders and of one 18-pounder in a gunboat. The *Blanche* and *Diadem* being to leeward, the former could not anchor until the vessels had struck; but the boats of all the ships were active in getting them off the shore, the enemy having cut their cables when they surrendered. The *Agamemnon's* masts, sails, and rigging are a little cut, but of no material consequence.

Not a shot all the time would Nelson allow to be fired from the *Agamemnon*, or any of his other ships, in reply to the Genoese fort, although its guns kept firing on the squadron. Remonstrated Nelson to the Genoese Government

During this contest, to my astonishment the Tower of L'Arena opened a fire on His Majesty's ships, having their colours flying. . . . I had every reason to expect an exact neutrality, and not that the Genoese fortress would have assisted the enemies of England.

Instead of replying to the cannonade, Nelson sent a flag of truce to the Genoese governor. Set forth Nelson in his protest to the authorities at Genoa:

So far from returning the fire to a fortress bearing the Genoese flag, and which had killed and wounded several of His Majesty's subjects, and fired through the *Agamemnon*, I patiently received the fire, and sent a boat, with an officer and a flag, to ask the reason of their firing on the English colours, and that if the governor continued to fire, I should most certainly return it.

The governor stopped the cannonade and apologized, sending back word that, to quote Nelson again:

. . . . he should fire no more, and hoped I would not fire on the fortress or the town; which I did not, although a heavy fire of musketry continued to be kept up on our boats from the houses, and which it was within my power to have destroyed in ten minutes.

The prizes proved a most important capture. Two were war vessels, one mounting three 18-pounders and four swivels, and being manned by sixty men; the other, a gunboat, carrying one 18-pounder, four swivels, and thirty men. The four transports were found, as Nelson had suspected would be the case, to be laden with part of Bonaparte's siege-train for the attack on Mantua, the chief Austrian fortress in Italy—the "Citadel of Italy "it was called. On board them were a number of heavy 24-pounder battering guns, large 13-inch mortars, gun-carriages, shells, and a siege-train equipment complete, and entrenching tools.

Nelson said:

> I took exactly one quarter of the battering, cannon, mortars, shells, shot, and every ordnance store intended for the siege of Mantua; for I have an exact list of every store intended for that siege, sent for Buona Parti, together with maps, an exact return of his army at the opening of the campaign, and such books as the Directory think it right he should read in his leisure hours.

Of such importance, in fact, did the seizure prove in its further effect that the attack on Mantua had to be suspended until fresh siege stores could arrive from France—most timely help being thereby rendered by Nelson to the Austrian army in the field. Unfortunately, it was not availed of, owing to the lack of energy of the Austrian generals.

A fifth transport, under Genoese colours, which lay at anchor nearby, was overhauled by one of the *Agamemnon's* boats, and found to be carrying 152 Austrian prisoners, taken in the late battle at Montenotte. It came out that they had been made over to a Spanish contractor for conveyance to Spain, where they were to be compulsorily enrolled in one of the foreign regiments attached to the Spanish Army. Reported Nelson to Sir John Jervis:

> Some hours later a boat came off from the shore with a Genoese master and crew of the vessel, and papers to say they were chartered by the Spanish consul at Savona to carry these troops to Barcelona for the Swiss regiment. I have examined some of the Austrians, who say that they were marched by a guard to the vessel, and, when on board, a person gave them thirty

sous each, and told them they were going to Spain, where they would find many of their comrades. The men say it was against their inclination, and that they wish to return to their own service, or serve with the English until there is an opportunity. Knowing, as I do that the French absolutely sell them to the Spaniards, I have no difficulty in keeping them, to be returned to their own sovereign whenever opportunities offer; and, if you approve, I shall discharge the Genoese vessel. They are, sir, as fine, healthy-looking men as ever I saw; the oldest of one hundred and fifty-two, is thirty-four years of age. I think, until we have an opportunity of sending them to General Beaulieu, they would add to the strength of our ships—five ships thirty each; this is submitted to your better judgement.

The Austrian prisoners rescued by Nelson were, indeed, as it would seem also, only a small portion of the unfortunates whom the French had sold. In a letter to Colonel Graham (the future victor of Barrosa, and later on Lord Lynedoch), then acting as British commissioner with the Austrian army, Nelson wrote:

> More than 2,000, these people say, have already been sold. They were marched by a French guard in the night in to the vessel. They were naked, and had to be clothed by the fleet in the red British marines' uniform, in which they proceeded to do duty on board our ships.

It was found impracticable to send the Austrians back to their own army, and they volunteered to do service in Jervis's fleet; most of them fighting on board our ships at St. Vincent, and some 50 of them, after that, in Nelson's squadron at the Nile.

The French tried, some little time afterwards, it may be mentioned by the way, to get Nelson's batch of Austrian prisoners back by negotiation with Jervis through two neutral intermediaries, only, however, to draw this protest from the indignant admiral:

> From a Swiss dealer in human flesh, the demand made upon me to deliver up 152 grenadiers, serving on board His Majesty's fleet under my command, is natural enough; but that a Spaniard, who is a noble creature, should join in such a demand, I must confess astonishes me; and I can only account for it by the Chevalier Camano being ignorant that the persons in question were prisoners of war in the last affair with General Beaulieu,

and are not deserters, and they were most basely sold by the French commissaries in the Western Riviera of Genoa to the vile crimps who recruit for foreign regiments in the service of Spain. It is high time that a stop should be put to this abominable traffic, a million times more disgraceful than the African Slave Trade; and I trust the strong remonstrances about to be made by the Court of Vienna to the Court of Madrid will produce the desired effect.

Nelson says this of his "find," on board one of the other transports, of the war library specially sent from Paris for Bonaparte's reading

> I have got the charts of Italy sent by the Directory to Buonaparte, also Maillebois' *Wars in Italy*, Vauban's *Attack and Defence of Places*, and Prince Eugene's *History*—all sent for the general. If Buonaparte is ignorant, the Directory, it would appear, wish to instruct him; pray God he may remain ignorant.

With that *coup* the *Agamemnon's* commission under Nelson terminated. The ship, by now, was barely seaworthy, in spite of all the endeavours to keep her going, and she was ordered home forthwith. Nelson turning over into the *Captain*, a seventy-four, whose commanding officer, Captain T. S. Smith, had been compelled by broken health to invalid and go home to England. Wrote Nelson at the close of his commission in the *Agamemnon:*

> Had all my actions been gazetted not one fortnight would have passed during the whole war without a letter from me.

He only parted from his men then because he could not help himself, in consequence of the ship's completely worn-out state. He had repeatedly refused the many offers made to him to exchange from the *Agamemnon* into a bigger and more powerful vessel, solely because he would not leave his Agamemnons until he must.

> Though I have been offered every 74 which has fallen vacant, yet I could not bring myself to part with a ship's company with whom I have gone through such a series of hard service, as has never before, I believe, fallen to the lot of any one ship.

Most of his *Agamemnon* officers Nelson took with him to his new ship, the famous *Captain*, destined to gain immortal renown at St. Vincent, thanks to Nelson; also as many seamen as the regulations allowed a captain to take with him on changing ships. "I have the officers and

The British Mediterranean Fleet off Gibralter 1798

many of the *Agamemnon's* crew with me," he wrote, on settling down in his new command, "and believe we can raise as good a name for the *Captain* as the *Agamemnon* possessed."

The officers who turned over to the *Captain* were these: Edward Berry (first-lieutenant), Peter Spicer, James Summers, James Noble, Henry Compton. Lieutenant Maurice Suckling, the *Agamemnon's* third-lieutenant, went home in the ship, having succeeded to some property in Suffolk, which necessitated his presence in England for a time. Of the *Agamemnon's* original officers, Lieutenants Hinton, Bullen, and Andrews had been promoted commanders, and now had ships of their own. Lieutenant Wenman Alison had gone home, to die of disease contracted on service.

The first-lieutenant at the close of Nelson's commission, Edward Berry, had joined in that capacity in May, 1796, less than a month before Nelson quitted the *Agamemnon*. Sir John Jervis, who knew Berry's capabilities, introduced him and strongly recommended him to Nelson. Berry proved his mettle in a boat affair within a few days of coming into the *Agamemnon*, and Nelson had already taken to him. He became one of the most devoted of "Nelsonians" in days to come. As a commander, and a "volunteer" in the *Captain*, Berry fought at Nelson's side at St. Vincent, and in the boarding episode personally helped Nelson across from the *San Nicolas* to the *San Josef*. As a captain, Berry was Nelson's flag-captain at the Nile, where he won a knighthood. He commanded his own and Nelson's old ship, the *Agamemnon*, at Trafalgar, and did good service on that supreme day. He lived to become, in after years, the only naval officer in possession of five gold medals for battle services in the Great War.

Lieutenants Spicer and Noble were both with Nelson at St. Vincent, where Lieutenant Noble, a heroic fellow to the end and becomingly named, led the first boarding party that set foot on the deck of the Spanish first-rates. Both these officers also won promotion to commander at St. Vincent. Lieutenant Summers, a *protégé* of old Commodore Locker, at whose suggestion Nelson received Summers in the *Agamemnon*, was also at St. Vincent with Nelson; as was Lieutenant Compton, who, further, saw service with Nelson in the boats of the *Theseus* at Teneriffe, and on board the *Vanguard* at the Nile. Compton and Berry were the last of the "Old Agamemnon" officers to do duty in the same ship with Nelson.

Midshipman Hoste, too, was with Nelson at St. Vincent and at Teneriffe, where the lad went through the cruel experience of seeing his ardently loved leader and friend return on board grievously maimed. Young Hoste, then a junior lieutenant in the *Theseus*, thus tells what he saw:

> At two (in the morning) Admiral Nelson returned on board, being dreadfully wounded in the right arm with a grape-shot. I leave you to judge of my situation when I beheld our boat approach with him, who, I may say, has been a second father to me; his right arm dangling by his side, while with the other he helped himself to jump up the ship's side, and with a spirit that astonished everyone told the surgeon to get his instruments ready, for he knew he must lose his arm, and the sooner it was off the better. He underwent the amputation with the same firmness and courage that have always marked his character.

"His gallantry," wrote Nelson of Hoste, three days after St. Vincent, "never can be exceeded, and each day rivets him stronger to my heart." Nelson had also previously said this, one day on board the *Agamemnon*: "Hoste is indeed a most exceeding good boy, and will shine in our service." It was a prophecy that was most completely fulfilled. Hoste became one of the finest captains the Royal Navy has ever had, and won perhaps the most dashing frigate battle ever fought—the brilliant victory off Lissa in 1811. He closed his heroic career as a baronet—an honour specially awarded him for war service—and K.C.B.

Midshipman Nisbet was also with Nelson at St. Vincent and at Teneriffe, where he caught his wounded stepfather in his arms, as Nelson, with his arm shattered, fell back off the mole landing-step. Then, laying him gently down in the bottom of the boat, he bandaged the lacerated blood-vessels with his silk neckerchief; young Nisbet's presence of mind and promptitude saving Nelson from bleeding to death.

Boatswain King also followed Nelson from the *Agamemnon* into the *Captain*; as did the detachment of the old 69th Regiment (now the second battalion of the Welsh Regiment), who today commemorate their services with Nelson by the battle-honour "St. Vincent" emblazoned on their colours. The detachment had been doing duty as marines on board the *Agamemnon* from the beginning of Nelson's commission. They joined the ship, fifty-five strong, with two officers, at Spithead, on April 29, 1793, and had served with distinction in the trenches before Bastia, where their commanding officer, Captain-Lieutenant John Clarke, had his arm shot off while standing by Nelson's side. Nelson specially took with him into the *Captain* the then commander of the detachment, Lieutenant Charles Pierson, a faithful follower of his, an English-born officer, originally in the Neapolitan service, who volunteered at Bastia into the British army, and was specially taken into the *Agamemnon* by Nelson.

Some forty of the Agamemnon's men, petty officers and seamen, also turned over into the *Captain*, twenty of them the regulation quota that the captain of a sixty-four, when changing ships, was permitted to take with him from his old command, and the others additional hands, drafted to fill vacancies in the *Captain's* complement. The entire crew of the *Agamemnon* practically had wanted to exchange *en bloc* with the *Captain's* men; but that, of course, was out of the question. That Nelson had made himself the idol of all long since goes, of course, without saying. As an officer wrote:

> On board ship he was almost adored; he had a kind word for everyone: even the powder-monkeys did not escape his pleasant smile.

Some of the "Old Agamemnons," as Nelson always affectionately called the men who were transferred into the *Captain* with him, were with him, among his barge's crew, at Teneriffe on the night that he lost his arm; and also at St. Vincent among the boarders who took the two Spanish first-rates.

One of these Old Agamemnons at St. Vincent, as Nelson tells the story, came forward:

> .... taking me by the hand on board the *San Josef*, saying he might not soon have such another place to do it in, and assuring me he was heartily glad to see me.

Two splendid Yorkshire lads, two brothers, William and John Kearney, were among other Old Agamemnons who stood at Nelson's side on board the Spanish prize, William Fearney being the sailor who, as fast as Nelson received the swords of the surrendered Spanish officers, took them and held them for him, tucking them up in a bundle under his arm.

> On the quarter-deck of a Spanish first-rate, extravagant as the story may seem, did I receive the swords of vanquished Spaniards; which, as I received, I gave to William Fearney, one of my barge-men, who put them with the greatest *sang-froid* under his arm. I was surrounded by Captain Berry, Lieutenant Pierson,

69th Regiment, John Sykes, John Thomson, Francis Cook, all Old Agamemnons, and several other brave men, seamen and soldiers.

Of those just named, Sykes was Nelson's coxswain, the magnificent fellow who, in Nelson's celebrated boat encounter with the Spanish launches off Cadiz in the following July, saved Nelson's life by parrying blows aimed at him. In the case of one blow, Sykes:

> .... actually interposed his own head to receive the full force of a Spanish sabre, which, fighting hand to hand, he could in no other way prevent from falling on Nelson.

It was proposed, indeed, to get Sykes a Lieutenant's commission as soon as he had served sufficient time. Wrote Nelson of him;

> His manners and conduct are so entirely above his station that Nature certainly intended him for a gentleman.

But the brave fellow, just before his service was complete, was accidentally killed by the bursting of a cannon, while acting as gunner of the *Amphion* and supervising the firing of a salute one day as his ship was entering Gibraltar Harbour.

"Glorious St. Valentine"—to quote the name given the battle by Nelson himself, when, within sight of the long-backed Cape St. Vincent, in Portugal, the British navy achieved, perhaps, one of the most "timely "of its victories—might, indeed, bear furthermore, printed in the calendar against the date, these words: "The Discovery of Nelson." Before February 14, 1797, Nelson, in spite of all he and his Agamemnons had done, was an unknown man—unknown to the public in England; unknown to the world at large; unknown outside the Navy and the immediate circle of his family and friends—as, indeed, he himself once said; while also to those who knew him, he was hardly more than a talented and fearless officer, one likely to rise perhaps to high command, but with little better prospects before him than had a dozen other distinguished officers of the hour. After St. Vincent it was that Nelson really became known; that he suddenly found himself famous, and all the world ringing with his name. What he did on that Valentine's Day battle led, as a fact, to everything for Nelson. It attracted royal notice to him, and brought about his momentous appointment to command the squadron which won the Battle of the Nile; after which the leadership at Trafalgar may be said to have followed for Nelson in natural sequence.

Another Old Agamemnon, John Lovell, one of those with Nelson at St. Vincent, but not named by him, was with his old captain in the night attack at Teneriffe, and was the sailor who, when Nelson fell with his arm shattered, "having torn his shirt into shreds, constructed a sling for the wounded arm."

One Old Agamemnon at least, also, should have been with Nelson on board the Victory at Trafalgar—Tom Allen, of Burnham Thorpe, a seaman on board the *Agamemnon* whom Nelson had made his personal attendant. In action in the *Agamemnon* he fought at one of the upper-deck guns, and he always claimed further to have been one of the men who were at Nelson's side when boarding the Spanish ships at St. Vincent. Tom Allen was with Nelson at both the Nile and Copenhagen. At the Nile, as Tom contended to the last day of his life, he prevented Nelson from going on deck for the battle dressed in a gleaming brand-new full-dress uniform, which, the old sailor used to say, would certainly have drawn the attention of the enemy's musketry on Nelson. With great difficulty, said Allen, he induced Nelson to keep on his old everyday uniform with its dull and faded gold lace.

Tom just missed accompanying Nelson to Trafalgar, to his lifelong regret. Had he been there, he would say, he would again never have allowed Nelson to put on his coat with the embroidered stars which Nelson was wearing when the French bullet struck him down. Tom Allen was at home at Burnham Thorpe when Nelson received at Merton the news that sent him to Trafalgar. He was written to, and directed to join Nelson at once; but Tom had just been married and was having his honeymoon. He delayed starting in consequence, and reached Portsmouth twenty-four hours after the *Victory* had sailed. A passage out had been bespoken for him in a frigate, but at the last moment the thought of his newly-married wife apparently held Tom back, and he returned instead to Burnham Thorpe. Thanks to Captain Hardy's compassionate offices in later years, Tom Allen, who had fallen on evil times and was in the depths of poverty, was found a special berth among the pensioners at Greenwich Hospital, where he ended his days with his wife in comfort. A memorial stone was erected to his memory by Hardy when governor at Greenwich.

Some others of Nelson's Agamemnons at Bastia and Calvi would seem to have continued in the old ship in after years, throughout her various commissions, to the very end. A number of them were on board, indeed, on that last tragic day which sealed the doom of their old captain's dearly loved ship, in June, 1809, when Nelson's *Agamem-*

non came to her end, wrecked on a sandbank off Maldonado on the coast of Brazil.

An elderly officer, Captain Jonas Rose, who, too, had served under Nelson's orders on board a frigate at Copenhagen, was then in command. His last farewell to the Agamemnons makes, perhaps, as pathetic a scene in its way as a man-of-war's quarter-deck ever witnessed.

It was found hopeless to save the ship, and orders were given that she was to be abandoned and left to break up.

Captain Rose, looking—as well he might, for his career also was wrecked for ever—utterly cast down and broken, was standing on the starboard poop-ladder when the men were reported ready to leave. "Send every soul aft," replied poor old Jonas sadly. The men came, kit-bags and hammocks in hand, their faces, so we are told, as gloomy and dejected as that of their captain.

An officer present relates:

> The dead silence was broken only by the moaning of the wind and the mournful splash of the waters in the hold, with the groaning of the vessel as she swayed with the swell. The rats, squeaking and gibbering, could be seen struggling through the water in black patches, swimming for life away from the ship to Goretta Beach. Poor old Rose, with a voice trembling with emotion and faltering, tried to bid his crew farewell. He began by recalling the past glories of the stricken ship, 'the days and deeds of old with Nelson in the Mediterranean, and the glorious victory of Trafalgar.' Then he bade all continue to do their duty as men, and after that was proceeding in broken accents, and almost inaudible, to allude again to 'this old ship that we must now quit,' when he broke down altogether. The poor old officer was only able to add, in a choking voice, 'Goodbye, Agamemnons. May God bless you all! Agamemnons, goodbye!'

Our eye-witness of the trying scene says:

> A few hats were raised as if to cheer, but not a sound was heard, and then the lifted hands dropped listlessly back again, while from many eyes in which no tear had been ever seen tears now welled up freely. For some moments after Captain Rose had ceased, not a man stirred; all seemed spellbound, overcome by grief. At last George Goldring, a veteran boatswain's mate, who as a powder-monkey had fought on board the *Agamemnon* with Nelson, stepped forward to reply, as spokesman for the

ship's company. 'God bless your honour,' he began, 'wheresoever you may be—' But the old sailor, too, stopped short in his turn, breaking down as he went on to speak of this 'ould craft in which many of us has served all through the war,' He could say no more, ending with a mournful shake of the head as he brushed his rough hand across his eyes, and drew back among his shipmates.

Silently, after that, all passed over the side, and half an hour later, as the shades of evening fell. Nelson's *Agamemnon* lay deserted—a doomed hulk. She was afterwards dismantled of her spars, and then left to settle down in the sand, or break up as she lay. Such was the last hour of Nelson's dearly-loved *Agamemnon*.

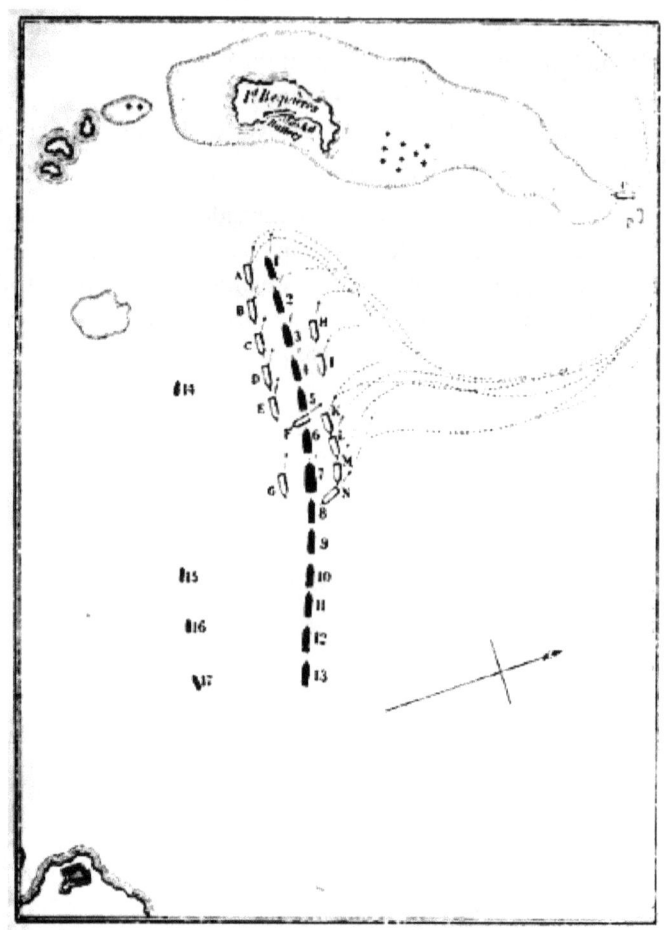

NELSONS ATTACK AT THE NILE
Drawn by one of the officers of the British Squadron

A. *Goliath* B. *Zealous* C. *Audacious* D. *Theseus* E. *Orion* F. *Leander*
G. *Alexander* H. *Vanguard* I. *Minotaur* K. *Defence* L. *Swiftsure*
M. *Bellerophon* N. *Majestic* O. *Culloden* P. *Mutine*

1. *Guerrier* 2. *Conquérant* 3. *Spartiate* 4. *Aquilon* 5. *Peuple Souverain*
6. *Franklin* 7. *Orient* 8. *Tonnant* 9. *Heureux* 10. *Mercure*
11. *Guillaume Tell* 12. *Génénereux* 13. *Timoléon* 14. *Sérieuse*
15. *Artémise* 16. *Diane* 17. *Justice*

Chapter 2

At the Nile

Nelson's Line of Battle

Ships.	Guns,	Commanders.
Vanguard	74	Rear-Admiral Sir Horatio Nelson, K.B.; Captain Berry.
Orion	74	Captain Sir James Saumarez.
Culloden	74	Captain Thomas Troubridge.
Bellerophon	74	Captain Henry d'Esterre Darby.
Minotaur	74	Captain Thomas Louis.
Defence	74	Captain John Peyton.
Alexander	74	Captain Alexander John Ball.
Zealous	74	Captain Samuel Hood.
Audacious	74	Captain Davidge Gould.
Goliath	74	Captain Thomas Foley.
Majestic	74	Captain George Blagdon Westcott.
Swiftsure	74	Captain Benjamin Hallowell.
Theseus	64	Captain Ralph Willet Miller.
Leander	50	Captain Thomas Boulden Thompson.
Mutine (brig)	—	Captain Thomas Masterman Hardy.

On That Wednesday Afternoon

At last the long and weary chase was over. From one end of the Eastern Mediterranean to the other, Nelson had been hunting for the enemy for the past eight weeks. Week after week, ever since June 7, the search had been in vain. The smartest squadron of men-of-war that the old British Navy ever had at sea had been baffled at every point. From off Toulon, round Corsica to Naples Bay, thence towards Malta and on to Alexandria, back after that along the Syrian coast to Syracuse for fresh provisions, and eastward once more to the coast of

Greece, and by Crete to Alexandria—so the fruitless, toilsome quest had shaped.

All the time, too, they knew that the huge French expedition must be somewhere within reach in those waters. At Naples they heard that the enemy they were seeking was off Malta and attacking the island fortress of Valetta, Then, that the enemy, after making themselves masters of all Malta, had gone off, steering to the east. After that all trace of the French had been lost until within the previous four days, when Nelson—at last—got definite news of the enemy's whereabouts.

A short while before, one day at sea, a French ship's lifebuoy, with a little tricolour pennon attached, and bearing painted on it *Artémise*, the name of a frigate known to be with the French fleet, had been picked up by the *Swiftsure*, and carried to the eager Nelson on board his flagship, the *Vanguard*. That served to revive the hopes of all, but the discovery had led to nothing. It was off the coast of the Morea, in the eighth week of the cruise, that the first intelligence of real value came to hand. The Turkish Bey in charge of the garrison at Coron, in the Morea, informed Captain Troubridge, of the *Culloden*, who had been sent into the port to make inquiries, that the French had been sighted passing Crete, heading to the south-east, undoubtedly making their way to Egypt. That news was obtained on July 28. Four days later the goal was reached.

The coast of Egypt came in sight during the morning of August 1. The minarets of Alexandria were in view a few minutes after noon. Two and a half hours later, the mystery of the French expedition had been solved. The enemy's fleet was discovered at anchor near the western mouth of the Nile. The French were within Nelson's reach at last.

One and all in the British squadron were on tenterhooks of excitement throughout that Wednesday forenoon—on the tiptoe of expectation. All were eager and excited with high hopes. Nelson himself was among the most excited. All that morning the admiral, we are told, was in a fever of anxiety; now restlessly pacing the quarter-deck, now hurrying up to the poop to clap his telescope to his eye—ever and again watching the mast-heads of the two leading ships, which were keeping a little ahead of the rest, on the lookout.

All through the forenoon the low Egyptian coast had been showing up more and more distinctly on the horizon ahead. Eight bells struck, twelve o'clock, noon; and a few minutes after that could be dimly discerned, rising above the sea-line afar, Pompey's Pillar and the loftiest minarets of Alexandria. It was the second time that the squadron had seen them in that cruise. Would it be now as it had been on the first occasion? At their former visit Alexandria Harbour had been absolutely empty, bare of shipping except for a single Turkish man-of-war and a few small craft—Egyptian coasters and fishing-boats.

No, it was not like that now.

Alexandria Harbour this time could be seen to be crammed with big vessels: a forest of masts filled the port, belonging to a huge crowd of ships all closely packed together. The nationality of the great assemblage of vessels was disclosed not many minutes later. The French tricolour could be made out at the mast-heads of the vessels everywhere, and also flying on the city walls.

All held their breath on board the British squadron. Where were the fighting ships of the French fleet; where were Bonaparte's men-of-war? That was the question all asked themselves. Every telescope was kept pointed at the mast-head of the leading British ship, Captain Samuel Hood's *Zealous*, which, with another seventy-four, the *Goliath*, close at hand, was in advance of all and nearest to the enemy.

The answer came from *Zealous* in due course. Three little balls of signal bunting, the rolled-up flags, went up, sliding swiftly to the mast-head of the *Zealous*. Then the bunting fluttered open, broken out; the signal was made. The flags flew out clear on the breeze; their colours and marking were plainly visible. The message they told was read off at once. There was a general groan of disappointment and disgust as the flags spelled out the words:

The enemy's fleet do not form part of the vessels at anchor.

Says one officer, Sir James Saumarez, captain of the *Orion*:

> When the reconnoitring ship made the signal that the enemy was not there, despondency nearly took possession of our minds. I do not recollect ever to have felt so utterly hopeless or out of spirits as when we sat down to dinner.

But all the story had not been told. Within half an hour the *Zealous* had discovered what was in Aboukir Bay. Another signal came this time. There was news indeed now. Describes Captain Saumarez again:

> As the cloth was being removed the officer of the watch hastily came in, saying, 'Sir, a signal has just now been made that the enemy is in Aboukir Bay.' All sprang to their feet, and only

Nelsons Flag-Captain
at the Nile:
Sir Edward Berry

The captain who
first reported the enemy:
Sir Samuel Hood

The Bayard of
the British Navy
Sir Thomas Troubridge
of the "Culloden"

The hardest fighter
at the Nile
Captain H. D. Darby
of the "Billy Ruff'n"

Four of Nelsons "Band of Brothers"

staying to drink a bumper to our success, we were in a moment on deck.

On the captain's appearance there, as we are told, his gallant men of the *Orion*,

> .... animated by one spirit, gave three hearty cheers, in token of their joy at having at length found their long-looked-for enemy, without the possibility of his again eluding their escape.

Another officer in another ship, First-Lieutenant Hawkins, of the *Theseus*, also tells us of the finding of the enemy.

> On the 1st of August, after sitting down quite disappointed at not finding the French fleet in Alexandria, the *Zealous* made a signal for its being at anchor in the Bay of Aboukir. The steward was decanting the last bottle of wine for the day, when the officer on watch sent down to tell me that the Zealous had made the signal. Joy was instantly seen to illuminate every countenance; I ordered my servant to bring me a clean shirt, and dressed immediately. A half-past three we saw them very plainly; at half-past four the admiral hailed us and desired we would go ahead of him; this order we cheerfully obeyed. He bowed to me as we passed him; I never saw him look so well.

This is how the *Zealous* came to have the honour of first discovering the enemy, as her captain relates. They had been keeping a sharp look out all the forenoon:

> At half-past ten, *Alexander* made the signal for the land; at half-past eleven we saw it was Alexandria, and as we approached we could plainly discern there were many more vessels in the port than were there before. The *Alexander* made signal for six French ships of war lying in the port, and we soon discovered that the enemy's fleet had been there.

Hood at once pushed on farther along the coast, suspecting—as was the fact—that the French men-of-war might well have found an anchorage in Aboukir Bay, some twenty miles to the east. Hood says:

> I immediately kept well to the eastward of the admiral, to try if I could make out anything at Aboukir, as did also the *Goliath*. At about half-past one o'clock, the man at the mast-head said he saw a sail, and, instantly, a fleet at anchor. I sent a glass up,

and they told me there were sixteen or eighteen large ships; they thought sixteen of the line. I immediately made the signal to the admiral.

As it happened, by chance, Captain Foley of the *Goliath* all but anticipated Hood. According to one of Foley's officers, the lookout actually caught sight of the enemy's ships from on board the *Goliath* first of all. Midshipman the Hon. George Elliot claims to have seen the enemy before anybody else in Nelson's squadron. He tells, too, how he caught sight of them and what happened:

> I, as signal-midshipman, was sweeping round the horizon ahead with my glass from the royal-yard, when I discovered the French fleet at anchor in Aboukir Bay. The *Zealous* was so close to us that, had I hailed the deck, they must have heard me. I therefore slid down by the backstay and reported what I had seen. We instantly made the signal, but the under-toggle of the upper flag at the main came off, breaking the stop, and the lower flag came down. The compass-signal, however, was clear at the peak; but before we could recover our flag, *Zealous* made the signal for the enemy's fleet; whether from seeing our compass-signal or not I never heard. But we thus lost the little credit of first signalling the enemy, which, as signal-midshipman, rather affected me.

Captain Miller of the *Theseus* writes in a letter:

> The *Zealous* announced to the admiral, at three-quarters past two, that sixteen sail of the line were at anchor, East by South; and in a few minutes afterwards we all discovered them.
>
> At three the admiral made a signal to prepare for battle; at twenty-five minutes past four, to prepare for battle with the sheet-cable out of the stern-port and springs on the bower-anchor, etc.; at fifty-four minutes past four, that it was the admiral's intention to attack the van and centre of the enemy; at forty minutes past five, to form the line of battle as most convenient, ahead and astern of the admiral. The *Goliath* was leading, the *Zealous* next, then the *Vanguard*. The *Theseus* followed close to her stern, having the *Bellerophon* close on her weather-quarter, and the *Minotaur* equally so on her lee-quarter. I do not recollect the order of the other ships.

The other ships were the *Defence, Orion,* and *Majestic,* with the fifty-gun ship *Leander.* At some distance off was Troubridge's *Culloden,* some way astern, towing a French brig, a prize laden with wine, which was to be divided among the different crews, grog having run short in the squadron. The *Alexander* and *Swiftsure* were cruising at a distance inshore, detached to reconnoitre the ships in Alexandria Harbour.

At no time, perhaps, in the naval history of England did a finer, a smarter, a more thoroughly efficient set of men-of-war sail the seas than the ships of Nelson's squadron at that moment. Nelson, we have it on the authority of Sir Edward Berry of the *Vanguard*, the flag-captain, speaking of the state of the squadron when it came first under Nelson's orders off Corsica:

> . . . . had the happiness to find that to the captains of his squadron he had no necessity to give directions for being in readiness for battle. On this point their zeal anticipated his most utmost wishes, for the decks of all the ships were kept perfectly clear day and night, and every man was ready to start to his post at a moment's notice. It was a great satisfaction to him, likewise, to perceive that the men of all the ships were daily exercised at the great guns and small-arms, and that everything was in the best state of preparation for actual service.

The finest set of captains who ever backed up a British Admiral on the day of battle were with Nelson on that Wednesday afternoon. The "Band of Brothers" Nelson himself called them, indeed. "I had the happiness to command a Band of Brothers," wrote Nelson to Lord Howe. "The Chosen Band" was their own name among themselves. They were all men in the prime of life, the oldest forty-one, the youngest about thirty. All, also, on one occasion or another, most of them on several occasions, had proved their mettle before the enemy: some of them had won special promotion for distinguished conduct in action—for hard fighting. More than half of them, as young officers, had seen active service with Hood and Rodney in the fierce West Indian battles of the American War.

Others had had their part in the even fiercer fighting in the East Indies, in the five desperate battles with the redoubtable Bailli de Suffren, the hardest hitting and toughest battle-leader the French Navy has ever known. One had captained a ship in Lord Howe's line of battle on the "Glorious First of June." Four had commanded ships at St. Vincent; one of these with surpassing merit, outdone on "Glorious

Valentine's Day" only by Nelson's marvellous achievement. Two others had been present in the same battle as volunteers.

Sir James Saumarez, of the *Orion*, the senior of the captains, one of Guernsey's noblest and most distinguished sons, had seen his first two battles at sea with grim old "Vinegar" Parker in his Kilkenny Cat fight off the Dogger Bank, and Kempenfelt in his dashing little victory in the Channel. Saumarez, after that, had fought with Hood in Frigate Bay, St. Kitts, and had commanded with distinction a ship of the line in Rodney's smashing conquest of De Grasse. Captain Thomas Troubridge, of the *Culloden*, the next in seniority, was the splendid officer whom Earl St. Vincent styled "The Bayard of the British Navy," and Nelson's oldest friend in the service, with an intimacy dating back from the time when they were fellow-midshipmen serving in the *Seahorse* in the East Indies. Troubridge had been present before that day at no fewer than seven fleet battles, in five of them as a lieutenant in the British flagship fighting Suffren.

As a captain and the leader of Jervis's fleet at St. Vincent, the fine manner in which Troubridge broke through the enemy's line had shown him as second to none in the Navy, except Nelson himself. Captain Henry D'Esterre Darby, of the *Bellerophon*, an Irish officer and gentleman of the best type of the old-time school, had made his mark as a bold frigate captain. Louis, of the *Minotaur*, a gallant son of Devon, had seen his first shot fired with Keppel. Captain John Peyton, of the *Defence*, a member of an old naval family, had, in like manner, learned his business under fire in the American War; as also had Captain Alexander John Ball, of the *Alexander*, a member of an old Gloucestershire family, at the outset of his service a lieutenant in Rodney's famous flagship, the *Formidable*, on Rodney's great day. Davidge Gould, of the *Audacious*, a Somersetshire man, born at Bridgwater, had also, as a young officer, fought under Rodney, and since then had distinguished himself with Nelson in Corsica. Another "old Rodney man" was Captain Ralph Willett Miller, of the *Theseus*, the son of an American loyalist, and born in New York, also destined to be Nelson's flag-captain at St. Vincent and at Teneriffe. Captain Thomas Boulden Thompson, of the *Leander*, too, had begun his active service career in battle under Rodney.

So also had yet another, Ben Hallowell, of the *Swiftsure*, as noblehearted a fellow as ever lived, a Canadian by birth, a man of gigantic frame and stature, and of brains a match for his bulk, who had once quelled a mutiny on board ship by himself with his fists. Lord Hood had specially promoted Hallowell captain for his services at Toulon; and he had been, with marked distinction, Nelson's close companion-in-arms on shore in Corsica, being further, after St. Vincent, publicly thanked by the commander-in-chief for his services as a "volunteer" on the quarter-deck of the *Victory*. Captain George Blagdon Westcott, of the *Majestic*, a second gallant Devonian in "The Chosen Band," was a Honiton baker's son originally, whose handiness and readiness of resource one day, when a boy and serving his apprenticeship to a local miller, proved the means of his being found a berth in a man-of-war. Promotion followed rapidly, and Captain Westcott had commanded the *Impregnable* in Lord Howe's line of battle on the "First of June." Captain Samuel Hood, of the *Zealous*, of the famous Somersetshire naval family, one of the most chivalrous of English gentlemen, had been a lieutenant in the *Barfleur* with his great kinsman in Rodney's fine victory; and, more recently, as captain of the frigate *Juno*, had made a name for himself in the Navy for coolness and nerve in a perilous adventure one night in the middle of the French fleet in Toulon Harbour.

Captain Thomas Foley, of the *Goliath*, a member of an old Welsh family, and a nephew of one of Anson's officers in the *Centurion*, had seen hard fighting in his young days against French and American privateers in the North Atlantic; and, at St. Vincent, had been captain of the *Britannia*, flagship of the admiral second in command. Sir Edward Berry, Nelson's flag-captain in the *Vanguard*, a Londoner by birth, as a youngster had been all through the fierce battles with Suffren in the East Indies, and as a lieutenant had seen service at Lord Howe's battle of Ushant. He had been Nelson's first-lieutenant in the *Agamemnon* for the last part of the commission, as has been said, and, as a volunteer, had been by Nelson's side at St. Vincent in the heroic boarding of the Spanish first-rates. Captain Thomas Masterman Hardy, the future captain of the *Victory* at Trafalgar, was in command of Nelson's only cruiser at the Nile, the little gun-brig *Mutine*.

Such were the captains who formed Nelson's "Band of Brothers" at the Battle of the Nile—old acquaintances of one another and personal friends most of them, all of them true-hearted, single-minded gentlemen, heroic fellows without a spark of jealousy or thought of self-seeking among them; rivals only in honour, their thoughts set only on doing their utmost for the credit of their country's flag.

All through the long pursuit, Nelson had been in the closest touch with all his captains, signalling for them, as we are told, every evening, whenever the weather permitted, to come on board the *Vanguard*. There, as Captain Berry tells us:

> ..... he would fully develop to them his own ideas of the different and best modes of attack, and such plans as he proposed to execute upon falling in with the enemy, whatever their situation or position might be, by day or night. There was no possible position in which they could be found that he did not take into his calculations.

In that way Nelson made sure of victory beforehand. In those informal talks, sometimes sitting together in the cabin of the *Vanguard*, sometimes walking up and down, side by side with one or other, on the quarter-deck. Nelson made everything straightforward as soon as the enemy came in sight. Each captain had learnt to know instinctively, as it were, what he would have to do; there was no need for Nelson to issue "Fighting Instructions." Says Captain Berry, who was beside Nelson at these conferences, and heard all that was said;

> Signals became almost unnecessary; much time was saved; and the attention of every captain could almost undistractedly be paid to the conduct of his own particular ship

—circumstances from which, upon this occasion, the advantages to the general service were most incalculable.

The going up of the flags to "Prepare for battle" was received throughout the fleet with a tremendous outburst of cheering. There was really next to nothing left to be done on board the ships. All through the cruise, as has been told, the squadron had been sailing ready, to all intents, for instant action by day or night. All that remained to be seen to was the final clearing up of decks for action, hardly more than a quarter of an hour's work. In less than fifteen minutes, on an average, on board every one of the ships the decks were all clear, fore and aft, and the men were standing at their guns ready to fire the first shot.

At once the drums clashed out the warning ruffle, the battle summons on board ship:

> R-r-r-ap, tap. R-r-r-ap, tap. R-r-r-ap, tap-tap-tap.
> Rap-a-tap—a-rap-a-tap—a-rap-rap-a-tap—a-tap-tap!

At once, everywhere, all sprang to their allotted duties.

The decks were quickly wetted and sanded over, for the grim

purpose of, as far as possible, preventing the planks from getting too slippery with blood. The great horn battle-lanterns were hooked up, one lantern swinging over each gun; the usual practice before action whether by night or day. In the low, confined space between decks, the thick powder-smoke rendered it impossible to do without them, poor as was the gleam they gave. The guns—all ready, of course, long since, loaded and double-shotted—were cast loose; the firing-locks, with fresh flints, were screwed or clamped on the vents. Match-tubs, each with a coil of lighted slow-match inside, were placed on deck near by the guns, one to each gun, so as to be available in case the vent-mechanism of the locks went wrong. Spare breechings and tackles, for running the guns in and out, were brought up from the hold and placed in readiness for use near the hatchways.

Pistols and boarding-axes—"tomahawks," the men called them—and half-pikes were stacked along the ship's side between the guns, ready to be picked up in an instant at any call of "Repel boarders!" A supply of cannon-shot, round-shot, sufficient for the first dozen rounds, were laid on the deck close by each gun, in rope grummets, to keep them from rolling about; and "bunches" of grape also. The cook's fires were drawn and swamped; the magazines opened and cartridges ranged, ready for instant serving out to the powder-boys, two of whom attended each gun's crew. Fire-screens of canvas, or "fearnought" (thick stuff like blanketing), were rigged at the hatchways and drenched with water as a precaution. Filled fire-buckets were ranged along various parts of the deck, and in the channels outside the bulwarks, where the shrouds were made fast to the hull; the lumbering, clumsy ship's fire-engine was hoisted up on to the poop and the hoses screwed on.

All bulkheads and cabin furniture and the gear not likely to be wanted was lowered down into the hold or else summarily thrown overboard, with spare casks and other impedimenta. These included, on that afternoon, a number of unfortunate bullocks, taken on board at Syracuse to be killed, as wanted, as food for the crews. The poor beasts had to be thrown overboard and left to drown, one ship—Hood's *Zealous*—so disposing, as the log tells us, of eight unfortunate bullocks. They could not remain on deck with the enemy's cannon-balls flying about, and there was nowhere below for them to be stowed. The yards aloft were lashed firmly and slung in chains to prevent them coming down, when struck by shot, on to the heads of the men fighting the upper-deck guns; splinter nettings were stretched over the upper deck, also, to catch heavy splinters from aloft and other minor wreckage that might fall in the same way. All that and more had to be done on board throughout the squadron in clearing for action. All was finished, and everything ready for firing the first shot on board in every ship in less than fifteen minutes.

The French fleet was lying in line-ahead formation, from west to east, extending over a mile and three-quarters from end to end, with intervals between the ships of about 160 yards. There were twelve two-deckers in the enemy's line, nine of them seventy-fours, three of them eighty-gun ships, with, in the centre, the French flagship, the most powerful man-of-war in the world at that time, a giant one hundred and twenty-gun ship—the three-decker, *L'Orient*.

To landward were the sands and shoals of Aboukir Bay, the beach being distant some three miles. Seaward, the anchorage was protected by the low, flat island of Aboukir, off Aboukir Point, which formed the western extremity of the bay, with a stretch of reefs and shoals between the island and the point. Beyond Aboukir Island, to the north, there extended a long shoal, impassable to anything of a deeper draught than a small coaster or a sloop. To the north-east, and away round to due east, in the direction of the Rosetta mouth of the Nile, it was open water. Admiral Brueys, the French commander-in-chief, had fortified Aboukir Island with a battery of twelve guns and two mortars. He had satisfied himself that his van was secured from serious attack by the island and the rocks between it and the point, and, consequently, anchored his least powerful ships at that end of the line—three old-type seventy-fours.

He placed *L'Orient* in the centre, at what seemed to him the point of greatest danger. His rear he considered as also open to attack, and to strengthen it he placed there his heavier and better ships—his three big eighty-gun ships. The admiral ranged his squadron so as to lie as close as possible along the fringe of shallow water which extended on the landward side along the shores of the bay. The French ships were anchored just beyond where the sand-banks shelved down into deep water, their line forming a slight curve from end to end. All were anchored sufficiently clear of the shoal to allow each vessel to swing with the tide without touching ground.

The British squadron drew near, with the leadsmen in the chains sounding carefully and continuously as the ships advanced. The water was steadily shoaling—fifteen, fourteen, thirteen, ten fathoms. There was no official chart available of Aboukir Bay; only a rough diagram of the anchorage, which had been found on board a captured trading vessel and taken to Nelson.

A chaplain on board one of Nelson's ships, the Rev. Cooper Willyams, of the *Swiftsure*, who was watching the scene from on deck, not having yet gone down to his station in the cockpit, wrote down in these words some of his impressions on that afternoon:

> Here true heroism was displayed in the prompt decision of Admiral Nelson. When his squadron was well collected around him, he determined, without loss of time, to attack the foe, formidable as their appearance was, superior their number, weight of metal, and size, night coming on, and an unknown navigation. Surely too much cannot be said of such magnanimity! His honour, character, and life were to be put to the decision of the enterprise, for it was well known that conquest or death was his determined object.
>
> His resolution was instantly formed, and his intentions made known to the fleet by the signal for the headmost ship to bear down and engage as she reached the van of the enemy, the next ship to pass by and engage the second ship of the line, and so on. With alacrity was this signal obeyed; the sure presage of victory sat on the brow of every Briton, and a general ardour pervaded all ranks. The commanders, with that courage which distinguishes men inured to danger, saw the hazard of the contest, and prepared to meet it: their ships were trained to every exercise of arms; all means of preservation from fire, leaks, and other casualties were arranged in order; a bower-cable was got out of the after-part of each ship, and bent forwards, that she might anchor by the stern; the dreadful engines of destruction ready primed and doubly loaded; the men at their quarters, waiting in silent expectation the orders of their superiors; the officers respectfully looking towards their captains, and waiting with firmness the awful moment.
>
> The enemy's line presented a most formidable appearance. It was anchored in close order, and apparently near the shore, flanked with gunboats, mortar vessels, and four large frigates, with a battery of mortars and guns on an island near which we must pass. This posture gave the most decided advantage to the French, whose well-known perfection and skill in the use of artillery has so often secured to them splendid victories on

shore. To that they were now to look for success, for each ship, being at anchor, became a fixed battery.

The British admiral, who saw all the advantages the enemy possessed, but saw them with a seaman's eye, knew that they must have room to swing the length of their cables, and, consequently, that there would be space enough for our ships to anchor between them and the shore.

Just before five o'clock, the signal went up at the mast-head of the *Vanguard*, "I intend to attack the enemy's van and centre." It was in itself a stroke of genius; it gave victory into Nelson's hand before a single shot had been fired. Nelson's masterly tactics meant that fourteen British ships—counting the fifty-gunship *Leander* in the fighting line—would oppose eight or ten French at most, these all anchored and immovable. With the wind blowing from the quarter that it was—the north-west—and the difficulty of any move forward owing to the shoals on either side, and the darkness of night soon coming on, it would be impossible for the remainder of the enemy, the powerful French ships in rear, to move up and assist the ships ahead before the van had been overpowered, if only by mere force of numbers.

About half-past five, or a little later, when they were getting close to the enemy, Nelson made signal for the squadron to take post in line of battle in the order that the captains found themselves at the moment.

It was after that, during the last half-hour, as they began to draw in towards the destined point of attack, that these incidents took place, as two of Nelson's captains relate. Describes Captain Miller of the *Theseus:*

> We wore gradually round preserving our order till we brought the wind on the starboard beam, when the admiral hove-to, to speak the *Mutine*, about three miles from the enemy, who were making signals and heaving on their springs. I took this opportunity to pass the admiral to leeward, and endeavoured to obtain the honour of leading the fleet into battle, as the *Culloden*, the only ship ahead of us in the regular line, was still considerably distant; but Captain Berry hailed as we passed, and gave me the admiral's order to become his second ahead, in consequence of which I hove-to close ahead of him, and the *Orion* and the *Audacious* passed us.

Captain Hood, in the *Zealous,* adds how Nelson, a few minutes afterwards, hailed across to him to ask a question about the soundings:

> As we got abreast of the end of the shoal at the entrance, being within hail of the admiral and of his lee bow, Sir Horatio asked me if I thought we were far enough to the eastward to bear up round the shoal. I told him I was in eleven fathoms, that I had no chart of the place, but if he would allow me I would bear up and try with the lead, which I would be attentive to, and lead him as close as I could with safety, it appearing to shoal regularly. He said he would be obliged to me. I then bore away and rounded the shoal, the *Goliath* keeping on my larboard bow, until I found we were advancing too fast from the admiral. I shortened sail soon after the ship's advancing, and the admiral only waiting to speak a boat, he made the signal for to proceed on.

Hood's first-lieutenant Lieutenant William Henry Webley, who was standing close beside his captain, says this of the incident:

> We were nearly past the island, and Lord Nelson hailed the *Zealous*, and asked if Captain Hood thought he might bear up for the enemy? Captain Hood replied, 'I cannot say; we have eleven fathoms of water, but if you allow me the honour of leading you into battle, I will keep the lead going.' He answered, 'You have my leave, and I wish you success,' and then took off his hat. Captain Hood, in endeavouring to do the same, let his hat fall overboard, and immediately said, 'Never mind, Webley! There it goes for luck! Put the helm up and make sail!' This was done directly, and was speedily followed by the *Goliath*, who, when the course was shaped, had the lead of the *Zealous* (in consequence of being inside) about a ship's length.

> The two ships continued to run in this way until they got within shot of the enemy, when Captain Hood said to me, 'I see Foley does not like to give up the lead; let him take it, he is very welcome to it; therefore shorten sail, and let him place himself. I suppose he will take the van ship.'

Just as the squadron was getting within range, once more signal flags ran up at the masthead of the *Vanguard*. They were two flags, a red pennant over a yellow and blue flag. The two flags made No. 5 in the *Signal Book*, Nelson's favourite battle-message—"Engage the enemy closer." Enthusiastic cheers from every ship in the squadron was the instant answer. Every captain meant to do so; one and all meant to give battle at the closest quarters.

It was just six o'clock when the first shots went off. The French began the firing—at the outset with shells from the mortars that Admiral Brueys had placed on Aboukir Island, near the western entrance to the bay. The practice, however, was bad. Not one of the French shells touched our ships. Nor, on board the British squadron, was any reply made to the firing; no notice was taken of it except that, as the first shells went off, every ship, all of them simultaneously, hoisted her colours, the White Ensign at the staff, together with three Union Jacks, one on each topmost stay. On board the *Vanguard* Nelson hoisted six Union Jacks.

The French van ships then began to fire, but still there was no answer from the British line.

One and all. Nelson's ships moved forward steadily, with imposing stillness. The only sounds on board were the droning chant of the leadsmen posted in the fore-chains, as they reported soundings; the straining and creaking of cordage and blocks overhead, or the flap of a sail; now and again a sharp *click! click!* from the marines' flint-locks, getting muskets ready; now and again a short, gruff order to men tending the braces in trimming yards, or aloft ready to furl sail. That was all: save for that the dead silence of the advance was unbroken. Marvellously impressive and awe-inspiring was Nelson's calm, unhesitating approach. It amazed the French, as their prisoners after the battle confessed, and of itself produced a disquieting and disheartening effect.

The British squadron were all under topsails now. That was sail sufficient to carry them into the battle; and it could be readily taken in, without embarrassment when the critical moment came, when each ship had to bring up sharply and let go anchor promptly alongside her destined opponent. They were moving through the water at six knots, with a breeze from the north-west blowing briskly.

The sun's rim was just touching the sea-horizon astern when the leading ship of the British squadron rounded the enemy's line and opened fire.

"Goliath" Strikes the First Blow

Midshipman Elliot, of the *Goliath*, whose account of how he sighted the enemy has been given, tells also how his ship led inside the French line and began the battle. The bearing of his narrative on the professional controversy is not our business here.

When we were nearly within gunshot, standing as *A.D.C.* close to Captain Foley, I heard him say to the master that he wished he could get inside the leading ship of the enemy's line (the *Guerrier*). I immediately looked for the buoy on her anchor, and saw it apparently at the usual distance of a cable's length—*i.e.*, 200 yards—which I reported. They both looked at it, and agreed there was room to pass between the ship and her anchor (the danger was the ship being close up to the edge of the shoal), and it was decided to do it. The master then had orders to go forward and drop the anchor the moment it was a ship's breadth inside the French ship, so that we should not actually swing on board of her. All this was exactly executed.

I also heard Foley say he should not be surprised to find the Frenchman unprepared for action on the inner side; and as we passed her bow I saw he was right. Her lower-deck guns were not run out, and there was lumber, such as bags and boxes, on the upper-deck ports, which I reported with no small pleasure. We first fired a broadside into the bow. Not a shot could miss at the distance. The *Zealous* did the same, and in less than a quarter of an hour this ship was a perfect wreck, without a mast, or a broadside gun to fire. By this time, having no afterbitts to check the cable by (which came in at the stern port), it kept slowly surging—*i.e.*, slipping—and at last the remaining stoppers broke (our sails had flown loose by the gear being shot away—we had not time to fold them), and it ran out to the clinch, and placing us a little past the second ship of the French line, so as to engage her and the third ship. We were just in this position when the leading ships of the body of our fleet came in.

Several of the French captains, those of the ships of the enemy's van, Midshipman Elliot further says, were not on board. They had not had time to return from their flagship, *L'Orient*, where they had been to receive instructions from Admiral Brueys, before the battle opened with the *Goliath's*, attack.

The French captains were all on board their admiral's ship, and did not expect us to come in that night. They had sent for their boats to return from the shore where they were procuring water. The senior officer of the van division, seeing us stand on under all sail, got anxious, and sent his own boat to hasten off the boats of his division without waiting to fill with water. She had not got back when we were getting very close, and as his own launch was passing the flagship, half-laden with water, he got into her, but she pulled up slowly against the fresh sea-breeze, and did not reach his ship till we had passed her. I saw him waving his hat, and evidently calling to his ship, when still at a considerable distance. An officer was leaning against his ensign staff listening. At last this officer ran forward to the poop and down to the lower deck. We knew what was coming, and off went their whole broadside, but just too late to hit us, and passed harmlessly between us and *Zealous*, and before he could give a second broadside *Zealous* was past his range. We therefore both got up to our places without injury of any sort, and were able to take up the exact positions we wished, neither ship returning a single shot.

The midshipman as well notes:

The sun's rim was just touching the horizon as our fire began. *Zealous* exactly followed *Goliah's* example, but the enemy being occupied, she furled her sails, and anchoring a little more to windward, veered into the place just left by the *Goliah*. [*Goliah* is Elliot's spelling of his ship's name all through, the sailors' usual rendering of the name.] From this moment the *Guerrier* never fired a shot, except from her stern guns; she had been practically destroyed in five minutes by her two opponents. As the *Goliah* passed her quarter the *Guerrier's* foremast fell by the deck, and five minutes after the main and mizzen fell, and also the main of the *Conquérant*. This was just as the *Orion* was passing inside the *Goliah* and the *Audacious*, coming to anchor on the inner bow of the *Conquérant*.

As the *Theseus* passed the *Goliah* in getting to her station she gave her three tremendous cheers. Returned by the *Goliah's* crew and an attempt made by the French to copy, but the effort was ridiculous, and caused shouts of laughter in our ships, loud enough to be heard by both sides. The French admitted that the enthusiastic cheers were very disheartening to them.

The *Goliath* fastened on the *Conquérant* and did not leave her until her colours—or rather her lights, for it was after dark when the duel was over—had come down in surrender, Captain Foley being materially aided by the *Audacious*. Adds Midshipman Elliot:

> The *Audacious* took possession of the second and third ships, neither the *Theseus* nor *Goliah* having a boat to swim.

After that the *Goliath* assisted the *Theseus* in engaging the *Spartiate* until that ship surrendered.

Midshipman Elliot was on the quarter-deck throughout, and was in a position to see all that was going on round him on every side. One of the men on board the *Goliath* at the Nile, John Nichol, "one of the gunner's crew" he describes himself, who went through the battle deep down in the depths of the ship, put some of his experiences in writing. There are not many such stories in existence. This is how Nichol tells his tale:

> The sun was just setting as we went into the bay, and a red and fiery sun it was. I would, if I had had my choice, been on the deck; there I would have seen what was passing, and the time would not have hung so heavy; but every man does his duty with spirit, whether his station be in the slaughter-house or in the magazine. (The seamen call the lower deck, near the mainmast, 'the slaughter-house,' as it is amidships, and the enemy aim their fire principally at the body of the ship.) My station was in the powder-magazine with the gunner. As we entered the bay we stripped to our trousers, opened our ports, cleared, and every ship we passed gave them a broadside and three cheers.
> Any information we got was from the boys and women who carried the powder. They behaved as well as the men, and got a present for their bravery from the *Grand Signior*. When the French admiral's ship blew up, the *Goliah* got such a shake we thought the after-part of her had blown up until the boys told us what it was. They brought us every now and then the cheering news of another French ship having struck, and we answered the cheers on deck with heartfelt joy.
> In the heat of the action, a shot came right into the magazine, but did no harm, as the carpenters plugged it up, and stopped the water that was rushing in. I was much indebted to the gunner's wife, who gave her husband and me a drink of wine every now and then, which lessened our fatigue much. There were some of the women wounded, and one woman belonging to

Leith died of her wounds, and was buried on a small island in the bay. One woman bore a son in the heat of the action; she belonged to Edinburgh.

When we ceased firing, I went on deck to view the state of the fleets, and an awful sight it was. The whole bay was covered with dead bodies, mangled, wounded, and scorched, not a bit of clothes on them except their trousers. There were a number of French, belonging to the French admiral's ship, the *L'Orient*, who had swam to the *Goliah,* and were cowering under her forecastle. Poor fellows! they were brought on board, and Captain Foley ordered them down to the steward's room, to get provisions and clothing.

One thing I observed in these Frenchmen quite different from anything I had before observed. In the American War, when we took a French ship, the *Duke de Chartres*, the prisoners were as merry as if they had taken us, only saying, 'Fortune de guerre—you take me today, I take you tomorrow.' Those we now had on board were thankful for our kindness, but were sullen and as downcast as if each had lost a ship of his own.

The only incidents I heard of are two. One lad who was stationed by a salt-box, on which he sat to give out cartridges, and keep the lid close—it is a trying berth—when asked for a cartridge, he gave none, yet he sat upright; his eyes were open. One of the men gave him a push; he fell all his length on the deck. There was not a blemish on his body, yet he was quite dead, and was thrown overboard. The other, a lad who had the match in his hand to fire his gun.

In the act of applying it, a shot took off his arm; it hung by a small piece of skin. The match fell to the deck. He looked to his arm, and seeing what had happened, seized the match in his left hand, and fired off the gun before he went to the cockpit to have it dressed. They were in our mess, or I might never have heard of it. Two of the mess were killed, and I knew not of it until the day after. Thus terminated the glorious first of August, the busiest night in my life.

Midshipman Elliot again mentions this interesting incident of the Nile:

What I suspect the public never knew was that the ships of our fleet were on the average 100 men short of their proper complement, which was then small, and of those on board a considerable number were foreigners or sick. In the *Goliah* we had about half a company of Austrian grenadiers (I think 50) and others of all nations.

(The Austrians were the soldiers rescued by Nelson in the last fight of his Agamemnons on May 31, 1796, the story of which has been told.)

We may break off at this point with a little story, by the way, which has to do with Midshipman Elliot personally on another occasion, as related by somebody else. In those days not many officers on board a man-of-war except the master had practical knowledge of navigation. Indeed, we are told "if a prize was taken it was a difficulty as to who to navigate her into port."

On board the *Goliath* was a young man, who had entered the Navy apparently as a "volunteer," among the ordinary seamen. He had been educated at Christ's Hospital, and had passed good examinations as a "mathemat." Getting to hear of his attainments, Captain Foley promoted the young fellow to act as "schoolmaster" and general "coach" in seamanship and navigation to the midshipmen. One day, when the *Goliath* was at sea, cruising with a squadron, the "schoolmaster" somehow fell overboard; whereupon young Elliot sprang in bravely after him, and managed to hold him up in the water—the schoolmaster could not swim—until a boat could be lowered from the ship to pick them both up. For this action the plucky young midshipman was tried by his brother-midshipmen at a gun-room court-martial, and ordered to be punished. "As there was no denial of the fact, he was found guilty of the aggravated offence of saving a schoolmaster, and sentenced to be 'cobbed.'" The sentence was duly carried out, young Elliot being stretched on his face on the table in the gun-room, and spanked with the leather sheath of a brother midshipman's dirk.

CAPTAIN SAMUEL HOOD TAKES THE FRENCH VAN SHIP

How Hood's well-trained men in the *Zealous*—the second ship in action—got to work promptly at the outset and did their part with signal success, taking the French van ship as their own prize, is best of all told by the captain; as he describes it in a private letter to his relative, Lord Hood.

The van ship of the enemy being in five fathoms water, expected the *Goliath* and *Zealous* to stick on the shoal every moment, and did not imagine we should attempt to pass within her. . . . Captain Foley, of course, intended anchoring abreast of the van ship; but his sheet-anchor (the cable being out of the stern port) not dropping the moment he wished it, (he) missed and brought up abreast of the second ship, having given the van ship his fire. I saw immediately he had failed in his intention; cut away the *Zealous'* sheet-anchor and came to in the exact situation Captain Foley intended to have taken; the van ship of the enemy having his larboard bow towards the *Zealous*, we having received very little damage, notwithstanding a fire from the whole van, island, etc., as we came in.

I commenced (such) a well-directed fire into her bow within pistol-shot a little after six that her foremast went by the board in about seven minutes, just as the sun was closing the horizon; on which the whole squadron gave three cheers; it happening before the next ship astern of me had fired a shot, and only the *Goliath* and *Zealous* engaged. And in ten minutes more her main and mizzen masts (went). At this time also went the main mast of the second ship, engaged closely by the *Goliaith* and *Audacious*; but I could not get her commander to strike for three hours, though I hailed him twenty times, and seeing he was totally cut up and only firing a stern gun now and then at the *Goliath* and *Audacious*.

At last being tired (of) firing and killing people in that way, I sent my boat on board her, and the lieutenant was allowed with the jolly-boat to hoist a light and haul it down to show his submission. From the time her foremast fell they had been driven from the upper decks by our canister and musketry; and I assure your Lordship from her bow to her larboard gangway the ports on the main deck are entirely in one, and her gunwale in that part entirely cut away, two of the main deck beams fallen on the guns in consequence. And (she) is so much cut up that we cannot move her without great detention and expense, so I fancy the admiral will destroy her. And in doing all this I have the pleasure to say the *Zealous* had only seven men materially wounded.

First-Lieutenant Webley summarizes the fight with the *Guerrier* in these words:

Captain Hood . . . placed the *Zealous* so well that in seven minutes her foremast was shot away, and in twenty she was totally dismasted, and about eight o'clock I took possession of her without the *Zealous* having lost *one man!*

Captain Hood in his letter goes on, speaking of how Nelson doubled on the French line:

> The admiral did not follow the van ship, as he was afraid he might lead the ships too near the shoals and dangerous reefs to windward, he having a very good chart of the place; and, of course, might have lost the assistance of some ships which we could ill afford, the night approaching fast. This, of course, caused some of our ships to fire into each other, the enemy being between and which could not be avoided. I am confident had I been in his situation, and so late in the evening, I should have acted the same way.

When, at noon next day, what was left of the French fleet—two line-of-battle ships, the *Guillaume Tell* of eighty-guns, and the *Généreux* of seventy-four guns with two frigates—made sail to escape, the *Zealous* tried to stop them single-handed. Hood attempted to close with the two bigger men-of-war:

> . . . . in the hope I should be able to bring them to action and disable them in such a manner as to allow our ships to come to my assistance (there being then none under sail), and that should I disable them at all they could not fetch out of the bay. I just weathered them within musket shot and obliged the *Guillaume Tell* to keep away to prevent my raking her; and, though I did them a great deal of damage, they were so well prepared as to cut every bowline, boom, topmast and standing rigging, sails, etc., away. I intended to have boarded the near frigate, but could not get the ship round for a short space of time; and when I was doing it Sir Horatio called me in by signal, seeing that I should only get disabled and not stop them with such a superior force. (He) called me in and thanked me most kindly for my conduct, on the opportunity I had of distinguishing myself, particularly on that occasion. I thought I only did my duty, and though the ship was a good deal cut in her sails and rigging, having by this last alone forty shot in the mainsail, I only had one man killed and none materially wounded.

With Nelson in the Flagship "Vanguard"

Nelson's Flag-Captain, Sir Edward Berry, of the *Vanguard*, himself tells how Nelson's own ship at the Nile took up her station and began her part in the battle.

> The *Goliath* and *Zealous* had the honour to lead inside, and to receive the first fire from the van ships of the enemy, as well as from the batteries and gunboats with which their van was strengthened. These two ships, with the *Orion*, *Audacious*, and *Theseus*, took their stations inside the enemy's line, and were immediately in close action. The *Vanguard* anchored the first on the outside of the enemy, and was opposed at within half pistol-shot to *Le Spartiate,* the third in the enemy's line. In standing in, our leading ships were unavoidably obliged to receive into their bows the whole fire of the broadside of the French line, until they could take their respective stations; and it is but justice to observe that the enemy received us with great firmness and deliberation, no colours having been hoisted on either side, nor a gun fired, until our van ships were within half gun-shot.

Another officer describes:

> The *Vanguard* steered for the *Spartiate*, the third ship of the enemy's line, already engaged from the inshore side by the *Goliath* on her larboard bow. After sustaining a raking fire from the three van ships, the *Vanguard*, at 6 h. 40 m., anchored by the stern in eight fathoms water, *outside* and distant from the *Spartiate* about 60 yards.

Captain Berry tells the story:

> At this time the necessary number of our men were employed aloft in furling sails, and on deck in hauling the braces, etc., preparatory to our casting anchor. As soon as this took place, a most animated fire was opened from the *Vanguard*, which ship covered the approach of those in the rear, which were following in a close line. The *Minotaur, Defence, Bellerophon, Majestic* . . came up in succession, and passing within hail of the *Vanguard*, took their respective stations opposed to the enemy's line. All our ships anchored by the stern, by which means the British line became inverted from van to rear.
>
> The action commenced at sunset, which was at thirty-one min.

Wounds received by Lord Nelson

His Eye in Corsica

His Belly off Cape S.t Vincent

His arm at Teneriffe

His Head in Egypt

Josumes for one War

FACSIMILE OF NELSON'S STATEMENT OF WOUNDS

past six p.m., with an ardour and vigour which it is impossible to describe. At about seven o'clock total darkness had come on; but the whole hemisphere was, with intervals, illuminated by the fire of the hostile fleets. Our ships, when darkness came on, had all hoisted their distinguishing lights by a signal from the admiral.

Before that, the *Vanguard* was in fierce fight with the powerful and well-manned antagonist it had fallen to the British flagship's lot to deal with. That was, as has been said, the *Spartiate*, which ship the *Theseus* was already attacking on the inner side of the enemy's line. Captain Miller, however, on seeing the admiral approach, quitted his opponent to find another elsewhere. The withdrawal of the *Theseus* at that moment, though, was by no means entirely an act of courtesy, of chivalrous consideration for the well-known susceptibilities of Miller's leader. There was in the captain's mind the thought that he would inevitably incur the grave risk of firing past the enemy's ship in the middle between the two British ships, his stray shots hitting and doing damage on board the *Vanguard*. Such a calamity did, in fact, happen with other ships on that night.

The *Aquilon*, for her part, while fighting the *Theseus* on one side, did her best to help the *Spartiate* against the *Vanguard* on the other, and immediately the *Vanguard* let go anchor attacked Nelson's flagship with a heavy raking fire that swept the vanguard's decks with devastating effect. The French captain swung his ship so as to be nearly across the bows of the *Vanguard*, by means of a spring on his cable—an extra cable, led out from one of the stern ports and made fast to the main cable at the bows by which the ship was anchored, enabling her, by hauling on the "spring," to be swung out at an angle to the general line. In that way the *Aquilon* was able to attack the *Vanguard* end-on and add the fire of her broadside guns to the continuous cannonading of the *Spartiate*.

So deadly was the raking fire from the *Aquilon* that the seven foremost guns in the *Vanguard* had all the men at them struck down, killed or wounded, three times over, "swept away as fast as the guns could be remanned," as is related by an eyewitness on board Nelson's ship. At another gun all the men were "shot down seven times," but fresh men were always ready to take the places of the fallen.

Fortunately for the gallant Vanguards in that part of the ship, the *Minotaur*, which anchored next beyond the flagship, compelled the

Aquilon to desist from her raking tactics and look after herself, after which the *Spartiate* was left to face the *Vanguard* as best she could unassisted.

The men at the guns of the *Spartiate*, however, were brave fellows, and took a good deal of beating. For two hours the gallant Frenchmen maintained their fight stout-heartedly, and kept their colours flying. As the *Vanguard's* log puts it, summing up two hot hours' work in one brief matter-of-fact sentence:

> 31 minutes past (6), opened our fire on the *Spartiate*, which was continued without intermission, until half past 8, when she struck to us.

The sequel is recorded in the next sentence:

> Sent Lieutenant Galwey with a party of marines to take possession of her.

Nelson was lying wounded in the bread-room adjoining the cockpit, at the time, and Captain Berry brought him the French captain's sword, which Lieutenant Galwey (the *Vanguard's* first-lieutenant) had sent back by the boat immediately on having it handed to him as he stepped on the deck of the *Spartiate*.

How Nelson was wounded over the right eye by a fragment of iron langridge—a charge made up of scraps of metal and fired like grapeshot among the men on an enemy's decks—and believed he was mortally injured, is, of course, a familiar tale as are most of the details of what took place that night in the *Vanguard's* cockpit when Nelson was taken below. This brief outline, therefore, will suffice.

In spite of his excruciating pain, Nelson, when the surgeon, on his being taken below, came hurrying to attend to him, waved the doctor aside, bidding him see first to those brought down earlier. "I will take my turn with my brave fellows," he said; and while waiting, convinced in his own mind that he had not long to live, he had a boat lowered and sent specially to fetch Captain Louis of the *Minotaur*, in order to thank him personally "before he died," as Nelson put it, for the assistance the *Minotaur* had given the *Vanguard*.

The surgeon, after dressing Nelson's wound, induced him to go and rest awhile in the bread-room, next to the cockpit; but Nelson would not remain quiet there, and sent for his secretary to take down an official dispatch. The secretary came, but was so much affected at the sight of the admiral's sufferings that he was unable to write. The

Vanguard's chaplain was sent for in his place, but he, too, seemed so unmanned that Nelson himself took the pen from him and tried, half blindly, to scrawl down a few words. As he was doing so, the news came down that one of the French ships was on fire. Nelson, forgetting his own terrible pain, stumbled up on deck again, helped by Captain Berry.

There, his first thought was for his endangered enemies, and he sent the only boat the *Vanguard* had left able to float to pick up as many as possible of the drowning Frenchmen. He remained on deck until the *Orient* blew up "with a tremendous explosion that shook the *Vanguard* to her keel." Nelson was then reluctantly persuaded to go below and lie down. His admiral's work was done. Six out of thirteen French ships had already surrendered; the French flagship had been destroyed; the remaining ships were apparently at the mercy of the victors, whatever further resistance they might make.

The first of the French ships to surrender was the luckless *Conquérant*, severely maltreated at the outset by the *Goliath* and *Theseus*, and then fastened on and finished off by Captain Davidge Gould's *Audacious*, to which ship the *Conquérant* struck her flag.

An incident by the way is this; it is one that surely is unique:

Captain Gould, apparently during the temporary cessation of firing that took place after *L'Orient* blew up, scribbled off a hasty note to Nelson, reporting the *Conquérant's* surrender, and sent it by a boat on board the Vanguard:

Audacious,
1st August, 1798.

Sir,

I have the satisfaction to tell you the French ship *Le Conquérant* has struck to the *Audacious*, and I have her in possession. The slaughter on board her is dreadful; her captain is dying. We have but one killed, but a great many wounded. Our fore and main masts are wounded, but I hope not very bad. They tell me the fore-mast is the worst. I give you joy. This is a glorious victory.

I am, with the utmost respect, yours in haste,

D. Gould.

The Battle of the Nile cost the *Vanguard* 3 officers and 27 men killed, and 7 officers and 68 men wounded: a total of 30 killed and 75 wounded.

Next morning early, before he began his official dispatch reporting the victory, Nelson, in his cabin on board the *Vanguard*, dictated his nobly worded order for a public thanksgiving to God:

> *Vanguard*,
> Off Mouth of the Nile,
> 2nd Day of August, 1798.
>
> Almighty God having blessed His Majesty's arms with victory, the admiral intends returning public thanksgiving for the same at two o'clock this day; and he recommends every ship doing the same as soon as convenient.

On board the *Vanguard* it was that Nelson received later on from Hallowell, of the *Swiftsure*, the gift of a coffin made from the mainmast of the French flagship *L'Orient*. The coffin was entirely put together out of wreckage picked up by a boat from the *Swiftsure* while floating in the sea a day or two after the battle, and was made on board by the carpenter of the ship. Every detail of it was constructed from materials which had been part of *L'Orient*. The staples, for instance, were formed from the spikes drawn from the cheeks of the mast, and when the lid was on, toggles, made similarly from *L'Orient*'s ironwork, were inserted in the staples to keep it down, so as to obviate the use of screws or nails. "I do hereby certify," wrote Hallowell, by way of attestation, on a paper that he pasted on the bottom of the coffin, "that every part of this coffin is made of the wood and iron of *L'Orient*, most of which was picked up by His Majesty's ship under my command in the Bay of Aboukir.—Ben. Hallowell." It is in that coffin, as the inner shell, that Nelson's remains rest in the tomb in St. Paul's.

The astonishment among the crew of the *Vanguard* when they saw the coffin being brought on board was long remembered by the officers. "We shall have hot work of it indeed," exclaimed one of the seamen; "you see, the admiral intends to fight till he's killed, and there he is to be buried!" On board the *Vanguard*, Nelson for a time kept the coffin standing on end, with the lid on, against the bulkhead at the back of his dinner-table chair in the main cabin; until, after some weeks, at the entreaties of Tom Allen, his Burnham Thorpe follower and personal attendant, he was prevailed on to permit it to be removed and stowed below.

In the Guildhall Museum, in London, is preserved the sword of the French admiral, second in command at the Battle of the Nile. This sword Nelson sent to the then lord mayor, and it was for a long time displayed in a place of honour in the Council Chamber. The blade is of fine workmanship, fluted and chased, and is inscribed, "*Vivre Libre ou mourir pour la Nation, la Loi, et le* ———." In the blank spot was originally the word "*Roi*," which had been erased at the Revolution. "The flag of the same French admiral (Blanquet Duchayla), together with the other trophy flags from the captured ships. Nelson sent to the Admiralty, with his original dispatch, by the Leander; but that ship being captured on the way to Gibraltar, none of those spoils ever reached England. The flag of Admiral Brueys, the French commander-in-chief at the Nile, disappeared during the burning of *L'Orient,* perishing probably in the flames. Admiral Brueys' sword lies at the bottom of Aboukir Bay, with the body of the ill-fated admiral, in or near the wreck of the blown-up French flagship.

The Captain of the "Orion" and his Men

Sir James Saumarez, one of the ablest and most distinguished of the many fine officers the Channel Islands have given to the Royal Navy, was captain of the *Orion*, as has been said. He had made his mark in the earlier part of the war as a bold and skilful frigate captain while in command of the *Crescent*—to such effect, indeed, that when, in March, 1795, Saumarez was promoted to a ship of the line, to the *Orion*, one of the best seventy-fours in the Navy, every officer and man of the *Crescent* volunteered to accompany their chief. A notable crew, too, were the *Crescent's*—half of them Guernseymen, who had come forward to follow the fortunes of a popular compatriot; half of them Devonshiremen, who, knowing of Saumarez by reputation as a dashing and successful officer, had volunteered for service under him. Taking with him as many of all ranks and ratings as he could, Saumarez found no difficulty in manning his *Orion* satisfactorily.

How the Orions did their duty at the Nile is told in the following account, written from information supplied by some of the officers:

> The batteries of the island of Bequir, or Aboukir, and the headmost ships (of the enemy) opened their fire as the leading ship approached; and they, in return, opened theirs on rounding the advanced ship of the enemy's line.
>
> The *Orion*, after giving that ship her broadside, passed round the *Zealous* and *Goliath*, and as she was passing the third ship of the enemy the French frigate *Sérieuse* approached, began to fire on her, and wounded two men. In reply to an observation of one of the officers, who proposed to return her fire immediately, Sir James said: 'Let her alone; she will get courage and

come nearer. Shorten sail!' As the *Orion* lost way by shortening sail, the frigate came up, and, when judged to be sufficiently advanced, orders were given to yaw the *Orion* and stand by the starboard guns, which were double-shotted. The moment having arrived when every gun was brought to bear, the fatal order to fire was given, when by this single but well-directed broadside, the unfortunate *Sérieuse* was not only totally dismasted, but shortly afterwards sunk, and was discovered next morning with only her quarter above water.

On discharging the fatal broadside, the helm was put hard a-starboard; but it was found that the ship would not fetch sufficiently to windward and near to the *Goliath* if she anchored by the stern. She stood on, and having given the fourth ship her starboard broadside, let go her bow anchor, and brought up on the quarter of the *Le Peuple Souverain*, which was the fifth ship, and on the bow of *Le Franklin*, the sixth ship of the enemy's line.

By the log of the *Orion*, it was forty-five minutes past six o'clock when the ship let go her anchor, and in 'tending' poured her starboard broadside into the *Franklin* and *L'Orient*. The fire was then directed on *Le Peuple Souverain*, until she cut and dropped out of line, totally dismasted and silenced.

At seven o'clock the headmost ships were dismasted; a fire-raft was observed dropping from them on the *Orion*. Her stern boat having been shot through, and the others being on the booms, it was impossible to have recourse to the usual method of towing it clear. Booms were then prepared to keep it off. As it approached, however, the current carried it about twenty-five yards clear of the ship.

About half-past eight, just as *Le Peuple Souverain*, which had been the *Orion's* opponent, had dropped to leeward, a suspicious ship was seen approaching the *Orion* in the vacant space which the vanquished one had occupied. Many on board were convinced of her being a fireship of the enemy, and Sir James was urged to allow the guns to be turned upon her. Happily, he himself had stronger doubts of her being such than those who pressed the reverse. He ordered a vigilant watch to be kept on her movements, and when the darkness dispersed she was discovered to be the *Leander*. Distinguishing lights were hoisted, and the *Orion* continued to engage *Le Franklin* from fifty minutes past six o'clock to a quarter to ten. The action was general, and kept up on both sides with perseverance and vigour, when the enemy's fire began to slacken, and the three-decker was discovered to be on fire.

At ten the firing ceased, the ship opposed to the *Orion* having surrendered; as also all the van of the enemy.

Preparations were now made to secure the ship from the effects of the expected explosion. The ports were lowered down, the magazine secured, the sails handed and water placed in various parts to extinguish whatever flames might be communicated. The unfortunate ship was now in a blaze; at half-past eleven she blew up, and the tremendous concussion was felt to the very keelsons of all the ships near her. The combatants on both sides seemed equally to feel the solemnity of this destructive scene.

A pause of at least ten minutes ensued, each side engaged in contemplating a sight so grand and terrible. The *Orion* was not far off, but being happily placed to windward, the few fiery fragments that fell in her were soon extinguished. Her vicinity to *L'Orient* was the happy means of saving the lives of fourteen of her (*e.g.*, *L'Orient's*) crew, who, trying to escape the flames, sought refuge in another element, and swam to the *Orion*, where they met a reception worthy of the humanity of the conquerors. The generous, warm-hearted sailors stripped off their jackets to cover these unfortunate men, and treated them with kindness, proving that humanity is compatible with bravery.

About the middle of the action. Sir James received a wound from a splinter, or rather the sheave from the heel of the spare top-mast on the booms, which, after killing Mr. Baird, the clerk, and wounding Mr. Miells, a midshipman, mortally, struck him on the thigh and side, when he fell into the arms of Captain Savage (of the marines), who conducted him under the half-deck, where he soon recovered from the shock it gave him; but although he acknowledged it was painful, and might in the end be serious, he could not be persuaded to leave the deck, even to have the wound examined; and the part was so much swelled and inflamed on the next day, that he was not able to leave the ship.

"A better young man I think never existed," was what Saumarez wrote to his wife, in announcing the death of the brave young midshipman Miells, the son of a Guernsey friend and neighbour. "He lived until this evening" (the evening of the day after the battle);

> .... and was the whole time perfectly resigned to his fate, saying, 'He died in a good cause.' His shoulder having been nearly carried off, and his life being despaired of, the surgeons were unwilling to put him to needless pain by amputation; but after some hours, finding he still lived, it was determined to give him a chance of recovery by removing the shattered limb. The operation was ably performed by Mr. Nepecker, the surgeon of the *Orion*, assisted by the surgeon of the *Vanguard*. The sufferer never uttered a moan, but as soon as it was over, quietly said, 'Have I not borne it well?' The tidings were instantly conveyed to his captain, whose feelings may be better imagined than described, and who could only fervently exclaim, 'Thank God!' But his joy soon received a check. Many minutes had not lapsed before he learnt that this able and promising youth had been seized with a fit of coughing and expired.

It is related:

> The *Orion* was the first to hoist the pendant at the mizzen-peak, and thereby to show an example to the fleet worthy of imitation, in returning thanks to the great Disposer of Events and Giver of all Victory for that which they had just obtained over their enemies. A discourse on this occasion was delivered by the clergyman of the *Orion*, which must have made a great and lasting impression on the hearers; but the circumstance, which is much easier to be imagined than described, of a ship's company on their knees at prayers, and offering up a most solemn thanksgiving for the Divine mercy and favour which had been so fully manifested towards them, must have excited feelings in the minds of the prisoners—the demoralized citizens of the French Republic—which had never before been known to them; and we understand that they did not fail to express their astonishment and admiration at a scene of that kind under such circumstances.

What the Captain of the "Theseus" saw and did

The *Theseus* went into the battle third ship from the head of Nelson's squadron, following the *Goliath* and *Zealous* inshore of the enemy's line at the opening of the attack. Captain Ralph Willett Miller, who commanded on board, gives a notable eyewitness's account of what took place in a letter to his wife, written a few days after the battle, entering into many remarkably interesting details. These are some of the incidents which he describes, for the most part having to do in particular with the men of his own ship.

The men of the *Theseus*, as their captain tells, began their work in this style on the French van ship, the *Guerrier*:

> In running along the enemy's line in the wake of the *Zealous* and *Goliath*, I observed their shot sweep just over us, and knowing well that at such a moment Frenchmen would not have coolness enough to change their elevation, I closed them suddenly, and running under the arch of their shot, reserved my fire, every gun being loaded with two and some with three round-shot, until I had the *Guerrier's* masts in a line, and her jib-boom about six feet clear of our rigging; we then opened with such effect that a second breath could not be drawn before her main and mizzen mast were also gone.

First-Lieutenant Hawkins says:

> We ran alongside of the *Guerrier* within seven yards of her; our first broadside carried away her main and mizzen masts. There was only one man left on her deck; he was on the starboard gangway.

Captain Miller continues:

> This was precisely at sunset, or 44 minutes past six. Then, passing between her and the *Zealous*, and so close as possible round the off-side of the *Goliath*, we anchored exactly in a line with her, and, as I have said before, abreast the *Spartiate*. The *Audacious*, having passed between the *Guerrier* and the *Conquérant*, came-to with her bower close upon the inner bow of the latter. We had not been many minutes in action with the *Spartiate* when we observed one of our ships (and soon knew her to be the *Vanguard*) place herself directly opposite to us on the outside of her. I desisted firing on her, that I might not do mischief to our friends, and directed every gun before the main-mast on the *Aquilon*, and all abaft on the *Conquérant*, giving up my proper bird to the admiral.

The captain of the *Theseus*, speaking of his nearest opponents, continues:

> The *Guerrier* and *Conquérant* made a very inefficient resistance, the latter being soon stripped of her main and mizzen masts. They continued for a considerable time to fire every now and then a gun or two, and about eight o'clock, I think, were totally silent. The *Spartiate* resisted much longer, and with serious effect, as the *Vanguard's* killed and wounded announces, who received her principal fire. Her larboard guns were fired upon us in the beginning with great quickness; but, after the admiral anchored on his starboard side, it was slow and irregular. Before or about nine o'clock she was silenced, and had also lost her main and mizzen masts; having the whole fire of the *Minotaur* on her starboard side, and, for some time, near half ours on her larboard bow.
>
> Not long after that, the fire (the third and fatal fire) on board the French flagship, *L'Orient*, attracted general attention in the *Theseus*.
>
> *L'Orient* caught fire on the poop, when the heavy cannonade from all the *Alexander's* and part of the *Swiftsure's* guns became so furious that she was soon in a blaze, displaying a most grand and awful spectacle, such as formerly would have drawn tears down the victor's cheeks; but now, pity was stifled as it rose by the remembrance of the numerous and horrid atrocities their unprincipled and bloodthirsty nation had and were committing.
>
> When she blew up, about eleven o'clock, though I endeavoured to stop the momentary cheer of the ship's company, my heart scarce felt a single pang for their fate. Indeed, all its anxiety was in a moment called forth to a degree of terror at seeing the *Alexander* on fire in several places; and a boat that was taking in a hawser, in order to warp the *Orion* further from *L'Orient*, I filled with fire-buckets, and sent instantly to her, and was putting the engine in another just returned from sounding, when I had the unspeakable happiness of seeing her get before the wind and extinguish the flames. There was now no firing, except towards the French rear, and that quite a broken, disconnected one.
>
> Just after *L'Orient* blew up, I discovered by the moonlight a dismasted frigate on our inner beam, and sent Lieutenant Brodie to take possession of her, if, on hailing, she surrendered; and, if not, to burn false fires, that we might compel her to it. The first took place, and he sent me the captain and three officers of

the *Sérieuse* frigate, which, having been severely handled by the *Orion*, had got aground and filled with water trying to escape, and all her masts gone; her crew, except thirty, had abandoned her. I, at this time, also perceived a group of the enemy's ships about a mile and a half within us, which must have moved there after the attack, and sent one of the mates to sound between us and them (the master being employed sounding with us, and examining the state of the *Sérieuse*). Being, as well as the officers and people, greatly fatigued, I was happy to snatch half an hour's sleep, from which, in a little time, I was roused by Captain Hood of the *Zealous*, who came to propose that our ships and the *Goliath* should go down to the group of ships.

The second phase of the engagement was now opening, and Captain Miller has something, too, to say of that.

We prepared for it, and were lifting our bower-anchor when an officer from the *Swiftsure* came to say the admiral wished us all to go to the assistance of the *Alexander* and *Majestic*, then exchanging an irregular fire with the enemy's rear. While we were lifting our stern-anchor for that purpose, a lieutenant of the *Alexander* came from the admiral to us, and any other ships that could renew the action, to desire us to go down to these ships, and slip our cables if necessary. All firing had now ceased about ten minutes. I therefore hove up the stern-anchor, and ran down under staysails, till I passed the *Majestic*, when we dropped our sheet-anchor; and, having run out a cable, let go our bower, so as to present our broadside to the enemy in a line with the *Alexander*, and leave a clear opening for the *Majestic* (who appeared to have suffered much) to fire through.

Adding a curious detail of that night's experience, Captain Miller relates:

My people were also so extremely jaded, that as soon as they had hove our sheet-anchor up they dropped under the capstan-bars, and were asleep in a moment in every sort of posture, having been then working at their fullest exertion, or fighting, for near twelve hours, without being able to benefit by the respite that occurred, because, while *L'Orient* was on fire, I had the ship completely sluiced, as one of our precautionary measures against fire or combustibles falling on board us when she blew up.

The *Theseus'* men had their part after that in the final episode of the Nile next day—in finishing off the remains of the French fleet.

At sunrise they exchanged a sharp cannonade with four of the French ships as these were moving farther off—the firing lasting until the French were out of range. The captain says:

> That over, we turned our whole fire upon the two line-of-battle ships that were on our quarter, and whom we had now long known to be on shore; the *Majestic* and *Alexander* firing a few shot over us at them, as the *Leander* may perhaps have done. In a short time we compelled *L'Heureux*, seventy-four, to strike her colours; and I sent Lieutenant Brodie to take possession of her, and from her to hail the other ship to strike immediately or she would else soon be involved in so much smoke and fire, that we, not being able to see her colours come down, might unintentionally destroy all on board her.

> Just as the boat got there, the *Goliath* anchored on our outer quarter and began to fire, but desisted on my hailing her; and, presently after, *Mercure*, of seventy-four guns, hauled her colours down; also as *l'Artémise*, thirty-six, after firing her guns shotted, had done just before, I sent Lieutenant Hawkins to take possession of *Mercure*, and Lieutenant Hoste of *Artémise*; the former, on a lieutenant of the *Alexander* afterwards coming, delivered her into his charge, and returned on board; and when the latter got within a cable's length of the *Artémise*, perceiving she was set on fire by a train, and that her people had abandoned her on the opposite side, he also returned on board. After burning about half an hour she blew up. This dishonourable action was not out of character for a modern Frenchman; the devil is beyond blackening.

> We were now thus situated in the *Theseus*: our mizzen-mast so badly wounded that it could bear no sail; our fore and main yards so badly wounded that I almost expected them to come down about our ears; without sail; the fore-topmast and bowsprit wounded; the fore and main sails cut to pieces, and most of the other sails much torn; nine of our main and several fore and mizzen shrouds and much of our other standing and running rigging shot away: 8 guns disabled, either from the deck being ploughed up under themselves, or carriages struck by shot, or the axle-trees breaking from the heat of the fire; and

four of them lower-deckers.

In men we were fortunate beyond anything I ever saw or heard of; for, though near 80 large shot struck our hull, and some of them through both sides, we had only 6 men killed and 31 wounded: Providence, in its goodness, seemed willing to make up to us for our heavy loss at Santa Cruz. Hawkins and myself were the only officers from whom blood was drawn, and that in a very trifling way.

Says First-Lieutenant Hawkins:

Providence was certainly very kind to us; our loss was but trifling. The poop was much shattered; and myself had one shot which knocked the plank from under us.

Once more the *Theseus* turned her attention to the four French ships she had exchanged fire with at sunrise.

The enemy was anchored again at the long range of shot, and many large boats from the shore were passing to and fro among them.

Captain Miller continues:

Hearing it was the enemy's intention to take their men out of their line-of-battle ships and set them on fire. I caused a cool and steady fire to be opened on them from our lower-deckers only, all of which, being admirably pointed by Lieutenant England, who commanded that deck, they soon drove the boats entirely away from all their ships, and doubtless hulled them frequently, particularly the *Timoléon*. The boats having abandoned them, the *Guillaume Tell*, the *Généreux*, the *Timoléon*, with the *Justice* and the *Diane* frigates, got under way, and stood out of the bay in line of battle. The *Timoléon*, being under our fire all the time, cast inshore and, after appearing to make another attempt to wear, stood directly for the shore, and, as she struck, her foremast went over the bow; the *Tonnant*, being dismasted, remained where she was. . . . I gave up all further thoughts of the *Tonnant*, except sending a boat to see if she had surrendered, which, being menaced by her guns, returned.

It was impossible for the *Theseus*, after her damages of the night, to follow the escaping French ships, who made off after a gallant effort to stop them by the *Zealous*, the only British ship able to get near.

Captain Miller goes on to say:

> In the evening I went on board the admiral, who I before knew was wounded. I found him in his cot, weak, but in good spirits, and, as I believe every captain did, received his warmest thanks, which I could return from my heart, for the promptness and gallantry of the attack. I found him naturally anxious to secure the *Tonnant* and *Timoléon*, and that the *Leander* was ordered to go down for that purpose in the morning; I told him that if there was any difficulty I would also go down in the morning, notwithstanding the state of the ship.

The *Tonnant* surrendered to the *Theseus* on Friday morning (August 3). This is how Captain Miller describes that closing event:

> Seeing the *Leander* get under way, we hove up to our best bower; sent our prisoners and their baggage, which lumbered our guns, on board the *Goliath*, and got a slip buoy on the end of the sheet cable. The *Swiftsure's* boat, returning from having been with a flag of truce to summons the *Tonnant*, informed us the answer of the captain was, that he had 1,600 men on board, and unless the admiral would give him a ship to convey them to Toulon, he would fight to the last man—a true French *gasconade*. We immediately slipped the sheet cable and hoisted our topsails, and seeing the admiral make the *Leander's* signal to engage the enemy, which must have been the moment of his receiving this French reply, we hove up our best bower and ran down directly for the *Tonnant*, with the master sounding in a boat ahead.
>
> As we cast so as to open the view of our broadside to her she hoisted true colours. When we got within a cable and a half of her, having only 25½ feet water, we let go our anchor, veered to within half a cable of her and hauled upon our spring, which was parted. It was now, however, of no consequence, as just after we came to, she allowed the *Leander's* boat, to come on board, and was soon after under English colours; the *Leander* had brought-to about two or three cables without us while we were going down. The *Timoléon*, being abandoned by her crew, was set on fire with her colours flying, and soon blew up.

The *Tonnant*, according to one account, after making a futile effort to get boats to take the remainder of her crew to Alexandria, made an attempt to get terms from the *Theseus*: equally in vain. "Your battle-flag or none!" was Captain Miller's sharp rejoinder in response to the *Tonnant's* attempt at parley by hoisting the flag of truce. The French ship's battle-flag was thereupon hoisted and formally hauled down, in token of surrender at discretion.

After that came the worthy *finale*, characteristic of a brave and God-fearing man: the holding on board the *Theseus* of a solemn service of gratitude and thanksgiving to Almighty God.

> There being no longer any enemy to contend with, we beat the retreat and solemnly returned thanks to Almighty God, through whose mercy we had been instrumental in obtaining so great and glorious a victory to His Majesty's arms; and I believe from a body of men more fervent gratitude never mingled in prayer. I had desired the chaplain to introduce a prayer for the slain, which was attended to with a degree of feeling that could not but delight every good heart. Previous to the public service, I had returned my own thanks to the officers and ship's company for their gallantry and good conduct; and, observing to them that our business was not finished till the prizes were fit for sea, exhorted them to obtain as much credit by their work as by their courage.

HOW THE "BILLY RUFF'NS" TACKLED MIGHTY "L'ORIENT"

The most ferocious fighting of all that night took place in the terrific duel between the famous *Billy Ruff'n* and the French flagship, *L'Orient*. It was fought out broadside to broadside from first to last, and carried through to a finish practically for the gallant British two-decker.

Captain Darby, in the *Bellerophon*, followed the *Defence* along the enemy's line into the battle. He came up a few minutes after seven, when it was nearly dark. Even as the *Bellerophon* neared the firing line, it had become thick from the cannon smoke of the ships engaged, which hung heavily over the water as the evening breeze began to drop. In the gathering gloom it was not easy for the Bellerophons to see what was in front of them. They stood on, passing round the *Defence*, to find that the most formidable task of all had fallen to their lot. The post of honour above all, perhaps, it was, offering the noblest of opportunities for distinction; but for a small third-rate, a small two-decker, it was a post of extreme peril. The *Ruff'n's* station was to be close to where the giant French flagship lay anchored, the huge one hundred and twenty-gun first-rate and three-decker, *L'Orient*.

Captain Darby was an Irishman, as bold and daring an officer as any, and the hot corner well suited with his mood. His fighting blood was up, and he gladly accepted the offer made him by the fortune of war, heading in his ship for his destined opponent with cheerful alacrity. At the same time, though, he was a man of common sense, and knew his business. Nelson, he was well aware, would never forgive a captain who sacrificed the lives of his men unnecessarily. Captain Darby had no idea of exposing his brave Bellerophons to more danger than he must. Nearing his antagonist to within a ship's length of the *Orient*, he let go anchor at the right moment, dropping it to take up a point of vantage on the bow of the three-decker.

But the anchor failed to hold; it dragged on the sandy bottom, and failed to bring up the ship. Before the impetus with which the *Bellerophon* was moving through the water could be checked, the ship had forged ahead until she came exactly opposite to *L'Orient*, bringing-to immediately facing the heavily armed triple batteries of the French giant.

The misadventure had immediate and well-nigh disastrous consequences. The French captain of *L'Orient*, Casabianca, the father of the "boy" who "stood on the burning deck," was quick to make the most of his opportunity. As the *Bellerophon* was in the act of coming to a standstill alongside, in quick succession he discharged into her two terrific broadsides. The British two-decker, on her side, had not yet had the chance of firing her first gun.

Fearful was the havoc that the crashing discharge made throughout the British ship; murderous its slaughter. Eight of the *Bellerophon's* guns were disabled, dismounted, and put out of action at one blow. Between sixty and seventy men were killed outright or badly wounded. Captain Darby was struck down on the quarter-deck with a bad wound in the head, and was carried to the cockpit stunned and bleeding. Lieutenant Daniell, the first-lieutenant, was severely gashed by a splinter, but the gallant fellow had the wound tied up on the spot, and bravely stayed at his post on deck. Lieutenant Lander, the second-lieutenant, badly wounded in like manner, also pluckily kept the deck at his post. The fourth-lieutenant, John Hadaway, struck down by a cannon-ball, had to be taken below to the surgeon. Lieutenant George Jolliffe, the fifth-lieutenant, was killed outright, as was also one of the senior midshipmen, Mr. Thomas Ellison. Mr. Edward Kirby, the master; the boatswain, Mr. Chapman; a midshipman, Mr. Nicholas Betson; and

Captain John Hopkins, of the marines, were also among the casualties—all struck down by those first two broadsides from *L'Orient*, two concentrated discharges from sixty cannon fired within fifteen yards.

There was not a moment's hesitation, though, no hanging back, no shrinking, among the gallant fellows who on that night manned the heroic *Billy Ruff'n*. First-Lieutenant Daniell, with his wound hastily bandaged, took Captain Darby's place on the quarter-deck, and gave orders to open fire. The two ships had already swung close together until the *Bellerophon's* gun-muzzles almost touched the planking of the three-decker's sides. They "came so close as almost to touch (*presque toucher*)," were the words used by Rear-Admiral Gantheaume, the French Captain of the Fleet (who was on board *L'Orient*, and afterwards escaped on shore), in his official report on the battle to Bonaparte at Cairo. Small ship as the *Bellerophon* was—her upper decks were twelve feet lower than those of *L'Orient*—the splendid *Bellerophon* stood up squarely to her antagonist, undauntedly bearing her heavy "punishment," striking back her hardest, replying with broadside after broadside into the ports of the French flagship as fast as the guns could be fired.

That was the case with the men in the batteries below.

On deck, on the forecastle, quarter-deck, and poop, they had to fight with small-arms as well; with muskets and pistols. The officers and marines and small-arms men—sailors using muskets—had a fierce fight with the French soldiers on *L'Orient's* deck, infantrymen (mostly of the 69th Demi-Brigade), and also with the French admiral and several of his staff officers. Admiral Brueys, Rear-Admiral Gantheaume, Captain Casabianca, Midshipman Casabianca, his son, and other officers, we are told, all hastened up to *L'Orient's* poop as the *Bellerophon* closed alongside, from there to fire down on her decks with hand weapons. In that fierce set-to at the outset Admiral Brueys received his first wounds that night—two bullet-wounds, one in the face and the second in the left hand. The brave man, though, would not turn away and go and have the wounds seen to. He continued firing off his pistols from the poop, all the time "trying to stanch the blood with his handkerchief."

First-Lieutenant Daniell met his death within the first half-hour. A cannon-ball shot off his right leg, and then, as he was being carried below to the cockpit in the arms of one of the seamen, a grape-shot struck him in the back, killing him, and at the same time the man who was carrying him. Lieutenant Lander, sent for from the lower-deck where he was in charge of the *Bellerophon's* heavy batteries, came up and took command of the ship.

Towards eight o'clock, by which time the Bellerophons had been upwards of three-quarters of an hour in hot action, the mizzen-mast, shot through close to the deck, of a sudden came down with a crash. A second misadventure, with even more disastrous results for some of those on board, came about just a quarter of an hour afterwards. The heavy main-mast, with its ponderous top-hamper of spars and sails and rigging, gave way without warning, and collapsed bodily; shot through, like the mizzen, close above the deck. It toppled over and came crashing down, falling lengthways, smashing all the ship's boats except one, with the wreckage lying all along the starboard gangway and across the forecastle.

All the *Bellerophon's* guns there were put out of action at a blow, and many men fighting the guns were struck down under the tangled mass of splintered wood and torn canvas and cordage. The fall of the main-mast killed Lieutenant Lander. It knocked him down, crushed and mangled, as he was in the act of shouting an order from the gangway through his speaking-trumpet.

Thus, within an hour, three officers successively in command of the *Bellerophon* had fallen.

The third-lieutenant, Robert Cathcart, had now to take charge, called up to the quarter-deck from superintending the guns on the main-deck. Captain Darby had regained consciousness, and his wound had been dressed, but he was not yet in a fit condition to leave the cockpit and resume duty.

As Lieutenant Cathcart came up to take command a fire broke out on board the *Bellerophon*. It was caused by an incendiary projectile flung in through one of the ports of the *Bellerophon* on to the lower-deck. Fortunately, the fire was quickly got under control, as was a second outbreak elsewhere on board a few minutes later. At that moment, too, a fire broke out on board *L'Orient*, on the upper deck amidships. One of the ship's boats, which were kept stacked there with the spare spars, caught fire and blazed up. Captain Casabianca himself rushed to the spot with a number of men, and had the blazing boat hauled across to the ship's side—the farther side, where as yet no enemy had attacked—and let drop, a mass of flames, into the sea.

Undauntedly the stubborn Bellerophons fought on—defiantly, doggedly—without slackening or relaxing their energies for an instant. They were plainly having the worst of it, for *L'Orient*, so far, seemed, outwardly at any rate, not greatly damaged in the encounter. Her masts and spars all stood, hardly injured, practically intact; no sign of weakening was apparent in the furious cannonading that burst in continuous sheets of flame from her triple row of ports, beating down a hell-fire without ceasing. The French weight of metal—the deadweight of the mass of cannon-balls hurled into the *Bellerophon* at every discharge of the heavy guns on *L'Orient's* lower-deck alone, leaving out of account her tiers of guns on the decks above—by itself exceeded the weight of the *Bellerophon's* entire broadside from every gun and carronade mounted on board the British ship. The *Bellerophon's* heaviest gun was a 32-pounder, fourteen of them on one broadside; on *L'Orient's* lower-deck were sixteen 42-pounders. Elsewhere on board the Bellerophons had to fight with fourteen 18-pounders against seventeen 28-pounders, and seventeen 12- and 9-pounders and carronades against twenty-seven 14- and 10-pounders.

Regardless of the terrible odds, they manfully stood up to the *feu d'enfer* for nearly an hour and a half; and, meanwhile, other French ships lying near *L'Orient*, the flagship's supporters ahead and astern (two big eighty-gun ships, the *Franklin* and *Tonnant*), persistently kept firing at them into their bows and stern.

Terrible was the scene of devastation on board the heroically fought British seventy-four.

> Let every man picture to himself this frightful carnage taking place in a space of less than a hundred yards square. Let him consider that the slain did not all die suddenly, nor by one manner of death; that some perished by steel, some by shot, some by water; that some were crushed and mangled by heavy weights; some trampled upon; some dashed to atoms by fiery explosions, and that this destruction was endured without shrinking.

So Napier writes of the horrors at the storming of the breach at Badajoz. His words might well apply to some of the things that happened that night on the decks of the *Bellerophon*.

> At one gun, every one of the fourteen men manning it was struck down, six of them killed on the spot, by a 42-pounder shot from *L'Orient*, which smashed into the upper part of the muzzle as the gun was being run out, shattering it, down to the trunnions, into fragments that acted like a bombshell. At another gun four men were killed outright by a similar shot, which crumpled up the muzzle in fragments, and jammed the

gun almost to the chamber.

No help was available for the Bellerophons from any of their friends in the squadron—had it indeed been possible, in the obscurity of a night battle, for their desperate position to be known on board any of the *Bellerophon's* consorts. As the fact, the nearest one of Nelson's ships at that moment was in almost as serious a case, almost as hard pressed. That was the *Majestic*, fiercely fighting just then at close quarters with one of the French eighty-gun-ships and two seventy-fours.

Never, perhaps, did the French fight harder in any sea-battle than they did on the night of the Battle of the Nile. Nor, too, did the crew of any French man-of-war, perhaps, fight more fiercely than did Admiral Brueys' men on board *L'Orient* in their duel with the Bellerophons on that night.

But all that heroic endurance could do for Darby's crew was to be of no avail. Unless help came, the *Bellerophon's* duel could have but one end. To surrender was, of course, unthinkable.

The end came between half-past eight and nine o'clock, a few minutes before the hour.

"Overwhelmed, but not subdued," as the historian Alison describes, "a glorious monument of unconquerable valour," the *Bellerophon* had to withdraw from the fight. She was, all the same, not beaten off at the last. The reason was quite otherwise. A second fire had broken out on board *L'Orient*, and it threatened to spread to the *Bellerophon*, lying close alongside, with sides almost touching. And, too, at the same time the *Bellerophon* herself was on fire in three different parts of the ship. These fires, as before, were got under control promptly; that on board *L'Orient* was more serious. "At 9," says the *Bellerophon's* log, "observing our antagonist on fire on the middle gun-deck, cut the stern-cable and ware clear of her by loosing the sprit-sail."

One of the midshipmen it actually was—John Hindmarsh by name, a lad of fourteen—who gave the order to sheer off. Lieutenant Cathcart was below at the moment, it would appear, otherwise occupied, and the midshipman was in charge on deck. "Thinking the fire in *L'Orient* would spread to the *Bellerophon*, he got some hands and cut her cable, and then had the sprit-sail set." Captain Darby, who was by now sufficiently recovered to return on deck, "came up immediately afterwards and approved of what had been done." The *Bellerophon*, however, had finished her work for that battle; as the ship was slowly moving away the foremast came down, her last mast remaining. The only thing to be done after that was to rig a jury-sail, as best might be managed, on the stumps of the masts, and let the ship drift away before the wind.

Midshipman Hindmarsh, as we are told, had been wounded earlier that night, "having received a blow on the forehead which later on cost him the loss of an eye," but the heroic lad refused to leave his post. For his plucky assumption of responsibility and prompt action in cutting the ship clear at so critical a moment the boy was publicly thanked on the quarter-deck by Nelson himself three days after the battle, when Nelson came on board the Bellerophon to congratulate Captain Darby and his officers and men with his own lips on the magnificent manner in which they had upheld the honour of the flag. In his address to the men, Nelson laid stress on what young Hindmarsh had done, and before everybody handed him his lieutenant's commission.

Nor, for his part, was Captain Darby backward. He introduced the boy to all the captains of the squadron when they came on board, during the week after the battle, to congratulate their brother captain—as the "Band of Brothers" nobly did—for the heroism of his ship's fight. The only one of them who could not come, Troubridge, unable to leave the half-wrecked *Culloden* during her repairs, wrote this instead to Captain Darby: "I envy you the magnificent conduct of the *Bellerophon*."

Nelson himself, in the duplicate of his official dispatch to Earl St. Vincent (the original, of course, was captured on board the *Leander*), published in the *London Gazette Extraordinary* of October 2, said this:

> The undaunted magnanimity with which the *Bellerophon* was placed alongside *L'Orient* excited at the moment the highest admiration, and the perseverance with which she retained her situation must ever be the theme of eulogium with every officer and man in the British squadron.

The Bellerophons, however, although they had done their work in the battle, had yet to meet experiences.

First, as they drifted slowly to the eastward, across Aboukir Bay, they had to run the gauntlet of the French rear ships, three eighty-gunships and three seventy-fours. The moon was rising by now, and gave sufficient light to show up the ship to the enemy as she passed by, though it was difficult to tell whether the dismantled wreck passing was a French or British ship. Everything above the deck practically, even the ensign staff, had been shot away. The four lanterns of the "distinguishing lights" had come down with the masts. Some of the French captains made up their minds that the strange vessel must be an enemy and fired at her. Others let her go by. Not a shot in reply came from the Bellerophons, fully occupied in getting jury-sails on the ship and attending to their most urgent damages.

Admiral Villeneuve, on board the *Guillaume Tell,* allowed the mysterious stranger to pass by quite close without firing at all. At first, as he said, he mistook the vessel for a dismasted French ship. But somebody on board had doubts about it, and, just as the *Bellerophon* was disappearing in the darkness, a few random shots were sent after her, none of which hit. The *Généreux,* the last ship in the French line, fired three or four shots as the drifting hulk was passing abreast of her. Getting no reply-fire, they concluded on board that the vessel had surrendered and a boat was hoisted out to take possession. The Frenchmen were so slow about it, however, that the boat was not in the water until after the *Bellerophon* had disappeared astern in the darkness, and on second thoughts it was considered better not to risk a possible mistake, and the taking prisoners of the boat's crew alongside in consequence.

That, though, was not all. After getting past the French, Captain Darby and his men had to meet a more serious danger still from one of their own friends—they narrowly escaped being sent to the bottom by another of Nelson's ships. As the dismasted hull was slowly drifting along, just distinguishable in the moonlight, it crossed the bows of the belated *Swiftsure,* at that moment hastening forward to take part in the battle. The *Swiftsure's* men at once, assuming the nearing vessel to be an enemy, quickly trained their guns on her. They were on the verge of opening fire, all impatiently awaiting the captain's word, when, providentially, something raised a doubt in Captain Hallowell's mind about the nationality of the strange ship. At the very last moment, just as the order to open fire was on his lips, a sudden thought caused Hallowell to pause. Intently examining the strange ship with his night-glasses, he made out that her sails, as they lay heaped amid the wreckage all over the deck, had, before they came down, all been loose.

That discovery made Captain Hallowell pause. The French ships were all at anchor; they had been so for some time past, and would have their sails furled and lashed fast. Before he gave the fatal order, the captain of the *Swiftsure* hailed across the water: "What ship is that?"

The answer—to Captain Hallowell's inexpressible relief—came back: "*Bellerophon,* going out of action disabled!"

Well might the *Swiftsure's* men give vent to a "loud sigh of relief"—as we are told they did. "Thank God we waited!" exclaimed they, one and all. After that, giving the gallant "Billy Ruff'ns" three ringing cheers, the *Swiftsure* passed on to anchor with the *Alexander*, and take up the fight with *L'Orient* where the *Bellerophon* had left it.

The *Bellerophon* continued to keep steerage way, under such sail as the ship could make. As soon as he was clear of the last of the French ships, Captain Darby tried to anchor, but it proved impossible. It was found that every one of their cables, ranged in the tiers of the hold, had been rendered unserviceable by *L'Orient's* shot. So they had to drift on, getting farther and farther from the battle, while the tired survivors of the crew set to work to splice together some of the least damaged lengths of cable.

They witnessed the fate of their late antagonist from on board the *Bellerophon* before they had got very far across the Bay. A tremendous glare and blaze suddenly began to show, coming from towards the rear of where the battle was still raging fiercely. What ship was on fire, whether it was friend or enemy, it was, of course, impossible for them to tell. And in their disabled and distressed condition little could be attempted in helping to save life; but all that was possible was done. The only boat the *Bellerophon* had left able to float was at once lowered and sent to row back as near as might be to the burning vessel, to pick up any men in the water that they could. The boat succeeded in rescuing two Frenchmen, found after the explosion clinging to a spar.

Drifting on slowly all night, it was not until the general firing had ceased, between three and four in the morning, that the *Bellerophons* were at last able to bring the ship up, with the only anchor they had left and a damaged cable spliced temporarily, in seven fathoms water, six miles from the battle.

They were, though, not to be left in quietude. Their ensign had been nailed to the stump of the mizzen-mast before they quitted the fighting. It now caught the eye of Admiral Villeneuve, looking round when daylight came to see what ships of his fleet yet remained untaken. At the rear of the French line with him were three French men-of-war which had not yet been seriously engaged. Villeneuve, catching sight of the *Bellerophon* away to leeward, sent off the French forty-gun frigate *Justice* to cross the bay and enforce the surrender of that apparently helplessly disabled British ship. But Captain Darby and his Bellerophons were not the men to yield however hopeless might appear their state.

The French frigate approached between seven and eight in the morning. It was just as the chaplain of the *Bellerophon*, with as many as could be got together of the survivors of the night, all standing round him bare-headed on the blood-stained upper-deck, was reading the burial service previous to the *Bellerophon's* dead being committed to the deep. For the moment no British ship was to be seen on the move to assist them. But they did not lose their heads. The service was solemnly and calmly brought to its close, and the bodies of the gallant dead were launched overboard to their final resting-place. All was done decently, reverently, and in order. Then the scene abruptly changed. Captain Darby once again gave the word to beat to quarters and to man the guns—all that were left serviceable—ready to fight on both sides of the ship. Sixteen guns were found to be completely disabled, but the rest were quickly manned, and once more the tired crew stood at their posts, prepared to deal with their oncoming antagonist.

It proved, however, happily not necessary to open fire. Nelson, from the *Vanguard's* quarter-deck, had marked Villeneuve's move. Before the *Justice* had quite got within range, one of the British seventy-fours from the squadron, Hood's *Zealous*, was seen to be following in the track of the French frigate, and on observing that the *Justice* turned away to see after herself.

Such was the end for the "Billy Ruff ns" of their part of the Nile. Their killed and wounded were officially returned at 197 officers and men (49 killed and 148 wounded) out of a total ship's company of 571, who, on the evening before, had gone into the battle.

THE BRITISH CAPTAIN WHO FELL AT THE NILE

One of Nelson's captains lost his life at the Battle of the Nile—the only officer of rank on the British side who fell in the action. He was the captain of the *Majestic*, Captain George Blagdon Westcott, the son of a baker of Honiton, in Devonshire, as has been said, whose abilities had raised him to post-rank. He had commanded the *Majestic* for the past four years. Captain Westcott brought his ship into action, the tenth from the van of Nelson's squadron, next in station to the heroic *Bellerophon*. Taking up their berths alongside the enemy in inverted order as the squadron did, the *Majestic* finally found herself in the forefront of the British fighting-line on the outer side, with three French ships firing on her, two of them seventy-fours—the *Heureux* and the *Mercure*—also a formidable 80-gun ship, the *Tonnant*.

The Majestics met with hard fortune at the outset. Relates an officer on board another ship in the squadron:

> The *Majestic*, whether owing to the thickness of the smoke at the shutting in of the evening, or that her stern-cable did not bring her up in time, ran her jibboom into the main rigging of *L'Heureux*, ninth (French) ship, and remained a long time in that unfortunate position suffering greatly: poor Westcott was almost the first that fell, being killed by a musket-ball in the neck.

Held fast and interlocked closely with the enemy's ship, the captain of which made several desperate attempts to board, the *Majestic*, in spite of every effort that her men made, remained held fast, unable to get clear, suffering terribly meanwhile. It was during this close-quarter fight, while the French soldiers on board the *Mercure* scoured her upper decks with musketry, that Captain Westcott fell, struck down dead by a bullet.

> She lay in that position for one hour, able to make use of but few guns, and the *Tonnant* firing into her quarter with her stern-chase, in addition to such guns as *L'Heureux* could bring to bear.

But without flinching the gallant Majestics stout-heartedly maintained the contest. Their brave first-lieutenant, Robert Cuthbert, worthily and well filled his captain's place, and carried on an exceptionally well-fought fight. "The loss," says the captain of another ship, referring to Captain Westcott's death in a letter, "was not felt. Her first-lieutenant, Cuthbert (who was in the *Montagu* in the West Indies), fought the *Majestic* most gallantly during the remainder of the action, as she had commenced."

When at length the *Majestic* got free, they first turned savagely on the *Mercure* and paid off their score against that antagonist with interest.

> She got disentangled, and brought her broadside to bear on the starboard bow of the *Mercure*, the tenth ship, on whom she took a severe revenge; having laid that bow almost open, she also had only a foremast standing at daylight.

The *Heureux*, meanwhile, had been keeping up a sharp fire on the *Majestic*, and all the time, also, Lieutenant Cuthbert and his men had to carry on a fight, within musket-shot range, with their big antagonist, the powerful 80-gun ship *Tonnant*, "an opponent that, although nominally a two-decker, was more than a match for a British 98." The men of the *Majestic* were soon engaging the *Tonnant* at closer quarters as their principal opponent, though still having to hold in check the incessant cannonading of the *Mercure*. The fierce duel went on without slackening, while *L'Orient* lay blazing nearby, the gunners on both sides pointing their guns by the glare of the flames. And after the French flagship blew up the fight went on, the *Majestic* being aided to some extent at that stage by the *Alexander* and the *Swiftsure*, which two ships on coming into action had taken up their positions not far off.

From ten o'clock until nearly three in the morning the Majestic and *Tonnant* continued to fire into one another as fast as ammunition could be brought to the guns. For four of the five hours the *Mercure* lent her assistance to the *Tonnant*—until two o'clock, when all three of the *Mercure's* masts came down and that enemy drifted off. The *Tonnant* was dismasted almost at the same moment, but she remained where she was and still maintained the battle. As the *Majestic's* log records:

> At 2 the ship on our starboard quarter left us, dismasted. A ship that was engaging us on the larboard beam—masts went by the board."

The Majestics turn to be dismasted came an hour later: "At 3, our main and mizzen masts went by the board." That put the *Majestic hors-de-combat* for the time being. Her fire had to cease until the wreckage could be cleared away—an hour's hard work.

> Left off firing. Employed cutting away the wreck. At a quarter past four, having got clear of the wreck, began action again.

So says the log.

The renewed battle lasted for two hours and a quarter, until half-past six, being mostly a long-range cannonade with the ships at the rear of the French line who had taken little or no part in the night battle. The *Tonnant* had shifted her berth by then, and had been towed away by her boats to gain the protection of the rear ships.

This was the appearance of the enemy when the *Majestic* finally ceased action, as the master witnessed the scene from on board, and recorded roughly in the log:

> At half-past six left off firing, 9 of the French ships having struck, 7 of which were dismasted. One frigate sunk. Another

frigate, after striking her colours, the crew left her in their boats and set fire to her, which soon blew up. One French ship run on shore with her colours (flying). The crew left her and set fire to her, which soon blew up also.

The captain's funeral took place close to the spot where his ship had fought, on the afternoon of the day following the battle. To quote the log again:

> At 4 p.m. committed the body of the deceased Captain Westcott to the deep, and fired 20 minute guns. Read to the ship's company Admiral Nelson's thanks for their gallant behaviour during the action, and Lieutenant Robert Cuthbert's commission to act as commander after the death of Captain Westcott.

Nelson sent Lieutenant Cuthbert his commander's commission, as a reward for the splendid manner in which he had done his duty, wording his letter in these words:

> In consequence of your gallant conduct in commanding His Majesty's ship *Majestic*, after the death of the brave Captain Westcott, you are therefore to act as commander of the *Majestic* until further orders.
> Given on board His Majesty's ship the *Vanguard*, off the mouth of the Nile, 2nd of August, 1798.
>
> Horatio Nelson.

In killed and wounded the *Majestic's* loss at the Battle of the Nile was the heaviest of all in the British fleet, next after the terrible casualty roll of the *Bellerophon*—194 officers and men.

A national monument was erected in St. Paul's, by vote of Parliament, to the memory of Captain Westcott, and he has also a memorial in his native town of Honiton in Devonshire. At Honiton, later on, Nelson himself, when visiting the West Country during his stay on shore at the time of the Peace of Amiens, presented his own medal for the Nile to the widow of his brave companion in arms. Having to stop for a night at an inn in the little town, he sent an invitation to the widow and daughter of Captain Westcott to breakfast with him.

During the breakfast he asked Mrs. Westcott if she had received the medal to which her husband would have been entitled had he lived. On her replying that none had been sent her. Nelson at once took off the gold medal for the Nile which he was wearing and handed it to her. "There," said he, "you will not value this medal the less because

Nelson has worn it." The medal is now in the possession of a descendant of Captain Westcott. Nelson, also, before leaving the town, paid a special visit to the aged mother of his captain, a woman then in very humble circumstances; showing her, we are told, every attention, and treating her with the utmost respect and deference, speaking to her also about her dead son in that tender, affectionate manner which was so peculiarly Nelson's own.

IN THE LAST HOUR OF THE FRENCH FLAGSHIP

Three men-of-war had their part in settling the fate of the French flagship at the Nile—the *Swiftsure*, Captain Ben Hallowell; the *Alexander*, Captain Alexander John Ball; and the *Leander*, Captain Thomas Boulden Thompson, The chaplain of the *Swiftsure*, the Rev. Cooper Willyams, in his narrative of the battle, tells this of the terrible episode, as he himself witnessed it from on board his ship.

Speaking of his ship's entry into the battle the chaplain says:

The *Alexander* and *Swiftsure* now came in for their share of glory. Having been . . . prevented assisting at the commencement of the battle, by bearing down to reconnoitre Alexandria, and afterwards being obliged to alter their course to avoid the shoal that had proved so fatal to the *Culloden*, it was eight o'clock before they came into action, and total darkness had enveloped the combatants for some time, which was dispelled only by the frequent flashes from their guns; the volumes of smoke now rolling down the line from the fierce fire of those engaged to windward rendered it extremely difficult for the rest of the British ships who came in last to take their station: it was scarcely possible to distinguish friend from foe.

The two ships, indeed, owed their preservation, and that they were able to take part in the battle, to the disaster that crippled the *Culloden*, astern of which they had been following with all sail set. The "frantic waving of a signal lantern" warned them of danger close ahead just in time.

Captain Troubridge says in a letter to Lord St. Vincent:

The misfortune befell the *Culloden* just as I got within gun-shot of the enemy. As we had no knowledge of the place, and the soundings continued regular as we stood in, I did not conceive the smallest danger; the man at the head calling out eleven fathom when she struck. The only consolation I have to support me in this cruel case is that I had just time to make the signal to the *Swiftsure* and *Alexander*, which saved them, or they must inevitably have been lost, as they would have been farther on the reef from their hauling considerably within me.

Realizing the situation and state of the battle, as it were intuitively, Captains Ball and Hallowell took their way into action and placed their ships just where their services were most needed. Chaplain Willyams relates:

> At three minutes past eight o'clock the *Swiftsure* anchored, taking the place that had before been occupied by the *Bellerophon*, and two minutes after began a steady and well-directed fire on the quarter of the *Franklin* and bow of *L'Orient*. At the same instant the *Alexander* passed under the stern of the French admiral, and anchored withinside on his larboard quarter, raking him and keeping up a severe fire of musketry on his decks. The last ship which entered the bloody conflict was the *Leander*. Captain Thompson . . . took his station with great judgment athwart-hawse of the *Franklin*, by which manoeuvre he was enabled to do considerable damage to the enemy without exposing his own ship to the greatest danger.
> In the van four of the French ships had already struck their colours to the British flag. The battle now raged chiefly in the centre. The *Franklin*, *L'Orient*, *Tonnant*, and *Heureux* were in hot action, making every exertion to recover the glory that had been lost by their comrades.

Then came about the catastrophe:

> At three minutes past nine o'clock a fire was observed to have broken out in the cabin of *L'Orient;* to that point Captain Hallowell ordered as many guns as could be spared from firing on the *Franklin* to be directed, and, at the same time, that Captain Allen, of the marines, should throw in the whole fire of his musketry into the enemy's quarter, while the *Alexander*, on the other side, was keeping up an incessant shower of shot to the same point.
> It was a painful but imperative duty, as the enemy was still unsubdued and there was no alternative.

In those terms another officer characterizes the measures that Captain Hallowell, one of the most generous-hearted and humane of men by nature, felt himself compelled to take.

At the same time, as we are also told, where resistance had ceased, every effort was made on board to save life.

> The men of the *Swiftsure* ... did all they could to rescue those of the crew who had committed themselves to the waves before the explosion, ropes, spars, gratings, everything buoyant, being flung to the men, and every endeavour made to save life.

A terrible scene, indeed, was that *sauve qui peut* effort on board the French flagship. Mr. Willyams says:

> Several of the officers and men seeing the impracticability of extinguishing the fire, which had now extended itself along the upper-decks and was flaming up the masts, jumped overboard, some supporting themselves on spars and pieces of wreck, others swimming with all their might to escape the dreaded catastrophe. Shot flying in all directions dashed many of them to pieces; others were picked up by boats of the fleet, or dragged into the lower ports of the nearest ships. The British sailors humanely stretched forth their hands to save a fallen enemy, though the battle at that moment raged with uncontrolled fury. The *Swiftsure*, that was anchored within half-pistol shot of the larboard bow of *L'Orient*, saved the lives of the commissary, first lieutenant, and ten men, who were drawn out of the water into the lower-deck ports during the hottest part of the action.

How the French first-lieutenant of *L'Orient* made his entry on board the *Swiftsure* is a curious little story. He swam across to the ship, clambered up her side, and presented himself on the quarter-deck, stark naked but with his cocked-hat on. Captain Hallowell, taken aback at the dripping apparition, could only exclaim: "Who the deuce are you, sir?"

"*Je suis de l'Orient, monsieur*," was the reply. Berthelot, as the French lieutenant was named, then told an extraordinary story of his adventure.

He had been quartered, he said, on the lower-deck of *L'Orient*, and had stayed there with his men, working at their guns "until the planking of the deck overhead was actually seen to be on fire." Then the lieutenant stripped and jumped overboard. In the water he suddenly bethought him that, even if he were observed by the English, he would not be recognized as an officer, and might be left to drown.

He turned back and swam to *L'Orient* again, then a blazing mass of flames from stem to stern, some five minutes before the explosion. He climbed in at a lower-deck port, groped his way through the smoke, all along the charred and burning deck, and so got to where he had taken off his clothes. Then, having got possession again of his cocked-hat, he jumped overboard once more, and swam to the nearest British ship, the *Swiftsure*.

Meanwhile the anxiously awaited moment of the blowing up of the French flagship, when the flames should reach the powder-magazine, was fast approaching. It was anticipated with very grave anxiety on board the British ships in the immediate neighbourhood of *L'Orient*. As our chaplain friend tells:

> The situation of the *Alexander* and *Swiftsure* was perilous in the extreme. The expected explosion of such a ship as *L'Orient* was to be dreaded, as involving all around in certain destruction. Captain Hallowell, however, determined not to move from his devoted station, though repeatedly urged to do so. He perceived the advantage he possessed of being to windward of the burning ship.

On seeing his ill-fated enemy hopelessly ablaze. Captain Hallowell ceased firing:

> All the ports were made fast and the hatchways closed, while a number of firemen with buckets of water were held in readiness."

On board the *Alexander*, to be ready for the explosion, every precaution was taken in like manner so as to safeguard the ship from being set on fire.

> All the shrouds and sails of the ship, not absolutely necessary for its immediate management were thoroughly wetted and so rolled up that they were as hard and as little inflammable as so many solid cylinders of wood. Every sailor had his appropriate place and function, and a certain number were appointed as firemen, whose duty it was to be on the watch if any part of the vessel should take fire, and to these men exclusively the charge of extinguishing it was committed.

So Coleridge the poet relates from what Captain Ball afterwards told him at Malta, where Coleridge for a time acted as Ball's secretary.

Mr. Peter Bruff, the master of the *Orion*, whose ship was one of the nearest to the doomed *L'Orient*, makes this note in his log:

> The fire having communicated fore and aft of the three-deck ship, secured the magazine, lowered down the ports, handed the sails, expecting every moment she would blow up.

Remarks Mr. Brodie of the *Theseus*, in the log of that ship:

> Observed the French admiral catch fire and burn with great rapidity sluiced the ship with water, and sent an additional quantity into the tops. Employed getting a hawser into the boats to bring to the *Orion*, to haul her farther ahead from *L'Orient*. An officer came alongside to request our assistance, but meanwhile, before the boat put off, the *Orient* blew up and set the *Alexander* on fire, to whom we sent our boat with fire-buckets, and shortly had the fire extinguished."

As recorded in the log of a third ship by Mr. Lawson, the master of the *Alexander:*

> With the explosion of the enemy's ship our jib and main-royal was set on fire; by cutting away the jib-boom and heaving the royal overboard, the fire was luckily extinguished. Served to the French prisoners saved from *L'Orient* when blown up, and came on board naked, shirts 28, trousers 28 pairs.

The proximity of the *Swiftsure* to *L'Orient* at the moment of the blowing-up saved that ship from serious harm.

> The explosion shook the *Swiftsure* to her keelson, opened her seams, and did her great damage; but, as expected by Captain Hallowell, the greater part of the flaming mass was driven by the explosion right over the ship. . . . Some of the wreckage from *L'Orient* fell in the *Swiftstire's* fore- and main-tops, but the fire was extinguished without injury.

Chaplain Willyams, in describing the scene during the conflagration, just before the *Orient* blew up, speaks of the:

> . . . . fine view of the two lines illumined by the flames of the ill-fated foe, the colours of the contending powers being plainly distinguished. The moon, which had risen, opposing her cold light to the warm glow of the fire beneath, added to the grand and solemn picture. The flames had by this time made

such progress that an explosion was instantly expected, yet the enemy on the lower-deck, either insensible of the danger that surrounded them, or impelled by the last paroxysms of despair and vengeance, continued to fire upon us.

Then, suddenly, all was over! Mr. Willyams continues:

> At thirty-seven minutes past nine the fatal explosion happened. The fire communicated to the magazine, and *L'Orient* blew up with a crashing sound that deafened all around her. The tremulous motion, felt to the very bottom of each ship, was like that of an earthquake; the fragments were driven such a vast height into the air that some moments elapsed before they could descend, and then the greatest apprehension was formed from the volumes of burning matter which threatened to fall on the decks and rigging of the surrounding ships.
> Fortunately, however, no material damage occurred. A port-fire fell into the main-royal of the *Alexander*, and she once more was in danger of sharing the same fate as the enemy; but by the skill and exertions of Captain Ball, it was soon extinguished. Two large pieces of the wreck dropped into the main- and fore-tops of the *Swiftsure*, but happily the men were withdrawn from those places.
> An awful silence reigned for several minutes, as if the contending squadrons, struck with horror at the dreadful event, which in an instant had hurled so many brave men into the air, had forgotten their hostile rage in pity for the sufferers.
> But, short was the pause of death; vengeance soon roused the drooping spirits of the enemy. The *Franklin*, now bearing the French commander's flag, opened her fire with redoubled fury on the *Defence* and *Swiftsure*, and gave the signal for renewed hostilities. The latter, being disengaged from her late formidable adversary, had leisure to direct her whole fire into the quarter of the foe, that had thus presumed to break the solemn silence; and in a very short time, by the well-directed and steady fire of these two ships, and the *Leander* on her bows, the *Franklin* called for quarter, and struck to a superior force.
> The *Alexander* and the *Majestic*, and occasionally the *Swiftsure*, were now the only British ships engaged; but the commander of the latter, finding that he could not direct his guns clear of the *Alexander*, who had dropped between him and the *Tonnant*,

and fearful lest he should fire into a friend, desisted, although he was severely annoyed by the shot of the *Tonnant*, which was falling thick about him. Most of our ships were so cut up in their masts and rigging that they were unable to set any sail or move from their stations. About three o'clock on the morning of the 2nd of August, the firing ceased entirely, both squadrons being equally exhausted with fatigue.

This story is told of the *Alexander* after the blowing up of *L'Orient*. Coleridge is the narrator, having been told about it by Captain Ball.

At the renewal of the battle Captain Ball, though his ship was then on fire in three different parts, laid her alongside a French eighty-four, and a second longer and more obstinate contest began. The firing on the part of the French ship at last slackened, and then altogether ceased; and yet no sign was given of surrender. The senior lieutenant came to Captain Ball, and told him 'the hearts of the men were as good as ever, but they were so completely exhausted they were scarcely capable of lifting an arm.' He asked whether, as the enemy had now ceased firing, the men might be permitted to lie down by their guns for a brief time. After some reflection Sir Alexander acceded to the proposal, taking, of course, the proper precautions to rouse them again at the moment he thought requisite. Accordingly, with the exception of himself, his officers, and the appointed watch, the ship's crew lay down, each in the place to which he was stationed, and slept for twenty minutes.

A somewhat similar incident, as we have seen, is described by Captain Miller as having taken place that night on board his ship, the *Theseus*.

The "Minutes of the Action," officially taken down on board Troubridge's unlucky *Culloden*, it may be added, record in two lines, in two consecutive entries, the fate of *L'Orient*, in the attack on which ship the *Culloden* would otherwise have had her part as one of the principal opponents of the French flagship, occupying much the same station that the *Swiftsure* took up:

9. 00. Observed *L'Orient* on fire.
9.55. Observed *L'Orient* blow up.

And that, practically, is all that is said of the actual battle in the "Minutes of the Action" noted on board Troubridge's unfortunate *Culloden*.

Captain Troubridge, indeed, was unable to get his ship off the reef until three o'clock on the following morning: after long hours of desperate energy and unfaltering effort in the darkness, and with the battle in full view all the time, raging furiously hardly two miles off. All through those bitter hours the gallant Cullodens, one of the very smartest and most efficient set of man-of-wars' men in the whole navy, had to toil on, laying out cables and anchors and heaving on them to try and haul their ship off by sheer muscular force; seconded by the strenuous aid that Hardy's lads in the *Mutine* exerted themselves to the utmost to render; also staving and emptying the water-casks in the hold, and flinging overboard tons of shot and provisions to lighten the ship. This was the state of things at midnight. In the words of the *Culloden's* log:

> People employed in throwing shot and provisions of all sorts overboard and sending some on board the *Mutine*. Found the ship make more water. Sent all hands to the pumps. Found the leak increasing. At this time five feet water per hour.

A heavy sea had got up, making the ship roll and thump dangerously on the rocks; at times, indeed, as though she must be shaken to pieces. The rudder was wrenched away, smashed off bodily, and the keel in parts had gone. It had begun to look, indeed, more than doubtful whether the *Culloden* could be saved at all.

Then, suddenly, the ship worked herself clear of the reef; between half-past two and three she swung free, snapping, like a piece of string, one of the cables laid out to haul her off.

> Parted the stream cable close to the end, and lost both anchor and cable.... At three, the ship struck three or four times very hard. Swung off the rock into five fathoms water, making at this time 7 feet water per hour.

So states the log. But the peril was still imminent. The *Culloden* remained in grave danger of foundering: "the ship leaking so much that all hands were continuously employed at the pumps." Troubridge wrote to Lord St. Vincent,:

> It was long doubtful whether I should be able to keep her afloat after I had got her off; the rudder was gone, and she was making seven feet water an hour. The false keel is gone, and probably part of the main, as she struck very hard for nine hours with a heavy swell. All the gripe (where the stem joins the keel) I can

see is off.

Troubridge hoped against hope and persevered, and in the end he saved his ship.

By great labour on the third day we got a new rudder made and hung, and with thrummed sails reduced the leak considerably. The rudder the ship's carpenters made out of a spare topmast; the fore top-gallant sail the sailmaker's crew 'thrummed,' or heckled, into a sort of thick mat which was lashed under the holes in the ship's bottom, checking the inflow of water.

Now, at last, there was hope for the *Culloden*. The captain wrote in his letter to Earl St. Vincent:

> I shall use every exertion, to patch poor *Culloden* up again, and I flatter myself I can still fight a good battle in her if opportunity offers. I am now fagging hard at the leak, and the first harbour we make I must and will patch the old ship up and make her last as long as your lordship has the command. Two pumps going I shall not mind; we are fully equal to that. I endeavour, and I believe succeed, in making my men believe that the leak is nothing; for they dance every evening as usual.

THE FATE OF NELSON'S NILE DISPATCH

The Battle of the Nile was fought on August 1. The news of the victory did not reach England until October 2, two months later, when Lieutenant Bladen Capel, who had been Nelson's signal-lieutenant in the *Vanguard*, arrived at Yarmouth with the duplicate copy of Nelson's dispatch. He had travelled overland from Naples by way of Vienna. Nelson's original dispatch, sent off on the day after the battle, never reached England at all. It lies at the bottom of the sea, off the coast of Crete; together with all the earlier letters from officers and men in the squadron to assure relatives and friends at home of their safety, and with also Nelson's chief personal trophy of the battle, the flag of the French admiral second in command—Admiral Brueys' flag, of course, perished in the blowing up of *L'Orient*.

Nelson's original dispatch and the squadron letter-bags, as well as the French flag, had to be thrown overboard with weights fastened to them to sink them and prevent their falling into the hands of the enemy. They had been sent off by the *Leander*, Captain T. B, Thompson, whom Flag-Captain Berry accompanied as bearer of the admiral's dispatch; but, on the way to Gibraltar, the *Leander* was fallen in with and attacked and taken, after as gallant a defence as perhaps any British man-of-war ever made, by a French seventy-four, the *Généreux*, one of the French rear ships, which had escaped from Aboukir Bay on the day after the battle. The *Leander* was a fifty-gun ship, with a crew of 300 all told, and 18-pounders and 9-pounders for her guns; the *Généreux* a seventy-four gun ship, with 900 men on board, and mounting 36-pounders and 18-pounders.

This is how one of the *Leander*'s men, Timothy Stewart by name, a sailor stationed at a gun on the main-deck, told the story of the desperate encounter in after days, when a pensioner at Greenwich Hospital:

> After the Nile action, our ship being in the best state, she was ordered to carry the account of the action to the admiral of the station, and Captain Berry, Lord Nelson's flag-captain, was sent on board with the dispatches, for a passage. Just eighteen days after the action, at daybreak in the morning, our ship was becalmed under the island of Candia, when we saw a large ship standing towards us with a light breeze. We soon made her out to be one of the Nile ships, because of the white patches over the shot-holes about her bows, and, accordingly, cleared for action. You see, we couldn't get away if we had tried, because the ship was land-locked; so the captain ordered the ship to be kept as she was going. We didn't take long to clear for action.
>
> We piped to breakfast at one bell in the morning watch. I suppose our captain thought the French wouldn't give us a belly-full; be that as it may, we went to breakfast upon cold water and biscuit, and many a poor fellow never had another. We had about fifteen hands wounded, lying in their hammocks, when we commenced the action, who got hurt at the Nile. Poor fellows! We had lost nearly a hundred men, killed and wounded, before we struck. Well, as soon as we had done breakfast—not long, you may be sure, when our enemy was in sight—the drum beat to quarters.
>
> I was doing quartermaster's duty at that time, though rather a young hand, and 'twas my watch on deck when we first made her out. When they beat to quarters after breakfast, I gave up the wheel to the captain's coxswain and went to my quarters on the main-deck. About one bell in the fore-noon watch, up

came the Frenchman, blazing away, right and left, long before she was in gunshot, and wasting the powder and shot which we wanted.

When she came pretty close, the word was passed to lie down at our quarters, as usual, to receive a broadside; and she began to hit us, but hurt no one. At last all as quiet below as house-breakers, we had the word of command given us—'Fire!' The Frenchman was close alongside, and we gave him as smart a broadside as our little guns, double-shotted, could throw. He then run us aboard by the fore-chains, and tried to board, but they got off with the worst of it. Our division of boarders was called up from below, to lend a hand to keep them off, and one fellow struck the point of a boarding-pike in my cheek—you can just see the mark.

Well, our mizzen mast was shot away, and a breeze coming off the land, the French ship got ahead of us, and we managed to get a chance of raking her. We poured every shot of our broadside into her cabin windows, and sent many a Johnny-Crappo to the bar of the other world. But it soon came to their turn, and they fired their whole broadside into us, within pistol shot. It shook us from stem to stern, and many a poor fellow lost the number of his mess.

We fought six hours; just think of that. Why, if she had handled her guns in a seamanlike manner, she ought to have sunk us in little more than six minutes. We had to cut through the main top-sail, lying over our larboard side, to make room for the muzzles of the guns, for our ship was quite a wreck—not a stick standing—but still the brave hearts wouldn't give in. Fore and aft there was no murmur heard, every man was ready to stick by the craft till she sunk; and once, when she (the *Généreux*) sheered off to repair some damages, we gave him three cheers, and turned-to, making cartridges, and refitting all we could to give him chase. We fired everything at him we could get hold of—crow-bars, nails, and all sorts. I saw one of the crow-bars sticking through her deck afterwards; and they never had a harder day's work in their lives than when they took the little *Leander*.

We killed nearly three hundred of them before we surrendered. But we lost two leftenants (*sic*), the master, the boatswain, and a third part of the crew; and the great lubberly hulk had taken up his berth under our stern, to give us another broadside, when our brave captain, thinking we had fought long enough, for it was now past five bells in the afternoon watch, ordered our colours to be hauled down; and the old English Ensign, all in strips, was struck. At the same time the dispatches and letters, in three large bags, were thrown out of the cabin windows with shot in them.

According to another account the *Leander* notified her submission by "holding a French jack out on a boarding pike."

Captain Thompson, for his part, writing to Nelson, while a prisoner of war, says this of how he had to surrender in the end:

> A most vigorous cannonade was kept up from the *Leander* without the smallest intermission until half-past three in the afternoon. All this time the enemy having passed our bows with a light breeze and brought himself on our starboard side, we found that our guns on that side were nearly all disabled by the wreck of our own spars, that had all fallen on this side. This produced a cessation of our fire, and the enemy took this time to ask us if we had surrendered? The *Leander* was now totally ungovernable, not having a thing standing but the shattered remains of the fore- and main-masts, and the bowsprit, her hull cut to pieces, and the decks full of killed and wounded.
>
> Perceiving the enemy, who had only lost his mizzen top-mast, approaching to place himself athwart our stern; in this defenceless situation I asked Captain Berry if he thought we could do more? He coincided with me that further resistance was vain and impracticable; and indeed, all hope of success having for some time vanished, I therefore now directed an answer to be given in the affirmative, and the enemy soon after took possession of his Majesty's ship.
>
> I should be wanting in justice if I did not bear testimony to the steady bravery of the officers and seamen of the *Leander* in this hard contest, which, though unsuccessful in its termination, will still, I trust, entitle them to the approbation of their country.

"Old Tim," of the *Leander*, our Greenwich pensioner, takes up the tale of what happened to his messmates afterwards:

> As soon as the Frenchmen saw we had struck, one of their midshipmen and two or three men swam on board of us (for

neither had a boat that could swim). They were stark naked, and they dived down below at once, and rigged themselves in any clothes they could get hold of. Not one of us offered the least resistance. At last the Frenchmen managed to mend one of their boats with tarpaulins, so as to get us aboard their ship. We had not many traps left us to take away, for lots of the Frenchmen soon swam aboard, and took care of our bags for us. Some of us thought it better to wear two shirts, but as soon as we got to the French ship, one of them was taken away.

Captain Jolly (Lejoille, of the *Généreux*) was a great scoundrel, and used our captain like a brute. His men in the *Leander* stole the doctor's instruments when he was going to dress the men's wounds; for the wounded men were all left aboard, and he (Captain Lejoille) kept him (the doctor) from coming aboard the French ship to our captain, who was badly wounded. We had nothing but oil and rice to eat, and they made us work and refit the ship. We fished his foremast (another shot would have knocked it down), and knotted all his shrouds, for which Captain Jolly promised us our liberty as soon as we got to Corfu; but as soon as we had done all the work, he started us down below, and kept us close till we got there. But we can't wonder at their being a little matter spiteful—see what a thrashing they got at the Nile, and we shouldn't have liked such a beating as that ourselves.

Well, when we got to Corfu, they sent us ashore to a dirty prison, where they used us as bad as they did in the ship, and it was two or three months before they sent some of us, and I among them, aboard a merchantman bound to Trieste. But as soon as we got out, we rose upon the crew, and made them take us to Naples, where we at last arrived, with hardly a rag to cover us, and half-starved.

Chapter 3

At Copenhagen

Nelson's Line of Battle

Ships	Guns	Commanders.
Elephant	74	Vice-Admiral Lord Nelson, K.B.; Captain Thomas Foley.
Defiance	74	Rear-Admiral Thomas Graves; Captain Richard Retallick.
Edgar	74	Captain George Murray.
Monarch	74	Captain James R. Mosse.
Bellona	74	Captain Sir Thomas B. Thompson.
Ganges	74	Captain Thomas F. Fremantle.
Russell	74	Captain William Cuming.
Agamemnon	64	Captain Robert D. Fancourt.
Ardent	64	Captain Thomas Bertie.
Polyphemus	64	Captain John Lawford.
Glatton	54	Captain William Bligh.
Isis	50	Captain James Walker.
Amazon	38	Captain Edward Riou.
Desirée	36	Captain Henry Inman.
Blanche	36	Captain Graham E. Hamond.
Alcmène	32	Captain Samuel Sutton.

At the Opening of the Campaign

The Battle of Copenhagen Nelson himself declared was his finest feat of arms. Captain Mahan says:

> The victory of Copenhagen was second in importance to none that Nelson ever gained, while in the severity of the resistance and in the attendant difficulties to be overcome the battle itself

The approaches to Copenhagen

was the most critical of all in which he was engaged. So conspicuous were the energy and sagacity shown by him that most seamen will agree in the opinion of a distinguished French admiral and naval writer, Jurien de la Gravière: 'They will always be in the eyes of seamen his fairest title to glory.'

From the outset of the cruise Nelson had set his mind on active measures. That, of course, was always his way. He gave a clear indication of his mood at the beginning of the Copenhagen campaign; on the first arrival of the fleet off Elsinore. Sir Hyde Parker, the admiral in chief command, a member of one of the most celebrated naval families of our eighteenth-century wars, was a veteran officer who had done good service in his day, but, with advancing years, the boldness and dash of former times had weakened. Fidgety, and inclined to be over-anxious at the responsibilities in front of him, he was nervous about undertaking an immediate advance into the Baltic. There were, in fact, three enemies to be dealt with in that quarter; the forces of the three nations who had banded together against England in the "Northern Confederacy," as it was styled—the Russians, the Danes, and the Swedes.

Sir Hyde could not make up his mind how to act. Which enemy should be dealt with first? how should the blow be struck? That was one question that it was for the Admiral in chief command to decide. Also there was this: to get at the enemy at all, the passage of the Sound, a narrow and intricate channel commanded by batteries and forts, Danish fortifications on one side and Swedish on the other, would assuredly have to be forced at the cannon's mouth.

Nelson urged on Sir Hyde Parker, as soon as the British fleet arrived off Elsinore (in March, 1801), that the Russians, as the principals of the coalition, should be attacked forthwith. A squadron detached from the fleet would, at the same time, suffice to deal with the Danes. The Russians, maintained Nelson, were by far the most formidable of the allies. To defeat the Danes, he said, would be like cutting a branch off a tree; to overpower the Russians would be felling the tree itself. "The measure may be thought bold," he declared, when laying his suggestions before Admiral Parker, "but I am of opinion that the boldest measures are the safest, and our country demands the most vigorous exertion of her force directed with judgment."

Sir Hyde Parker, however, did not agree. He refused to accept Nelson's proposal in regard to the Russians. Only with difficulty could the admiral be induced to strike forthwith at the Danes. He yielded in the end to Nelson's insistence as to undertaking that; but immediately afterwards his mind became obsessed with the natural difficulties in the way of the first step—as to how the approach to Copenhagen should be made. Apparently what his pilots said—they were mostly the skippers of merchant vessels trading to the Baltic, men chiefly concerned, as Nelson put it, "to keep their silly heads out of shot"—what these pilots told Sir Hyde about the intricacies of Baltic navigation, got on the old admiral's nerves.

There were two routes available for the fleet. The longer, but easier, was by the Great Belt. The more direct was by the Sound; but on that route the fortifications would need to be reckoned with.

Nelson, at Admiral Parker's Council of War, protested hotly against wasting precious time in talk. The Danes, he pointed out, were, it was common knowledge, hard at work strengthening their defences everywhere; the whole populace of Copenhagen were working on the fortifications by night and day. "Let it be by the Belt, by the Sound, or anyhow," he angrily exclaimed, "only lose not an hour!"

He had, before that, written this to the admiral:

> The more I have reflected, the more I am confirmed in opinion that not a moment should be lost in attacking the enemy. They will every day and hour be stronger; we never shall be so good a match for them as at this moment.

Sir Hyde Parker, after some demur, said that he would take the direct route by the Sound, which Nelson had pressed on him instead of the longer way by the Belt. Nelson, indeed, had made that proposal first of all, couching his advice in these words:

> To pass Cronenburg, taking the risk of damage, and to pass up the deepest and straightest channel above the Middle Grounds, and coming down the Garbar, or King's Channel, to attack their floating batteries, etc., etc., as we find it convenient. It must have the effect of preventing a junction between the Russians, Swedes, and Danes, and may give us an opportunity of bombarding Copenhagen.

But again after that the admiral's resolution began to waver. Within a short time the timid representations of the pilots induced Sir Hyde to alter the plan of advance to which Nelson had got him to agree. One of the officers in the fleet writes:

Scarcely had the admiral declared his intention of forcing the passage of the Sound, when he was induced to relinquish it by the suggestions of some ignorant and designing pilots, who, from motives of fear or interest, had considerably exaggerated the difficulties and dangers of the enterprise, and had represented, as much more practicable and less hazardous, the circuitous The 26th, at daybreak, the fleet got under weigh and stood to the westward, for the purpose, as it was generally believed, of passing the Great Belt. Captain Murray of the *Edgar*, an active and intelligent officer, who, the preceding summer, had surveyed this entrance to the Baltic with a degree of accuracy hitherto unknown, proffered his services to lead the fleet. It was now concluded, from the high opinion entertained of this officer's professional abilities, and the facility with which the passage might be effected in a place where the Danes had but one guardship, his offers would be accepted; but they were not.

Then Admiral Sir Hyde Parker changed his mind once more: before they had gone far he brought-to the fleet, and sent the captain of his flagship to tell Nelson, who was leading the advanced squadron, of his latest idea. He intended now, explained Sir Hyde, to go by the Sound. Nelson's reply was to lose his temper over his chief's vacillation, and swear. "I don't care a damn," he told Captain Otway, the captain of the London, on hearing the commander-in-chief's message, "by what passage we go, so that we fight them!"

It was, though, all the same, in no hot-headed spirit that Nelson had urged the attack on Copenhagen. Nelson had fully weighed the difficulties to be encountered. At the outset of the campaign he had frankly stated them to the admiral. He had said this:

> If the wind be fair, and you determine to attack the ships and Crown Islands, you must expect the natural issue of such a battle—ships crippled, and perhaps one or two lost; for the wind which carries you in will most probably not bring out a crippled ship.

Nelson decided to go back with Captain Otway to Parker's flagship, and talk to the admiral again. He was hot with excitement—and anger—and would not wait an instant. To save time in going off, "and in consequence of the wind blowing fresh," he had himself "hoisted out in one of the boats." The interview ended satisfactorily; Sir Hyde Parker made up his mind, finally and definitely, to proceed by the

Sound. He did not want another interview with his fiery subordinate; there was henceforward no further alteration of plans.

The decision to go by the Sound came with immense relief to the fleet in general. Yet greater pleasure was given by the announcement which soon followed that Nelson himself would lead them past the Danish forts. Says the officer who has been quoted:

> The order given on the 28th to prepare for battle, an order always received by British tars with acclamation of joy, at length relieved us from a state of despondency; and, together with some previous manoeuvres of the admiral, convinced us that the passage of the Sound was decided upon. Nothing but the appointment of a popular leader was now wanting to maintain and direct to the accomplishment of the enterprise that spirit of heroic enthusiasm which seemed to pervade every bosom; and, fortunately for the English nation, this service was allotted to the hero of the Nile, who had so often led the British tar to glory.
>
> The afternoon of the 29th was principally employed in clearing the ships for action, which was done with an alacrity and expedition unexampled in the history of naval events; and it now only remained to overthrow by the force of cannon a popular error, which all the power of reasoning could never have removed. It had long been a received opinion in Europe that the possession of Cronenburg Castle gave to the Danes an uncontrolled command of the passage of the Sound.
>
> The wind being as favourable as the most sanguine expectation could desire, the Admiral, to the inexpressible joy of the whole fleet, made, on the morning of the 30th, the signal to weigh and form the order of battle. The nomination of the Conqueror of Aboukir to lead the Van Division seemed already a happy presage of victory, and diffused a spirit of confidence and emulation which the name alone of Nelson never fails to excite among British seamen. Sir Hyde Parker acted with his division in the rear, as a corps of reserve.
>
> Such was the promptitude displayed in executing the orders to form the line and to engage, that at half-past six the *Monarch*, appointed to lead the fleet, was so far advanced that the enemy commenced a heavy and well-supported fire from the whole line of their positions, which was instantaneously returned from the leading ships, and of some of those of the centre and rear divisions.

There proved, however, actually to be little difficulty in forcing the passage through the Sound. The forts on the Swedish side remained silent. They were incomplete, and had only a few small guns mounted. To the general surprise not a shot came from them. The Danish batteries opposite blazed away furiously, but the British fleet, by keeping well over to the Swedish side of the channel, were able to make their way past, quite unharmed. "The Danish shot," says an officer, "fell in showers, but at least a cable's length from our ships." As another officer relates:

> At half-past ten every ship had passed the Sound without loss, except six or seven men killed or wounded on board the *Isis*, by the bursting of one of her lower-deck guns.

They were off Copenhagen at noon, and after a reconnaissance of the approach and fortifications by Sir Hyde Parker and Nelson, with other officers, the plan of attack was arranged at a council of war held in the *London*. At it, says an account of what passed during the council, which purports to have been written by an officer present:

> Lord Nelson offered his services, requiring ten line-of-battle ships and the whole of the smaller craft. The commander-in-chief, with sound discretion and in a handsome manner not only left everything to Lord Nelson for this detached service, but gave two more line-of-battle ships than he demanded. During this council of war, the energy of Lord Nelson's character was remarked; certain difficulties had been started by some of the members, relative to each of the three Powers we should either have to engage, in succession or united, in those seas. The number of the Russians was in particular represented as formidable. Lord Nelson kept pacing the cabin, mortified at everything that savoured either of alarm or irresolution. When the above remark was applied to the Swedes, he sharply observed, 'The more numerous the better;' and when to the Russians, he repeatedly said, 'So much the better; I wish they were twice as many; the easier the victory, depend on it.'

It only remained now to set to work.

During the night of March 30 soundings were taken by several of the officers, and buoys were laid down along the edge of the great shoal in front of Copenhagen. Additional soundings were taken during the afternoon of March 31 and the following night—this time, we are told, "under Nelson's immediate directions." Says Surgeon Ferguson of the *Elephant*, to which two-decker Nelson had shifted his flag for the coming battle, as drawing less water than his appointed flagship, the *St. George*, a big three-decker:

> I could only admire when I saw the first man in all the world spend the hours of the day and night in the boats, and wondered when the light showed me a path marked by buoys which was trackless the preceding evening.

This was the scene on board Nelson's ship, the *Elephant*, on the night of April 1, when the detached squadron of two-deckers and frigates had moved out from the main fleet and was about to take post in readiness to open the bombardment early next morning.

Colonel the Hon. William Stewart, of the Rifle Brigade, who was eyewitness of everything, and was on the quarter-deck close beside Nelson throughout the battle, tells us of what passed in the cabin of Nelson's temporary flagship on the night before the attack. Nelson, as has been said, had come on board the *Elephant*, as being a ship of lighter draught than the *St. George*, and, consequently, more suitable for the intricate navigation of the narrow channel among the shoals in front of Copenhagen. Captain Hardy accompanied Nelson from the *St. George*, but with no special duties, the command in the *Elephant* remaining in the very capable hands of Captain Thomas Foley, the captain of the ship, the same fine officer who, in the *Goliath*, had so brilliantly led Nelson's squadron into action at the Battle of the Nile. Relates Colonel Stewart:

> As soon as the fleet was at anchor, the gallant Nelson sat down to table with a large party of his comrades in arms. He was in the highest spirits, and drank to a leading wind, and to the success of the ensuing day. Captains Foley, Hardy, Fremantle, Riou, Inman, his Lordship's second-in-command. Admiral Graves, and a few others to whom he was particularly attached, were of this interesting party, from which every man separated with feelings of admiration for their great leader, and with anxious impatience to follow him to the approaching Battle. The signal to prepare for action had been made early in the evening. All the captains retired to their respective ships, Riou excepted, who, with Lord Nelson and Foley, arranged the order of battle, and those instructions that were to be issued to each ship on the succeeding day.
>
> These three officers retired between nine and ten to the after-

cabin, and drew up these orders that have been generally published, and which ought to be referred to as the best proof of the arduous nature of the enterprise in which the fleet was about to be engaged. From the previous fatigue of the day, and the two preceding, Lord Nelson was so much exhausted while dictating his instructions, that it was recommended to him by us all, and, indeed, insisted upon by his old servant, Allen, who assumed much command on these occasions, that he should go to his cot. It was placed on the floor, but from it he still continued to dictate. Captain Hardy returned about eleven, and reported the practicability of the Channel and the depth of water up to the ships of the enemy's line. Had we abided by this report, in lieu of confiding in our master's and pilot's, we should have acted better. The orders were completed about one o'clock, when half a dozen clerks in the foremost cabin proceeded to transcribe them.

Lord Nelson's impatience again showed itself, for instead of sleeping undisturbedly, as he might have done, he was every half-hour calling from his cot to these clerks to hasten their work, for that the wind was becoming fair: he was constantly receiving a report of this during the night. Their work being finished about six in the morning, his Lordship, who was previously up and dressed, breakfasted, and about seven made the signal for all captains. The instructions were delivered to each by eight o'clock, and a special command was given to Captain Riou to act as circumstances might require.

Another eyewitness's narrative, from one of Riou's men, a sailor on board the *Amazon*, Riou's ship, conveniently takes up the tale:

None of us could guess why our captain remained away from his ship so long during the night, at a time when so much danger was to be apprehended to the boats from the masses of floating ice. The morning's light told the grand secret. That path which but on the night before was trackless, was now distinctly marked out by buoys, this being accomplished by Riou and Hardy and a few others.

The only point on which the masters and pilots disagreed was the cast of the middle ground shoal and the deep-water line in St. George's Channel. Captain Hardy had taken soundings and reported the channel practicable, and Captain Riou's opinion was the same. We had an old Scotchman on board who had often passed the Sound, and he declared it would be a shame if Captain Hardy's track was not followed. He was confident the pilots had mistaken their bearings, for he declared there was no fear of shoaling water on the larboard shore. And he was right. Had the British ships approached nearer to the enemy's line they would have found deep water, whereas, when the pilots found the lead at a quarter less five, they refused to approach nearer. We profited by Hardy's plan, as the sequel will show.

By Nelson's Side on the Quarter-deck

An eyewitness's account from Nelson's flagship opens the story of the bombardment of Copenhagen—Colonel Stewart, of the Rifle Brigade, who was on board the *Elephant*. The gallant colonel tells the story in these words:

> The action began at five minutes past ten. In about half an hour afterwards the first half of our fleet was engaged, and before half-past eleven the battle became general. The *Elephant's* station was in the centre, opposite to the Danish commodore, who commanded in the *Dannebrog*, 62, Commodore Fischer, Captain F. Braun. Our distance was nearly a cable's length, and this was the average at which the action was fought; its being so great caused the long duration of it. Lord Nelson was most anxious to get nearer, but the same error which had led the two ships on the shoal, induced our master and pilots to dread shoaling their water on the larboard shore; they, therefore, when the lead was a quarter less five, refused to approach nearer, and insisted on the anchor being let go. We afterward found that had we but approached the enemy's line, we should have deepened our water up to their very side, and closed with them: as it was, the *Elephant* engaged in little more than four fathom. The *Glatton* had her station immediately astern of us, the *Ganges*, the *Monarch*, and *Defiance* ahead, the distance between each not exceeding a half-cable.
>
> The judgement with which each ship calculated her station in that intricate channel was admirable throughout. The failure of the three ships that were aground, and whose force was to have been opposed to the Trekroner battery, left this day, as glorious for seamanship as for courage—incomplete. The lead was in many ships confided to the

master alone, and the contest that arose on board the *Elephant* which of the two officers who attended the heaving of it should stand in the larboard chains, was a noble competition, and greatly pleased the heart of Nelson as he paced the quarter-deck. The gallant Riou, perceiving the blank in the original plan for the attack of the Crown Battery, proceeded down the line with his squadron of frigates, and attempted, but in vain, to fulfil the duty of the absent ships of the line. His force was unequal to it, and the general signal of recall, which was made about mid-action by the commander-in-chief, had the good effect of at least saving Riou's squadron from destruction.

Colonel Stewart continues:

> About 1 p.m., few if any of the enemy's heavy ships and *praams* had ceased to fire. The *Isis* had greatly suffered by the superior weight of the *Provestein's* fire, and if it had not been for the judicious diversion of it by the *Desirée*, Captain Inman, who raked her, and for other assistance from the *Polyphemus*, the *Isis* would have been destroyed. Both the *Isis* and *Bellona* had received serious injury by the bursting of some of their guns. The *Monarch* was also suffering severely under the united fire of the *Holstein* and *Zealand*, and only two of our bomb-vessels could get to their station on the middle ground and open their mortars on the arsenal, directing their shells over both fleets. Our squadron of gun-brigs, impeded by currents, could not, with the exception of one, although commanded by Captain Rose in the *Jamaica*, weather the eastern end of the middle ground, or come into action.
>
> The division of the commander-in-chief acted according to the preconcerted plan, but could only menace the entrance of the harbour. The *Elephant* was warmly engaged by the *Dannebrog*, and by two heavy *praams* on her bow and quarter. Signals of distress were on board the *Bellona* and *Russell*, and of inability from the *Agamemnon*. The contest, in general, although from the relaxed state of the enemy's fire it might not have given much room for apprehension as to the result, had certainly, at 1 p.m., not declared itself in favour of either side. About this juncture, and in this posture of affairs, the signal was thrown out on board the *London* for the action to cease.

It was from Colonel Stewart that the world first learnt the story of how Nelson received the order to withdraw in the middle of the battle. The colonel was beside Nelson at that moment.

Lord Nelson was at this time, as he had been during the whole action, walking the starboard side of the quarter-deck, sometimes much animated, and at others heroically fine in his observations. A shot through the main-mast knocked a few splinters about us. He observed to me with a smile, 'It is warm work, and this day may be the last to any of us at a moment,' and then, stopping short at the gangway, he used an expression never to be erased from my memory, and said with emotion, 'but, mark you, I would not be elsewhere for thousands.' When the signal, No. 39, was made, the signal-lieutenant reported it to him. He continued his walk, and did not appear to take notice of it. The lieutenant, meeting His Lordship at the next turn, asked 'whether he should repeat it?'

Lord Nelson answered, 'No, acknowledge it.' On the officer returning to the poop, His Lordship called after him, 'Is No. 16 still hoisted?' The lieutenant answered in the affirmative.

Lord Nelson said, 'Mind you keep it so.' He now walked the deck considerably agitated, which was always known by his moving the stump of his right arm. After a turn or two, he said to me in a quick manner, 'Do you know what is shown on board of the commander-in-chief—No. 39?' On asking him what he meant, he answered, 'Why, to leave off action! Leave off action,' he repeated, and then added with a shrug, 'Now, damn me if I do.'

He also observed, I believe to Captain Foley, 'You know, Foley, I have only one eye—I have a right to be blind sometimes;' and then, with an archness peculiar to his character, putting the glass to his blind eye, he exclaimed, 'I really do not see the signal.' This remarkable signal was, therefore, only acknowledged on board the *Elephant*, not repeated. Admiral Graves did the latter, not being able to distinguish the *Elephant's* conduct; either by a fortunate accident, or intentionally, No. 16 was not displaced.

This, again, is how "the gallant, good Riou," met his fate, as his death was reported on board the flagship and told to Nelson.

The squadron of frigates obeyed the signal, and hauled off. That brave officer. Captain Riou, was killed by a raking shot when the *Amazon* showed her stern to the *Trekroner*. He was sitting on a gun, was encouraging his men, and had been wounded in the head by a splinter. He had expressed himself grieved at being obliged to retreat, and nobly observed, 'What will Nelson think of us?' His clerk was killed by his side, and by another shot several of the marines, while hauling on the main-brace, shared the same fate. Riou then exclaimed: 'Come, then, my boys, let us die all together!' The words were scarcely uttered, when the fatal shot severed him in two. Thus, in an instant, was the British service deprived of one of its greatest ornaments, and society of a character of singular worth, resembling the heroes of romance.

The action now continued with unabated vigour. About 2 p.m. the greater part of the Danish line had ceased to fire, some of the lighter ships were adrift, and the carnage on board of the enemy, who reinforced their crews from the shore, was dreadful. The taking possession of such ships as had struck was, however, attended with difficulty, partly by reason of the batteries on Amak Island protecting them, and partly because an irregular fire was made on our boats, as they approached, from the ships themselves. The *Dannebrog* acted in this manner, and fired at our boat, although that ship was not only on fire and had struck; but the Commodore, Fischer, had removed his pennant and had deserted her.

A renewed attack on her by the *Elephant* and *Glatton*, for a quarter of an hour, not only completely silenced and disabled the *Dannebrog*, but, by the use of grape, nearly killed every man who was in the *praams* ahead and astern of that unfortunate ship. On our smoke clearing away, the *Dannebrog* was found to be drifting in flames before the wind, spreading terror throughout the enemy's line. The usual lamentable scene then ensued, and our boats rowed in every direction to save the crew, who were throwing themselves from her at every port-hole; few, however, were left unwounded in her after our last broadsides, or could be saved. She drifted to leeward, and, about half-past three, blew up.

The time of half-past two brings me to a most important part of Lord Nelson's conduct on this day, and about which so much discussion has arisen: his sending a flag of truce on shore. To the best of my recollection the facts were as follows: After the *Dannebrog* was adrift and ceased to fire, the action was found to be over along the whole of the line astern of us, but not so with the ships ahead and with the Crown Battery. Whether from ignorance of the custom of war, or from confusion on board the prizes, our boats, as before mentioned, were repulsed from the ships themselves, or fired on from Amak Island. Lord Nelson naturally lost temper at this, and observed, 'that he must either send on shore, and stop this irregular proceeding, or send in our fire-ships and burn them.' He accordingly retired into the stern gallery, and wrote with great dispatch that well-known letter, addressed to the Crown Prince, with the address: 'To the Brothers of Englishmen, the brave Danes,' etc.; and this letter was conveyed on shore through the contending fleets by Captain Sir Frederick Thesiger, who acted as His Lordship's *aide-de-camp*.

★★★★★

The firing from the Crown Battery and from our leading ships did not cease until past three o'clock, when the Danish adjutant-general, Lindholm, returning with a flag of truce, directed the fire of the battery to be suspended. The signal for doing the same, on our part, was then made from our ship to those engaged. The action closed, after five hours' duration, four of which were warmly contested.

Says Colonel Stewart further in regard to the historic incident of Nelson's insistence on having the letter to the crown prince sealed with wax:

> In order to show that no hurry had ensued on the occasion, he sent for a candle to the cockpit that he might affix a larger seal than usual. The letter being written and carefully folded, he sent for a stick of sealing wax; the person dispatched for the wax had his head taken off by a cannon-ball, which fact being reported to the admiral, he merely said, 'Send another messenger for the wax.' It was observed to him that there were wafers on his table. 'Send for the sealing wax,' he repeated. It was done, and the letter sealed with a large quantity of wax and a perfect impression.

Colonel Stewart asked Nelson immediately afterwards why he had been so insistent on the use of wax.

"May I take the liberty of asking why, under so hot a fire, and after so lamentable an accident, you have attached so much importance to a circumstance apparently trifling?" The colonel gives this as Nelson's answer:

Had I made use of a wafer, the wafer would have been still wet when the letter was presented to the crown prince; he would have inferred that the letter was sent off in a hurry, and that we had some very pressing reasons for being in a hurry. The wax told no tales.

Mr. Thomas Wallis, purser of the *Elephant*, who was at Nelson's elbow all the time, adds this by way of corroboration:

> Lord Nelson wrote the note at the casing of the rudder-head, and as he wrote I took a copy, both of us standing. The original was put into an envelope, and sealed with his arms; at first I was going to seal it with a wafer, but he would not allow it to be done, observing that it must be sealed, or the enemy would think it was written and sent in a hurry.

Nelson, who never forgot a friend, wrote to the captain of the *Elephant* some time after the battle:

> My Dear Foley,—
> I should be most ungrateful if I could for a moment forget your public support of me in the day of battle, or your private friendship.

So highly, indeed, did Nelson esteem Captain Foley's administrative abilities that in September, 1805, when about to set out for Trafalgar, on finding that the state of health of his former captain of the fleet, Sir George Murray, would not permit that distinguished officer to take up the post again, he offered it to Captain Foley. But Foley also unfortunately was in ill-health at the time, and he had to decline the brilliant offer. Thus it came about that Captain Hardy, a junior captain, had in the Trafalgar campaign to combine the double offices of captain of the fleet and captain of the flagship.

The captain of the *Elephant* at Copenhagen cherished to the last an extremely affectionate regard for his ship in that battle, and he now rests in the Garrison Chapel at Portsmouth in a coffin made from the quarter-deck timbers of the *Elephant*. He was commander-in-chief at Portsmouth when he died, in January, 1833—Admiral Sir Thomas Foley, G.C.B.—and Nelson's *Victory*, as his flagship, fired the minute guns while the imposing naval funeral procession escorted his remains from Government House in the dockyard to the place of interment. The *Elephant* had been taken to pieces three years before, in 1830, just at the time that the admiral took up his command—in itself the highest active-service post that a naval officer can aspire to. Mindful, it may be, of Nelson and his historic trophy-coffin, and with a natural desire that the timbers of the most famous ship he ever commanded should enshrine his body, Foley ordered part of the *Elephant's* quarter-deck planking to be reserved for him and made into his own coffin, which was done forthwith.

WITH NELSON'S SECOND IN COMMAND

Rear-Admiral Thomas Graves, a member of a fine old Irish family, several generations of whose sons have rendered distinguished service to the British Empire at sea, had the honour of being Nelson's second in command at Copenhagen. The *Defiance* was his flagship, and her station in the battle was abreast of the crown battery—a very formidable work—which mounted thirty-six heavy 42-pounder guns, and was fitted up with furnaces for red-hot shot. Owing to the *Bellona*, *Russell*, and *Agamemnon* getting aground, the *Defiance* had to face a heavy cross-fire, and her gallant crew suffered in consequence very severely, the ship being set on fire several times by the red-hot shot. When Sir Hyde Parker made the signal to discontinue the action, which Nelson refused to see, Rear-Admiral Graves was obliged to hoist it. He repeated the signal from the lee main-topsail yard-arm, whence it was not visible on board the *Elephant*. That was a chivalrous act of good feeling, typical of Admiral Graves, and was meant to spare Nelson's feelings.

A most interesting letter describing the battle was written by Rear Admiral Graves to his brother in England. The original is in the possession of Sir C. Graves-Sawle, Baronet, a descendant of the distinguished officer with Nelson on April 2, 1801.

> Yesterday was an awful day for the town of Copenhagen. Eleven sail of our ships under the command of Lord Nelson, under whom I served that day, attacked the floating batteries, ships, gun-vessels, and their works on shore, which lasted five hours, with as many hard blows and as much obstinacy as has ever been known, and with great loss on both sides, but finally ended in the complete overthrow of their outer defence. We have now eleven sail of their vessels in our possession. Two ran on shore, one sank, and one was blown up in the action. It was certainly a most gallant defence, and words cannot speak too high of the boldness of the attack, considering all the difficulties we had to struggle with, and their great superiority in number

and weight of guns.

I think we were playing a losing game in attacking stone walls, and I fear we shall not have much to boast of when it is known what our ships suffered, and the little impression we made on their navy. Lord Nelson tells me I shall be made a baronet, but I shall only ask for justice being done to my two brothers. Lord Nelson was appointed to command this attack, and he asked for me to serve with him; if not, you may depend on my not staying behind when anything was to be done. I think yesterday must prove that the enterprise of the British is invincible. Our loss in killed and wounded was only *ninety*. Lord Nelson's ship not thirty, but the *Monarch* that was next to us in the attack, and not so much exposed to the great crown batteries, lost between two and three hundred men killed and wounded. Boys escaped unhurt.

I am told the battle of the Nile was nothing to this. I am happy my flag was not a month hoisted before I got into action, and into the hottest one that has happened during the whole of the war. Considering the disadvantages of navigation, the approach to the enemy, their vast number of guns and mortars on both land and sea, I do not think there was a bolder attack. Some of our ships did not get into action, which made those who did feel it the hotter. In short, it was worthy of our gallant and enterprising little Hero of the Nile. Nothing can exceed his spirit. Sir Hyde made the signal to discontinue the action before we had been at it two hours, supposing that our ships would all be destroyed.

But our little Hero gloriously said, 'I will not move till we are crowned with victory, or that the commander-in-chief sends an officer to order me away.' And he was right, for if we had discontinued the action before the enemy struck, we should have all gone aground, and have been destroyed. As it was, both Nelson's ship and the *Defiance* got aground in coming off. Lord Nelson sent for me at the close of the action, and it was beautiful to see how the shot beat the water all round us in the boat. Give my love to my dear daughter. She has ever the most ardent prayers for her happiness. The destruction among the enemy is dreadful. One of the ships that was towed into the fleet yesterday had between two and three hundred dead on her decks, besides what they had thrown overboard.

As a reward for his share in winning the victory the honour of a knighthood of the Bath was conferred on Nelson's gallant second in command at Copenhagen, who had been promoted to Vice-Admiral shortly after the battle. His investiture took place on board Nelson's flagship, the *St. George*, in Kioge Bay, to the south of Copenhagen, the ceremony being performed with an elaborate state display by Nelson himself on June 14.

One or two points from the official narrative of what took place, as set forth in the *London Gazette*, may be noted here. To represent the throne on the occasion, one of the admiral's chairs, covered with a union flag, was placed on the quarter-deck, with the royal standard suspended above it. Nelson stood by the side of it throughout, having first made three reverences to the throne as he came on deck. A guard of honour of marines and men of the Rifle Corps (now the Rifle Brigade), in full-dress uniform, stood, with presented arms, drawn up at either side of the quarter-deck.

The sword which the captains at the Battle of the Nile presented to Nelson (its golden hilt was in the shape of a crocodile) did duty as the sword of state in the ceremony. With it the accolade, in the name of King George, was bestowed on the new knight as he knelt before the throne. It was this sword that some scoundrel stole one night in December, 1900, from the Painted Hall of Greenwich Hospital. Captain Hardy, together with Admiral Graves's flag-captain, Captain Retallick, helped Nelson, who was unable to manage it with his one hand, in placing the ribbon of the order over the shoulder of the new knight and pinning the star of the order on his breast.

Finally, as the act of investiture concluded, the whole fleet fired a royal salute of twenty-one guns.

IN THE VERY HOTTEST OF THE BATTLE

The famous old *Monarch*, one of the toughest of the hard-fighting seventy-fours of Nelson's time, the oldest line-of-battle ship in the world in commission in 1801, in the forty-first year of her existence afloat, also King George III.'s favourite man-of-war, as having been launched on the day of his Majesty's accession, was in the thick of the battle. The *Monarch* was in the very hottest of the fighting, and she had her captain, James Robert Mosse, killed, in addition to suffering among her crew the heaviest loss ever borne in battle by any British man-of-war of Nelson's day. An old naval officer of those times describes:

The *Edgar*, *Isis*, and *Polyphemus* dropped anchor in their appointed places; but, as the *Ardent* and *Monarch* had to pass several unengaged ships, to take up their appointed berths, they became exposed to a destructive cannonading. Proceed, however, they did; and the *Monarch*, anchoring between the *Indosforethen* (an old, condemned two-decker, cut down and dismantled, of 64-guns, with a crew of 390 men), and the *Holstein*, of 60-guns, and four hundred men, became exposed to a destructive fire from both; in addition to which, she was greatly exposed to the fire of the Trekroner battery. It was nearly an hour before the remaining British ships could take up their allotted places; and, when they did, they afforded little or no assistance to the *Monarch*. It is not to be wondered at, therefore, that her loss was greater than that ever sustained in later times (for we must except the old Dutch wars, where the slaughter was often truly awful) by a two-decked ship.

One of the *Monarch's* officers. Midshipman Millard, who was stationed on the quarter-deck for most of the battle, gives this vividly dramatic picture of what he and his shipmates went through.

> The hammocks were piped up at six, but having had the middle watch I indulged myself with another nap, from which I was roused by the drum beating to quarters. I bustled on deck, examined the guns under my directions, saw them provided with hand-spikes, spare breechings, tackles, etc., and reported accordingly. About seven the vice-admiral made the signal for all captains, when he delivered to each a card containing a copy of his instructions, his situation in the line, etc. Few as these instructions were, they were amply sufficient, and no general signal was made during the action, except No. 16—'To engage the enemy as close as possible;' this the vice-admiral kept at his mast-head the whole time.
> As soon as the reports had been delivered from all parts of the ship that everything was prepared for action, the men were ordered to breakfast. As the gunners' cabin, where I usually messed, was all cleared away, I went into the starboard cockpit berth, where I found one of the pilots that had been sounding the night before. He told us that they had pulled so near the enemy's ships as to hear the sentinels conversing, but returned without being discovered. Our repast, it may fairly be supposed, under

these circumstances was a slight one. When we left the berth, we had to pass all the dreadful preparations of the surgeons.

One table was covered with instruments of all shapes and sizes, another, of more than usual strength, was placed in the middle of the cockpit. As I had never seen this produced before, I could not help asking the use of it, and received for answer 'that it was to cut off legs and wings upon.' One of the surgeon's men (called Loblolly Boys) was spreading yards and yards of bandages, about six inches wide.

Very shortly after that came on the hour for the opening of Nelson's attack.

Soon after breakfast the vice-admiral made signal to weigh and prepare for battle, anchoring with the sheet-cable out at the stern port.

The ships nearest the enemy were ordered to lead in and anchor abreast of the southernmost of the enemy's line, the others to follow them and pass in succession, so that our line became reversed or inverted. The *Monarch* being the last but two or three in the line, we had a good opportunity of seeing the other ships approach the enemy to commence the action. A more beautiful and solemn spectacle I never witnessed. The *Edgar* led the van, and on her approach the battery on the Isle of Amak, and three or four of the southernmost vessels, opened their fire upon her. A man-of-war under sail is at all times a beautiful object, but at such a time the scene is heightened beyond the powers of description. We saw her pressing on through the enemy's fire, and manoeuvring in the midst of it to gain her station; our minds were deeply impressed with awe, and not a word was spoken throughout the ship but by the pilot and the helmsmen, and their communications being chanted very much in the same manner as the responses in our cathedral service, and repeated at intervals, added very much to the solemnity.

The *Edgar* was followed by the *Isis* and *Russell*, accompanied by the *Desirée* frigate. As our line extended to the northward, more of the enemy's ships opened their fire, and so on down their line, till lastly the Crown batteries got to work, and the action became general along the whole lines.

★★★★★

We continued firing all the way down between our own ships,

and when abreast of the vice-admiral gave him three hearty cheers, which compliment was returned by his men at their guns. We anchored about ten, but not precisely in the station originally intended: for this reason, that two of the ships stationed by Lord Nelson ahead of us never made their appearance. One of them, the *Bellona*, ran aground; the *Polyphemus*, which was the other, took the place of the *Agamemnon*, per signal, who remained at her anchorage, 'being unable' (says Lord Nelson's letter) 'to weather the shoal.' This brought us much nearer the Crown Islands, and last but one (the *Defiance*) in the line.

As has been said, the *Monarch*, as she came into action, had to run the gauntlet of a heavy fire from several unengaged Danish ships; but Captain Mosse held on his way with firm determination. Then she let go anchor between a 54-gun ship and a 60-gun ship, facing a tremendous fire from both, while the great Trekroner, or Three Crowns, batteries assailed her pitilessly at the same time.

The *Monarch's* gallant captain met his death almost at the beginning of the battle. Describes our midshipman eyewitness:

> When the ship came-to, I was on the quarter-deck, and saw Captain Mosse on the poop; his card of instructions was in his left hand, and his right was raised to his mouth with the speaking trumpet, through which he gave the word, 'Cut away the anchor.' I returned to my station at the aftermost guns, and in a few minutes the captain was brought aft, perfectly dead. Colonel Hutchinson (of the 49th Regiment, a detachment of which was serving in the *Monarch* as marines) was with the men, and was asked if he thought it right that the captain should be carried below; he answered that he saw no sign of life, and it would only damp the spirits of the men. He was then laid in the stern walk, and a flag thrown over him. Colonel Hutchinson turned round and exclaimed, with tears in his eyes, 'Poor man! he has left a wife and family to lament him.' I did not see the captain fall, but I understood afterwards from the quartermaster at the gun (Edward Kilgore) that he had left the poop, and fell on the quarter-deck on the very spot where I stood when the anchor was cut away.

Midshipman Millard had charge of five of the quarter-deck guns, and relates some of his personal experiences among his men:

I pulled off my coat, helped to run out the guns, handed the powder, and literally worked as hard as a dray-horse. Every gun was supplied at first with a portion of shot, wadding, etc., close by it; and when these were expended, we applied to a reserved place by the main-mast. It immediately occurred to me that I could not be more usefully employed than conveying this supply, which would enable the stronger ones to remain at their guns, for the men wanted no stimulus to keep them to their duty, nor any directions how to perform it.

The only cautions I remember to have given were hinted to me by the gunner before the action—*viz.*, to worm the guns frequently, that no fire might remain from the old cartridge, to fire two round-shot in each gun, and to use nothing else while round-shot was to be had. The men remained at the wheel for a very considerable time after the ship was anchored, in order to steady her, for the shock of bringing up so suddenly occasioned a very considerable 'oscillation' (if I may apply that term). As I was returning from the main-mast, and was abreast of the little binnacle, a shot came in at the port under the poop ladder, and carried away the wheel, and three out of the four men stationed at it were either killed or wounded, besides one or two at the guns.

The detachment of soldiers, part of the 49th Foot (now the 1st Battalion Royal Berkshire Regiment), served as marines on board the *Monarch* at Copenhagen, as has been said, and did their duty nobly. In commemoration of their services in the action the regiment now bears the name "Copenhagen "inscribed on the colours as a battle honour. Most of the soldiers and their officers were stationed on the poop and quarter-deck. Midshipman Millard tells this about two of the officers:

> Lieutenant Dennis, of the 49th (Grenadier Company), had just come up the companion ladder, and was going aft; the splinters shattered his sword, which was in the sheath, into three pieces, and tore off the finger-ends of his left hand. This, however, he scarcely seemed aware of, for, lifting up the sheath with his bloody fingers, he called out: 'Look here, colonel!' On being reminded by Colonel Hutchinson of his wounded hand, he twisted his handkerchief round it, and set up a huzza, which was soon repeated throughout the ship. Dennis, though he could not act against the enemy, found means to make himself use-

ful: he flew through every part of the ship, and when he found any of his men wounded, carried him in his arms down to the cockpit. When the carnage was greatest he encouraged his men by applauding their conduct, and frequently began a huzza, which is of more importance than might be imagined, for the men have no other communication throughout the ship; but know when a shout is set up, it runs from deck to deck, and that their comrades are, some of them, in good spirits.

Lieutenant-Colonel Hutchinson, being commanding officer of this detachment, did not leave the quarter-deck, but walked backward and forward with coolness and composure, till at length, seeing the improbability of being ordered away, he begged I would employ him if I thought he could do any good. I was at that time seated on the deck, cutting the wads asunder for the guns, and the colonel, notwithstanding the danger attending his uniform breeches, sat himself down and went to work very busily. Indeed, afterwards I was often obliged to leave the charge of my guns to the colonel, for I was now the only midshipman left upon the deck, and was therefore employed by Mr. Yelland, the commanding officer, as his *aide-de-camp*, and dispatched occasionally into all parts of the ship. On my return, the colonel made his report of what had passed in my absence.

Our midshipman then has something to say of his own personal adventures, and something of his brother-officers on board.

Our signal-midshipman (the Honourable William Bowes) was bruised from head to foot with splinters in such a manner as compelled him to leave the deck; Mr. Levescombe, another midshipman, who was my companion on the quarter-deck, and who was as cool and apparently unconcerned as usual, shared the same fate. I attended him to the lower-deck, but could not prevail upon myself to set foot upon the cockpit ladder, so there I left him to make the best of his way. As the splinters were so plentiful, it may be wondered how I escaped; the fact is, I did not escape entirely. When the wheel was shot away, I was in a cloud; but, being some little distance from the wheel, I did not receive any of the larger pieces.

When I passed backwards and forwards between my quarters and the main-mast, I went on the opposite side to that which was engaged, and by that means probably escaped a severe wound, for as I was returning with two shot in one hand and a cheese (or packet) of wads in the other, I received a pretty smart blow on my right cheek. I dropped my shot, just as a monkey does a hot potato, and clapped my hand to the place, which I found rather bloody, and immediately ran aft to get my handkerchief out of the coat pocket. My friend, Colonel Hutchinson, came to me immediately, to return the compliment I had paid him when passing the castle, and seemed really afraid lest my jaw was broken; however, after having felt it and found it all right, he let me return for my burthen.

Towards the close of the action the colonel reported to me that guns wanted quill or tin tubes (which are used as more safe and expeditious than loose priming), and wanted me to send someone, adding, 'his own men were too ignorant of the ship, or he would have sent one before my return.' I told him, 'I knew no one that could so well be spared as myself.' He, however, objected to my going, and as I was aware of the dreadful slaughter which had taken place in the centre of the ship, I was not very fond of the jaunt; but my conscience would not let me send another on an errand I was afraid to undertake myself, and away I posted towards the fore-magazine.

When I arrived on the main-deck, along which I had to pass, there was not a single man standing the whole way from the main-mast forward, a district containing eight guns on a side, some of which were run out ready for firing; others lay dismounted, and others remained as they were after recoiling. . . I hastened down the fore-ladder to the lower-deck, and felt really relieved to find somebody alive; from thence I reached the fore-cockpit, where I was obliged to wait a few minutes for my cargo; and after this pause, I own I felt something like regret, if not fear, as I remounted the ladder on my return.

This, however, entirely subsided when I saw the sun shining and the old blue ensign flying as lofty as ever. I never felt the genuine sense of glory so completely as that moment; and if I had seen any one attempt to haul that ensign down, I could have run aft and shot him dead in as determined a manner as the celebrated Paul Jones. I took off my hat by an involuntary motion, and gave three cheers as I jumped on to the quarter-deck.

Colonel Hutchinson welcomed me at my quarters as if I had

been on a hazardous enterprise and had returned in triumph. Mr. Yelland also expressed great satisfaction at seeing me in such high spirits and so active. The brave veteran had taken care to have the decks swept, and everything clean and nice before we went into action. He had dressed himself in full uniform, with his cocked hat set on square, his shirt-frill stiff starched, and his cravat tied tight under his chin as usual. After the fall of our poor captain, he sent me down to desire the lieutenants from the different quarters to come on deck, when he informed them of the captain's death, and appointed himself, of course, commanding officer; the remaining officers having, as it were, sworn fealty to him, returned to their different stations. How he escaped unhurt seems wonderful. Several times I lost sight of him in a cloud of splinters; as they subsided I saw first his cocked hat emerging, then by degrees the rest of his person, his face smiling, so that altogether one might imagine him dressed for his wedding-day....

Soon after my return from the magazine, Mr. Ponsonby (midshipman), who had been quartered on the forecastle, came on to the quarter-deck, his face and collar of his coat partly covered with a coagulated compost of human blood and brains. He presented himself and three of his men to Mr. Yelland as all that were left, and requested he would apply them where he thought proper, as they were of no longer service by themselves. There were two other officers quartered on the forecastle; the boatswain, who was very dangerously wounded in the body, and Mr. Morgan (midshipman), who had both feet shot off; and I suppose twenty men, of whom only three remained with poor Ponsonby. Mr. Yelland shook his head at Ponsonby's relation, and begged, as he had fought so gallantly, that he would attach himself and men to whatever quarters he thought proper; so they remained where they were on the quarter-deck.

The exceptionally severe casualty list of 240 killed and wounded (out of 600 on board) answers for the *Monarch's* part at Copenhagen—56 killed and 184 wounded, several mortally, according to the statement and numbers given in the ship's log. No British man-of-war, probably, ever lost so heavily, even in battle under Nelson.

This little item, showing something of the *esprit de corps* among the *Monarch's* men, may be added from a sailor's letter.

The *Monarch*, having somehow got foul of the rigging of the *Ganges*, one of the seamen who had been engaged in clearing the two ships, finding himself on board the *Ganges* as she moved away, jumped overboard and swam towards the *Monarch*, swearing that he would never desert his ship. A boat was instantly put off which saved the man's life.

The collision with the *Ganges* took place just after the battle ceased. We are told:

> Lord Nelson hoisted the signal for the *Monarch* and other ships to weigh; and accordingly the *Monarch* cut her cable, and was proceeding down the channel when she grounded on a shoal; but the *Ganges* striking her in mid-ships, drove her (butted her, so to speak) over the bank into deep water, and in the course of a short time she brought up, out of the range of the enemy's batteries.

The body of the dead captain of the *Monarch* was buried at sea off Copenhagen on the morning of the day following the battle. First-Lieutenant Yelland records the funeral in his journal in these words:

> April 3. At eight, committed the body of the deceased Captain J. Robert Mosse to the deep with the proper deference to the rank.

Said Nelson, in notifying the death to Sir Hyde Parker:

> Amongst other brave officers and men who were killed, I have, with sorrow, to place the name of Captain Mosse of the *Monarch*, who has left a wife and six children to lament his loss."

How One of Nelson's Old Messmates Had His Share

Captain Thomas Bertie, one of Nelson's old fellow-midshipmen on board the *Sea-Horse* in the East Indies, a lifelong friend and an officer with whom Nelson ever maintained terms of the closest affection and intimacy, was at Copenhagen on board the *Ardent*, and did brilliant service that day. Captain Bertie's ship had her post as second in the advance to the attack, following Murray in the *Edgar* (Nelson's future captain of the fleet on board the *Victory* during the two years that preceded Trafalgar), whose magnificent leading of the line on that day "set," in Nelson's words, "a noble example of intrepidity."

"My dear Tom," was Nelson's usual familiar mode of address to his old messmate when they were together. "Believe me ever, with the greatest affection, your old and attached friend," is the subscription of one of Nelson's letters to Captain Bertie. In Nelson's original scheme of attack on the Danish batteries, before he decided to assume the direction of everything himself, Captain Bertie was to have had charge of the division of ships told off to undertake the work.

This is by the way. In one of Nelson's letters to Captain Bertie, written at the time of the trial by court-martial of the captain of the *Agincourt* for misconduct before the enemy at Camperdown, are these characteristic expressions of Nelson's opinion:

> Upon the general question that if a man does not do his utmost in the time of action, I think but one punishment ought to be inflicted. Not that I take a man's merit from his list of killed and wounded, for but little may be in his power, and if he does his utmost in the station he is placed, he has equal merit to the man who may have his ship beat to pieces, but not his good fortune.

> Upon officers going into action, I would have every man believe, 'I shall only take my chance of being shot by the enemy, but if I do not take that chance I am certain of being shot by my friends.'

Captain Bertie, as it so happened, had not before fought under Nelson's leadership. He had, though, on his own account, an excellent battle-service record, under Keppel and Rodney, in the old days of the American War; and more recently he had done notable work in the North Sea Fleet, under Duncan. The Royal Navy owes to him the introduction of lifebuoys, first brought into the service through Captain Bertie, while a lieutenant in the Channel Fleet. To him, also, the Navy of Nelson's day owed a very important improvement in the mounting of carronades, which enabled the heaviest types of "smasher," as that deadly weapon was commonly called in the fleet, to be worked more quickly and efficiently than before; also by only four men, as compared with the fifteen or eighteen who were needed to man the heavier broadside guns of corresponding calibres; and firing projectiles of similar weight.

At Copenhagen, as an account written soon afterwards tells us:

> Captain Bertie particularly distinguished himself, compelling four sail of the Danish flotilla, large and small, to strike to the *Ardent*, which had also been engaged with the Lunette Quintus (one of the fortifications on shore). On this occasion, the *Ardent* expended 2,464 cartridges, and 2,693 shot of different descrip-

tions, and she had 130 men killed and wounded.

Put in the words of the *Ardent's* log, as written on the evening of the battle, this summarizes what it fell to Captain Bertie and his men to do:

> At 11, we began to fire on the enemy. Ran between the *Edgar* and the Danish batteries, and brought up with a stream anchor. Engaged with five of the enemy's floating batteries. At Noon, warmly engaged with the enemy's floating batteries. At 2, one of them struck, and 10 minutes after two more hauled down their colours. At half-past two, ceased firing, having silenced the enemy.

Here is something else that is told of the captain of the *Ardent* at Copenhagen:

> In this action, while the *Danneborg*—the ship of the Danish commodore, Fischer, who had quitted her some time before—was on fire, Captain Bertie sent an officer in the *Ardent's* launch, with orders to save as many of her crew as possible, but not to go alongside, lest the boat should be swamped or overset. The captain of the *Danneborg*, named Bramme, who was severely wounded at the time, hailed the launch to ascertain the name of the English ship and captain who had sent her; and, on receiving the information, he paid a handsome compliment to the gallant commander of the *Ardent*, adding that he should make a point of acquainting the Prince of Denmark with his generous attention and humanity. The launch returned with this message, having picked up twenty-three of the *Danneborg's* crew. That ship soon afterwards blew up, with all the killed, wounded, and sick on board, amounting to upwards of 200 persons.

How Nelson thanked his old messmate is another story which a contemporary writer tells:

> Early on the following morning (April 3) Lord Nelson, and his captain, the present Sir Thomas Hardy, went on board the *Ardent* to thank Captain Bertie, his officers and people, for their conduct and exertions on the preceding day—a compliment which was returned with six cheers on their leaving the ship.

We are also told this about the chivalrous captain of the *Ardent*. Two days after the battle:

He went on board the *London*, taking with him one of the Danish captains (the other three having been killed or severely wounded) and the lieutenants of the four ships which had struck to the *Ardent*, together with their swords, which, from the bravery of their late owners, Captain Bertie much wished to return. Sir Hyde Parker not opposing this generous request, Captain Bertie had the happiness, in restoring their swords to his prisoners, to express his admiration of the able and gallant manner in which they had been used.

A summary of the severe damage that the *Ardent* sustained at Copenhagen is given in an account from one of the officers. These details, taken from it, will help to form an idea of the battering that the ship underwent.

It was, by the way, the second severe mauling that the same crew had had within four years. At Camperdown, where for part of the battle they had five of the enemy on them at once, the Ardents came out of action with a casualty list of 40 killed and 96 wounded, their master and the heroic Captain Burgess (he has a monument in St. Paul's) being among the dead.

These damages, among others, are recorded in the Copenhagen statement:

Most of the quarter-deck guns disabled and rendered useless; and two-thirds of the guns on the main-deck rendered useless. Above the water-line on the port side (that facing the enemy), there were seventy-eight shot-holes through the ship's side; besides several shot-holes through the sides of the deck and cabin; and sixteen more low down between wind and water. Some of the Danish cannon-balls smashed their way right across the ship, and shattered holes through the starboard, or farther side, besides doing considerable additional damage—planks and timbers cut and started, etc. The portholes were much damaged by shot, beams and standards badly wounded in several places; in addition to many iron knees broke. Below the water-line, the orlop-deck planking was cut through in several places, and one beam much damaged. The jib-boom was shot away, and the bowsprit wounded.

Aloft, this was some of the damage that the *Ardent* suffered: The foremast shot through in different places, and in others very badly wounded; the mainmast shot through in many places, and many other parts badly wounded; the mizzen-mast shot through and badly wounded; the fore-top-gallant-mast wounded and shot away; the fore-yard—both arms shot away, and in other places badly wounded; the larboard-arm of the fore-topsail yard shot away; one of the fore cross-trees shot away.

Other entries are these: every main-shroud shot away, except one on the larboard side; most of the fore-shrouds shot away; most of the running rigging cut by shot—one hundred and thirty-eight holes in the fore-sail, and sixty-seven in the fore-topsail—the main-top-sail much torn by shot—almost to pieces—the mizzen-topsail and other sails much cut—the best bower-cable cut—the sheet cable shot away and the anchor gone overboard during the action—a cutter alongside of the ship sunk, and another boat and pinnace rendered unserviceable by shot.

The statement closes with a note of the killed and wounded:

Length of the action in *Ardent*, 4 hours and 50 minutes. Twenty-eight men killed and one midshipman; two others died of their wounds. Sixty men badly wounded, of whom eighteen amputations were made in arms and legs. Forty men lightly wounded, doing their duty.

The Hard Luck of the Bellonas

The *Bellona*, one of Nelson's seventy-fours, to which «hip had been given the honour of leading the flagship *Elephant* into battle as Nelson's "second ahead," had an unfortunate time at Copenhagen. Just as the battle was opening she got aground, in a position where the Danish batteries were able to cannonade her at long range and maul her severely; and the *Bellona* had to remain there to the end, exposed to a pitiless cross-fire all through the battle. Her captain, a very highly distinguished officer, one of the keenest of "Nelsonians," Captain Sir Thomas Boulden Thompson (of whose splendid fight in the *Leander* against the big French 80-gun ship *Généreux*, while carrying Nelson's dispatches after the Nile, something has been said), was severely wounded and put *hors de combat* at the beginning of the battle. Two of *Bellona's* biggest guns burst when the action was at its hottest, with terribly destructive effect; striking down men on all sides, killed and wounded, disabling other guns, and blowing up part of the deck. Yet the gallant Bellonas stood manfully to their work and did their duty, until the nearest of the Danes firing on them hauled down their colours.

Mr. Alexander Briarly, the master of the *Bellona* (he had served under Nelson, as the master of the *Audacious*, at the Nile), tells the story of his ship's day at Copenhagen in the journal he kept, wording it in a plain and matter-of-fact way, but characteristic and sufficiently clear. This is how he puts it:

> The *Isis* and *Edgar* had opened their fire on the enemy's *floating* and shore batteries, which kept up a constant heavy fire of shot and shells on our fleet. At 11, being within long range of the enemy's shot, and passing the *Isis*, who had just anchored by the stern, the captain ordered the lower-deck guns to be well pointed and fired. We now perceived the ship had struck the ground. General signal to 'Engage Closer.' At ½ past 11 the captain, standing on the 3rd gun on the quarter-deck, received a shot which took off his left leg. He was carried off the deck, and the 1st Lieutenant, by his directions, took the command. Finding the ship fast on shore, the 1st Lieutenant made signal to the admiral, 'The ship on a shoal.'
>
> At 1, broke off part of the people from the guns to lay the stream anchor out on the larboard bow, which we effected. Manned the capstan and hove; but finding the anchor come home, held all fast and went to the guns. At this time engaging two of the enemy's floating batteries. At 2, the fourth gun on the lower-deck burst, by which there were several men killed and wounded, among the latter two lieutenants and two midshipmen; one of the main-deck beams broke, and part of the main-deck gangway blown up.
>
> At 3, the 14th gun on the lower-deck burst, by which several men were killed and wounded, a great part of the main-deck blown up, and 3 of the main-deck guns disabled aloft and 2 forward, by the 1st gun. Prior to these accidents the commander-in-chief made the signal to discontinue the action, which was not obeyed by our squadron, several of them being aground at the time. 3.15, observed the 3 floating batteries we and the *Isis* had engaged haul down their colours and strike. At this time all the line-of-battle ships of the enemy engaged to the northward, and struck their colours and were taken possession of. 3.30, the enemy having hoisted a general flag of truce on shore, the firing ceased.

It was not until eight in the evening, and with the aid of the *Isis* as well, that they were able to get the *Bellona* afloat again. Notes Mr. Briarly at that time:

The vice- and rear-admirals, besides two line-of-battle ships, still aground.

One of the *Bellona's* midshipmen, Edward Daubeny, writing to his father, a clergyman in Gloucestershire, two days after the battle, among other things says this:

> After five hours' engagement gave them enough; great slaughter, I am very sorry to say, on both sides, particularly on the enemy's. Some of their ships were manned three times; eight hundred were killed and wounded in one of their ships, and almost as many in their others. Our ships suffered very much from the enemy's shot. We got on shore in going in, and of course stood all their shot; it may perhaps be lucky, as we were a mark to our other ships. Captain Thompson was wounded in the beginning of the action, I believe badly, though not dangerously; he bears it well. We have besides about 80 killed and wounded, by the bursting of our guns. I am, thank God, only slightly burnt by the bursting of one; don't be at all alarmed when you see my name amongst the wounded in the papers; to be sure I am weak, but that is occasioned by the length of the engagement, and I was not very well before. Should we come to action again, I am ready for them.

Referring to the exceptional severity of the losses on both sides, another young officer, Midshipman T. S. Asperne, of the *Jamaica*, a twenty-four gun corvette, at the head of Nelson's flotilla of gun-brigs, in a letter to his father, adds his testimony:

> The enemy made a very obstinate resistance, and fought like brave men. I need not inform you the English did the same; the action was kept up without a moment's ceasing for five hours. Most of our ships are very much cut up, more especially the *Defiance, Monarch*, and *Isis*: our number, killed and wounded, amounts nearly to 1,000 men. This severe loss was much occasioned by the *Bellona* and *Russell* being ashore, and the *Agamemnon* not being able to get up her anchor, which hindered them from taking their allotted stations; but our loss is nothing comparable to what the Danes have suffered. Their killed alone, by accounts from the Danish officers (of whom we have three on board, besides ninety-three men), must be near 3,000, and the vessels which have been captured are perfect sieves, there

not being hardly a single plank in any of them but what has at least ten shot-holes in it.

In fact it is thought to be the hardest fought action in the annals of history.... Lord Nelson, in the *Elephant*, fought nobly; really, to endeavour to make comments on his conduct would be impossible.... The Danish *Commodore* took fire, and blew up with a tremendous explosion within half a cable's length of the saucy *Jamaica*.... The impediments to the bombardment of Copenhagen are now removed, and our bombs are placed so that, if the Danes are not sensible of their situation, the town and arsenal will be very soon reduced to ashes.

Captain Thompson, writing to young Daubeny's father, some three weeks after Copenhagen, to say that the lad was getting over his injuries well, speaks with pathetic despondency about himself.

For myself, I am lain down, having patiently to wait my cure or dissolution, as it shall please God. I am now totally disabled and my career is run through, only at the age of 35. God bless you, my good sir. I write in great pain and under every disadvantage."

It is from a letter written by Mr. Briarly, of the *Bellona*, to his wife, that this fine little story of Nelson comes. The date of the incident is April 19, between two and three weeks after the battle. Mr. Briarly at the time was acting as pilot to Nelson, on board the *St. George*. It was he, who, on the day of the battle had been selected specially to navigate the squadron in front of the batteries.

This day the *St. George* got her guns aboard an American ship for the purpose of going over the grounds to the southward of Copenhagen, where Sir Hyde Parker with the Fleet had sailed two days before; but the wind being foul prevented us moving. At six p.m., Lord Nelson received advice, per letter from Sir Hyde Parker, of a Swedish squadron being seen by one of our lookout frigates. The moment he received the account he ordered a boat to be manned, and without even waiting for a boat-cloak (though you must suppose the weather pretty sharp here at this season of the year), and having to row about twenty-four miles with the wind and current against him, jumped into her, and ordered me to go with him, I having been on board that ship, to remain until she had got over the grounds.

All I had ever seen or heard of him could not half so clearly prove to me the singular and unbounded zeal of this truly great man. His anxiety in the boat for nearly six hours (lest the fleet should have sailed before he got on board one of them, and lest we should not catch the Swedish squadron), is beyond all conception. I will quote some expressions in his own words.

It was extremely cold, and I wished him to put on a great-coat of mine which was in the boat: 'No, I am not cold; my anxiety for my country will keep me warm. Do you think the fleet has sailed?'

'I should suppose not. My lord!'

'If they are, we shall follow them to Carlscrona in the boat, by God!'

I merely state this to show how his thoughts must have been employed. The idea of going in a small boat, rowing six oars, without a single morsel of anything to eat or drink, the distance of about fifty leagues, must convince the world that every other earthly consideration than that of serving his country was totally banished from his thoughts. We reached our fleet by midnight, and went on board the *Elephant*, Captain Foley, where I left His Lordship in the morning and returned to my ship.

The story is characteristic of Nelson, undoubtedly, but it rests entirely on Mr. Briarly's authority; on the word of a gentleman who had rather a name in the service for tall-yarn spinning. He was the same officer who had been the master of the *Audacious* at the Nile, and his *sobriquet* at that time in the squadron, and in after-years throughout the navy, of "Audacious Briarly" is said, by one of those who was in the ship with him, to have been given, not so much because of Mr. Briarly's connexion with the *Audacious*, but rather for his talents as an after-dinner story-teller in the ward room.

The Officer Who Carried Nelson's Letter to the Crown Prince

As gallant a deed as any done that day was performed by Sir Frederick Thesiger, the officer who carried Nelson's letter to the crown prince of Denmark. He was acting as one of Nelson's *aides-de-camp* on the quarter-deck of the *Elephant*, and volunteered for the dangerous duty. How he performed the duty is told in these words by a naval writer of the day.

He nobly volunteered his services to proceed with the flag of truce to the Prince Royal of Denmark.... Entering fully into the feelings and views of his noble chief and commander, and perceiving how importantly necessary it was to reach the shore with as little delay as possible, instead of rowing a circuitous route, which would have occupied the greater part of an hour, but in pursuing which he would have been out of reach of the Danish fire, he rushed impetuously forward, encouraging his men to persevere, through the cloud of smoke and the heavy fire which prevailed—the flag of truce not being either seen or respected—and landed safely at Copenhagen, without the least injury to himself or any of his boat's crew.

The crown prince, immediately acquiescing in the terms proposed by Lord Nelson, sent off with Sir Frederick a flag in return, and instantly gave orders for the firing to cease in every direction. As many of the batteries, however, were at a considerable distance from the capital, Captain Thesiger had got half way back to the British fleet before the orders could be thoroughly attended to; and before he joined his ship several of our fleet had grounded.

These circumstances evince the merit he possessed, in braving all danger to reach the shore in the quickest manner that was possible; for, had he proceeded by the circuitous and safe way, the situation of the English ships might have been perceived before he could have landed, and the consequences might have been incalculably fatal to the interests of this country. A portion of public praise and gratitude is therefore due to Captain Thesiger for having so fully performed his duty on that ever-memorable day.

The crown prince's adjutant-general, Lindholm, returned in the boat with Commander Thesiger, who, after the Danish officer's interview with Nelson as to the British leader's intention in sending the message, went back again to the crown prince with Nelson's reply.

> Lord Nelson's object in sending the flag of truce was humanity; he therefore consents that hostilities shall cease, and that the wounded Danes may be taken on shore; and Lord Nelson will take his prisoners out of the vessels, and burn and carry off his prizes as he shall think fit.
>
> Lord Nelson, with humble duty to His Royal Highness the Prince of Denmark, will consider this the greatest victory he

has ever gained, if it may be the cause of a happy reconciliation and union between his own most Gracious Sovereign and His Majesty the King of Denmark.

For Commander Thesiger it was an adventure in keeping with a career full of many adventures and under two flags. Copenhagen, as a fact, was the eighteenth sea-action in which Commander Thesiger had taken part. Transferring himself at an early age from the mercantile marine of the East India Company to the service of the crown, he fought his first battle as a midshipman on the quarter-deck of the famous "saucy" *Arethusa*. Next, Midshipman Thesiger found his way into Rodney's fleet, and won his Lieutenant's commission while serving under that brilliant leader. He had his part, indeed, as one of Rodney's *aides-de-camp*, on the "glorious 12th of April," 1782, in the great battle of the Saintes, by Dominica, in the West Indies, when Rodney dealt the *coup de grace* to French visions of dominion in the West Indies.

As the guns ceased firing at the close of the twelve hours' fight, he was told off, one of the first officers sent, to take possession of the grand prize of victory, the famous French flagship, *Ville de Paris*. Afterwards, impatient at the enforced idleness of half-pay life in England during the years of peace that followed the American War, Lieutenant Thesiger, with several other British officers of adventurous turn, took service in the Russian Navy, at the invitation of the Empress Catherine, and his brilliant battle-services, as captain of a Russian seventy-four in the war with Sweden of 1790, gained him a Knighthood of St. George and a sword of honour from the empress.

In one fierce fight, five out of six British captains present in the battle met their deaths, Captain Thesiger alone coming through the day alive, but with splinter wounds all over his body. The formation of Tsar Paul's "Northern Confederacy" against England brought Thesiger—Sir Frederick he was now, by virtue of his Russian knighthood—back to London. He had to escape from St. Petersburg by stealth. On arrival in England, his knowledge of the Baltic and thorough acquaintance with the Russian and Danish languages being considered at the Admiralty likely to be useful, he was sent, with the rank of a commander in the British Navy, to do duty on the staff in Sir Hyde Parker's fleet. Volunteering to act as one of Nelson's *aides-de-camp* on board the *Elephant* in the attack on Copenhagen, he comes into the story of the battle.

Commander Thesiger, it may be added, went ashore again from

the fleet at Copenhagen, on the occasion of Nelson's first visit to the crown prince; as one of the admiral's suite, to act as interpreter if necessary. Of the scene at Copenhagen on the occasion the accounts differ curiously. According to Colonel Stewart:

> A strong guard secured his safety, and appeared necessary to keep off the mob, whose rage, though mixed with admiration at his thus trusting himself amongst them, was naturally to be expected.

This account, from a Danish gentleman who was present, is probably the most accurate:

> On his landing, he was received by the people neither with acclamations nor with murmurs; they did not degrade themselves with the former, nor disgrace themselves with the latter. The admiral was received as one brave enemy ought ever to receive another—he was received with respect. A carriage was provided for his lordship, which he, however, declined, and walked amidst an immense crowd of persons, anxious to catch a glimpse of the British hero, to the palace of the Prince Royal.

Commander Thesiger accompanied Nelson also on his second visit a week later. Nelson this time:

> . . . . was escorted to the palace, surrounded by an immense crowd, who showed more satisfaction on this occasion than on the preceding one.

ON BOARD SIR HYDE PARKER'S FLAGSHIP

The *London*, together with the other ships of the fleet remaining in reserve with Sir Hyde Parker—another three-decker, Nelson's original flagship the *St. George*, four seventy-fours, and two sixty-fours—was by arrangement to have weighed anchor the moment Nelson stood in to begin his attack. The heavier ships were to menace the great Trekroner Fort, guarding Copenhagen on the northern sea-front, as well as four Danish ships of the line which protected the approach to the arsenal; besides covering any of Nelson's disabled ships which might need support or be forced to withdraw out of action.

As it befell, however, the wind and the tide, while they suited Nelson, were dead against Sir Hyde Parker's squadron. After working up towards the enemy as far as they could, the reserve ships had to anchor at some distance beyond gunshot. They weighed anchor again, and tried again to approach, but were still some three or four miles from the enemy when the Danish flag of truce ended the fighting.

It was, of course, a great disappointment to the gallant fellows so left out of the battle, for all in the squadron had fully expected that they would have a part, and have a glorious day before the enemy. Every preparation in anticipation of hot work had been made, as the journal of the surgeon of the flagship *London*, till recently kept at the Record Office, testifies. The journal details the very complete arrangements that were made for the reception and treatment of the wounded, and the provision of bandages, dressings, and so forth. Not only, indeed, is the journal a curious document in itself, but also, as a fact, it is the only surgeon's journal out of the two thousand odd stored at the Record Office which deals with and describes the arrangements on board an old-time man-of-war in the cockpit before a battle.

Nelson and the "Detached Squadron" weighed anchor for the attack at half-past nine on the morning of "Bloody Monday"—as the Danes to this day call April 2, 1801—and at a few minutes past ten the battle opened, to go on without slackening in its fury for over three hours.

The commander-in-chief, we are told, watched the battle with increasing anxiety, which became intensified after noon had passed. Nelson had told Sir Hyde Parker, so it is said, that an hour would probably suffice to subdue the Danish southern defences, after which he would move up and deal with those to the north, in co-operation with the commander-in-chief's reserve squadron. It proved "a devilish long hour," to use Sir Hyde Parker's own words, and still the Danes everywhere remained unsubdued. More than that, three of Nelson's ships were ashore. They had got aground at the outset, and remained hard and fast aground. The others were facing a tremendous fire from both the batteries on shore and the vessels of the Danish fleet, some eighteen men-of-war, armed hulks, and floating batteries, all ranged in close line.

So far there was no sign of giving in among the Danes that Sir Hyde could discover; no slackening on their side in the fierce and destructive cannonade that was beating down heavily on the detached squadron at every point. It was the harder to see how things were going, for the breeze blew the smoke from Nelson's guns right over the enemy's position, shrouding it to a large extent from Parker's view. All they could make out from on board the *London* was that the Danish fire did not seem to be slackening, while Nelson's own time-limit had long passed. Sir Hyde Parker began more and more to fidget and get apprehensive as to the serious risk that Nelson appeared to be incurring. He doubted, indeed, the possibilities of the ships with Nelson being able to stand up much longer against the terrific cannonade that they were facing; and, more than that, would Nelson, supposing he had to retire before the enemy were subdued, be able to withdraw his damaged ships under fire, and thread his way safely through the intricate channel among the shoals in front of the batteries?

Overcome by anxiety as to what was happening, Sir Hyde decided at noon to send an officer to see what the situation really was in the firing-line. His captain of the fleet, Captain Domett, was to have taken the message to Nelson: but he had been called below a moment before, and the captain of the *London*, Captain Robert Waller Otway, was sent instead. He had a hard row, "for the last mile through a hailstorm of shot that lashed the water all round the boat into foam;" but the boat managed to make its way without being seriously damaged. Captain Otway got on board Nelson's flagship, the *Elephant*, to find that the signal to discontinue the engagement had been made from the *London* while he was on his way, and had been received by Nelson in the manner Colonel Stewart has placed on record.

4
At Trafalgar

NELSON'S LINE OF BATTLE

Ships	Guns.	Commanders
Victory	100	Vice-Admiral Viscount Nelson, K.B.; Captain Thomas Masterman Hardy
Royal Sovereign	100	Vice-Admiral Cuthbert Collingwood; Captain Edward Rotherham.
Britannia	100	Rear-Admiral the Earl of Northesk; Captain Charles Bullen.
Téméraire	98	Captain Eliab Harvey.
Prince	98	Captain Richard Grindall.
Neptune	98	Captain Thomas Francis Fremantle,
Dreadnought	98	Captain John Conn.
Tonnant	80	Captain Charles Tyler.
Belleisle	74	Captain William Hargood.
Revenge	74	Captain Robert Moorsom.
Mars	74	Captain George Duff.
Spartiate	74	Captain Sir Charles Laforey, Baronet.
Defiance	74	Captain Philip Charles Durham.
Conqueror	74	Captain Israel Pellew.
Defence	74	Captain George Hope.
Colossus	74	Captain James Nicoll Morris.
Leviathan	74	Captain Henry William Bayntun.
Achille	74	Captain Richard King.
Bellerophon	74	Captain John Cooke.
Minotaur	74	Captain Charles John Moore Mansfield.
Orion	74	Captain Edward Codrington.
Swiftsure	74	Captain William George Rutherford.

Peace with honour: the "Victory" in Portsmouth harbour

Ajax	74	Lieutenant John Pilfold (Acting-Captain).
Thunderer	74	Lieutenant John Stockham (Acting-Captain).
Polyphemus	64	Captain Richard Redmill
Africa	64	Captain Henry Digby
Agamemnon	64	Captain Sir Edward Berry.

FRIGATES

Euryalus	Captain the Hon. Henry Blackwood.
Naiad	Captain Thomas Dundas.
Phoebe	Captain the Hon. Thomas Bladen Capel.
Sirius	Captain William Prowse.

SCHOONER

Pickle — Lieutenant John Richards Lapenotière.

CUTTER

Entreprenante Lieutenant Robert Benjamin Young.

GOING DOWN TO BATTLE

This was the scene as the morning of Trafalgar opened, and the magnificent spirit of absolute confidence in which Nelson's men went down into the battle. Says one of the officers of the *Belleisle:*

> As the day dawned the horizon appeared covered with ships. The whole force of the enemy was discovered standing to the southward, distant about nine miles, between us and the coast near Trafalgar. I was awakened by the cheers of the crew and by their rushing up the hatchways to get a glimpse of the hostile fleet. The delight manifested exceeded anything I ever witnessed, surpassing even those gratulations when our native cliffs are descried after a long period of distant service.

Midshipman Badcock of the *Neptune* gives this description of what he saw from his ship:

> It was my morning watch, I was midshipman of the forecastle, and at the first dawn of day a forest of strange masts was seen to leeward. I ran aft and informed the officer of the watch. The captain was on deck in a moment, and ere it was well light the signals were flying through the fleet to bear-up and form the order of sailing in two columns.

We have this also from one of the sailors of the *Revenge*:

On the memorable 21st of October, 1805, as the day began to dawn, a man at the topmast-head called out, 'A sail on the starboard bow,' and in two or three minutes more he gave another call, that there was more than one sail, for indeed they looked like a forest of masts rising from the ocean, and as the morning got light we could plainly discern them from the deck, and were satisfied it was the enemy, for the admiral began to telegraph to that effect.

Surgeon Beatty, on board the *Victory*, presents his account of Nelson's doings on that Monday morning in these words:

His Lordship came upon deck soon after daylight: he was dressed as usual in his admiral's frock-coat, bearing on the left breast four stars of different orders, which he always wore with his common apparel. He displayed excellent spirits, and expressed his pleasure at the prospect of giving a fatal blow to the naval power of France and Spain, and spoke with confidence of obtaining a signal victory, notwithstanding the inferiority of the British fleet, declaring to Captain Hardy that 'he would not be contented with capturing less than twenty sail of the line.'

He afterwards pleasantly observed that 'the 21st of October was the happiest day in the year among his family,' but did not assign the reason of this. His Lordship had previously entertained a strong presentiment that this would prove the auspicious day, and had several times said to Captain Hardy and Dr. Scott (chaplain of the ship, and foreign secretary to the commander-in-chief, whose intimate friendship he enjoyed), 'The 21st of October will be our day.'

The wind was now from the west, but the breeze was very light, with a long, heavy swell running. The signal being made for bearing down upon the enemy in two lines, the British fleet set all possible sail. The lee line, consisting of thirteen ships, was led by Admiral Collingwood in the *Royal Sovereign*, and the weather line, composed of fourteen ships, by the commander-in-chief in the *Victory*.

His Lordship had ascended the poop, to have a better view of both lines of the British fleet, and while there gave particular directions for taking down from his cabin the different fixtures, and for being very careful in removing the portrait of Lady Hamilton: 'Take care of my Guardian Angel!' said he, addressing

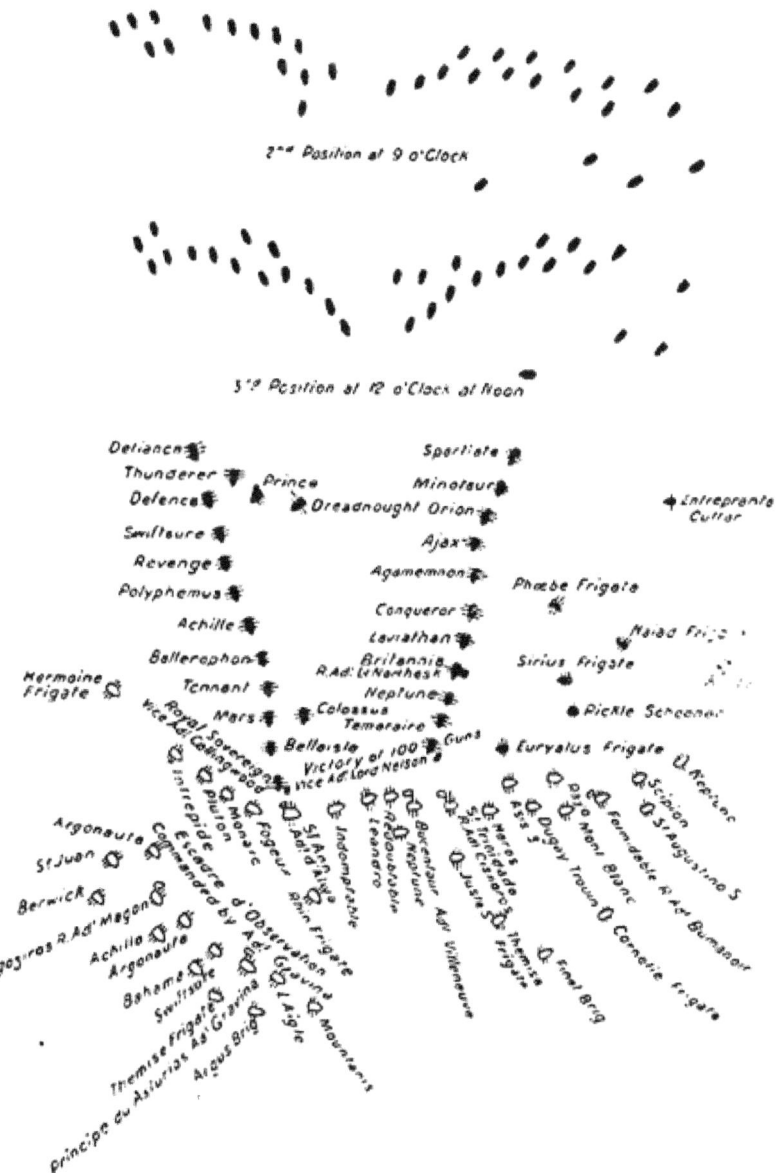

COLLINWOOD'S PLAN OF THE BATTLE OF TRAFALGAR
Reproduction of the plan sent to the Admiralty with Collingwood's dispatch, as corrected for the positions of the ships of the Combined Fleet by Villeneuve's Flag-Captain, a prisoner of war in the *Euryalus*.

himself to the persons to be employed in this business.
Immediately after this he quitted the poop, and retired to his cabin for a few minutes; where he committed to paper the following short but devout and fervent ejaculation, which must be universally admired as truly characteristic of the Christian hero, and the codicil to his will, which follows it:

> May the great God whom I worship grant to my country, and for the benefit of Europe in general, a great and glorious victory, and may no misconduct in anyone tarnish it, and may humanity after victory be the predominant feature in the British fleet! For myself individually, I commit my life to Him that made me, and may His blessing alight on my endeavours for serving my country faithfully! To Him I resign myself, and the just cause which is entrusted to me to defend. Amen, Amen, Amen.

Nelson was seen on his knees, writing down his prayer, by Flag-Lieutenant Pasco, who had gone down to make a report to the admiral, and mention a certain personal matter, a grievance of his own. Though senior lieutenant in the *Victory*, Pasco had been told off to act as signal-lieutenant—ordinarily the junior-lieutenant's post. It was in accordance with a practice Nelson had of making the officer whose name stood first on his list for promotion—as Pasco's did—do duty with the signals, regardless of his relative standing in the ship. Pasco came to urge that if kept to that duty his prospects might suffer after the battle, as actually happened; for Lieutenant Quilliam, who acted as first-lieutenant for the day, though junior to Pasco, was made a post-captain by the Admiralty, while Pasco, having lost his patron, was ignored, and treated as though he had been at his regular post, and only got promotion to commander. Pasco intended to seize the opportunity of having a report to make to lay his grievance before Nelson, but he could not bring himself to do so when he saw how Nelson was occupied.

> I waited until he rose and communicated what I had to report, but could not at such a moment disturb his mind with any grievances of mine.

Several officers describe what took place on board their ships in the course of that morning, as the two fleets neared one another.

This account, for one, is from Lieutenant Nicholas Harris Nicolas' vivid and detailed narrative of the day's doings on board the *Belleisle*:

> There was a light air from the north-west with a heavy swell. The signal to bear-up and make all sail, and to form the order of sailing in two divisions, was thrown out. The *Victory*, Lord Nelson's ship, led the weather line, and the *Royal Sovereign*, bearing the flag of Admiral Collingwood, the second-in-command, the lee line. At eight the enemy wore to the northward, and owing to the light wind, which prevailed during the day, they were prevented from forming with any precision, and presented the appearance of a double line, convexing, to leeward. At nine we were about six miles from them, with studding-sails set on both sides, and as our progress never exceeded a mile and a half an hour, we continued all the canvas we could spread until we gained our position alongside our opponent.
>
> The officers now met at breakfast, and though each seemed to exult in the hope of a glorious termination to the contest so near at hand, a fearful presage was experienced that all would not again unite at that festive board. One was particularly impressed with a persuasion that he should not survive the day, nor could he divest himself of this presentiment, but made the necessary disposal of his property in the event of his death. The sound of the drum, however, soon put an end to our meditations, and after a hasty and, alas! a final farewell to some, we repaired to our respective posts.

Speaking of the *Belleisle's* men, as he saw them a short time later, Lieutenant Harris Nicolas tells us this as well:

> The determined and resolute countenance of the weather-beaten sailor, here and there brightened by a smile of exultation, was well suited to the terrific appearance which they exhibited. Some were stripped to the waist, some had bared their necks and arms, others had tied a handkerchief round their heads, and all seemed eagerly to await the order to engage.

Second-Lieutenant Ellis of the marines of the *Ajax* gives from his ship another very interesting glimpse of the spirit in which the men went into action at Trafalgar:

> I was sent below with orders, and was much struck with the preparations made by the bluejackets, the majority of whom were stripped to the waist; a handkerchief was tightly bound

round their heads and over the ears, to deaden the noise of the cannon, many men being deaf for days after an action. The men were variously occupied; some were sharpening their cutlasses, others polishing the guns, as though an inspection were about to take place instead of a mortal combat, whilst three or four, as if in mere bravado, were dancing a hornpipe; but all seemed deeply anxious to come to close-quarters with the enemy. Occasionally they would look out of the ports, and speculate as to the various ships of the enemy, many of which had been on former occasions engaged by our vessels.

Our sailor on board the *Revenge* again has this to say of what he saw:

> During this time each ship was making the usual preparations, such as breaking the captain's and officers' cabins, and sending all lumber below. The doctors, parson, purser, and lob-lolly men were also busy, getting the medicine-chest and bandages out, and sails prepared for the wounded to be placed on, that they might be dressed in rotation as they were taken down to the after-cockpit.
>
> In such a bustling, and, it may be said, trying as well as serious time, it was curious to notice the different dispositions of the British sailor. Some would be offering a guinea for a glass of grog, whilst others were making a sort of mutual verbal will, such as: 'If one of Johnnie Crapeau's shots (a term given to France) knocks my head off, you will take all my effects; and if you are killed and I am not, why I will have all yours'; and this was generally agreed on.

A seaman of the *Tonnant*, one John Cash, in a letter to his brother in England, says this of his messmates:

> Our good captain called all hands and said: 'My lads, this will be a glorious day for us, and the groundwork of a speedy return to our homes for all.' He then ordered bread and cheese and butter and beer for every man at the guns. I was one of them, and, believe me, we ate and drank, and were as cheerful as ever we had been over a pot of beer.

For an outside view, we have from Midshipman Badcock of the *Neptune*, looking on the general scene from the quarter-deck of his ship, near the head of Nelson's line, this telling picture of the scene all round, as it displayed itself before his eyes. First there was this little episode. He said:

> About ten o'clock, we got close to the *Victory*, and Captain Fremantle had intended to pass her and break the enemy's line; but poor Lord Nelson himself hailed us from the stern-walk of the *Victory*, and said, '*Neptune*, take in your stun'sls and drop astern; I shall break the line myself.' A signal was then made for the *Téméraire* (98) to take her station between us and the *Victory*, which consequently made us the third ship in the van of His Lordship's column.

Looking about him after that, the midshipman describes what he saw on the enemy's side at the outset:

> At this period the enemy were forming their double line in the shape of a crescent. It was a beautiful sight when their line was completed: their broadsides turned towards us showing their iron teeth, and now and then trying the range of a shot to ascertain the distance, that they might, the moment we came within point-blank (about six hundred yards) open their fire upon our van ships—no doubt with the hope of dismasting some of our leading vessels before they could close and break their line.
>
> Some of the enemy's ships were painted like ourselves—with double yellow sides, some with a broad single red or yellow streak, others all black, and the noble *Santissima Trinidada* (138) with four distinct lines of red, with a white ribbon between them, made her seem to be a superb man-of-war, which, indeed, she was. Her appearance was imposing, her head splendidly ornamented with a colossal group of figures, painted white, representing the Holy Trinity, from which she took her name. This magnificent ship was destined to be our opponent. She was lying-to under topsails, top-gallant-sails, royals, jib, and spanker; her courses were hauled up, and her lofty, towering sails looked beautiful, peering through the smoke as she awaited the onset. The flags of France and Spain, both handsome, chequered the line, waving defiance to that of Britain.

Turning after that to his own fleet near at hand, our observant young officer takes things in on the British side:

> In our fleet Union Jacks and ensigns were made fast to the fore

and fore-topmast-stays, as well as to the mizzen rigging, besides one at the peak, in order that we might not mistake each other in the smoke, and to show the enemy our determination to conquer. Towards eleven our two lines were better formed, but still there existed long gaps in Vice-Admiral Collingwood's division. Lord Nelson's van was strong: three three-deckers—*Victory*, *Téméraire*, and *Neptune*—and four seventy-fours, their jib-booms nearly over the others' taffrails. The bands playing 'God Save the King,' 'Rule Britannia,' and 'Britons, Strike Home,' the crews stationed on the forecastles of the different ships, cheering the ship ahead of them when the enemy began to fire, sent those feelings to our hearts that insured victory. About ten minutes before twelve, our antagonists opened their fire upon the *Royal Sovereign* (110), Vice-Admiral Collingwood, who most nobly, and unsupported for at least ten minutes, led his division into action, steering for the *Santa Anna* (112), which was painted all black, bearing the flag of Admiral Gravina, during which time all the enemy's line that could possibly bring a gun to bear were firing at her. She was the admiration of the whole fleet.

To show the great and master-mind of Nelson, who was thinking of everything, even in the momentous hour of battle, when most minds would have been totally absorbed in other matters, it was remarked by him that the enemy had the iron hoops round their masts painted black. Orders were issued by signal to whitewash those of his fleet, that in the event of all the ensigns being shot away, his ships might be distinguished by their white masts and hoops.

Another eyewitness (Midshipman Hercules Robinson, of the frigate *Euryalus*) notes also, as something of a curiosity, what the little sloop-of-war. *Pickle*—the smallest vessel but one on either side at Trafalgar—looked like, as she sailed gaily towards the foe, midway between the two lines of big ships, all advancing in stately array, with canvas packed from decks to masthead.

Even the saucy little schooner *Pickle*—a tiny thing, too small except to make herself useful to Blackwood's frigates—tried to look fierce and threatening, with a confident assumption ridiculous to witness. She took post between the stately lines of the towering three and two-deckers, cleared for action fore and aft in ludicrous imitation of them, with her small boarding-nettings triced up, and her 4-pounder popguns—about as large and as formidable as two pairs of jack-boots—double-shotted and run out.

The fleet held steadfastly on its course in grim silence that was unbroken save for, now in one ship, now in another, a gruff, hoarse-toned order, short and sharp, or the chirp of a bo'sun's whistle, the creaking of a spar, or flap of a sail. Lieutenant Hoffman of the *Tonnant* tells us:

> The wind was very light, and it was nearly noon before we closed with the enemy. We remarked they had formed their ships alternately French and Spanish. All our ships that had bands were playing 'Rule Britannia,' 'Downfall of Paris,' etc. Our own struck up 'Britons, Strike Home.' We were so slow in moving through the water, in consequence of the lightness of the wind, that some of the enemy's ships gave us a royal salute before we could break their line, and we lost two of the band, and had nine wounded, before we opened our fire.

The *Belleisle*, a faster ship, passed the *Tonnant* at the last moment, cutting her out for second place in Collingwood's line. Lieutenant Harris Nicolas, of the *Belleisle*, best tells the story of what occurred as his ship went by her consort.

> Our ship's superior sailing caused an interchange of places with the *Tonnant*. On our passing that ship the Captains greeted each other on the honourable prospect in view. Captain Tyler exclaimed, 'A glorious day for old England! We shall have one apiece before night!' This confidence in our professional superiority—which carries such terror to other nations—seemed expressed in every countenance, and as if in confirmation of this soul-inspiring sentiment, the band of our consort was playing 'Britons, Strike Home.'

"ENGLAND EXPECTS THAT EVERY MAN WILL DO HIS DUTY"

It was a little before twelve o'clock that Nelson signalled his historic message to the fleet.

The *Victory* at the time was about a mile and a half from the enemy's line, slowly forging ahead before the faint breeze under every sail she could set. On the flagship's quarter-deck Nelson and Captain Blackwood were walking together, watching the long, straggling array of French and Spanish ships as they slowly drew across the course of the British advance.

The message went up in twelve separate hoists, Nelson's words being rendered according to the numbers of Sir Home Popham's telegraphic code, which he had insisted on having supplied to the fleet before leaving England, using with it the numerical flags of the current Admiralty Day Signal Book:

253	269	863	261	471	958
"ENGLAND	EXPECTS	THAT	EVERY MAN		WILL
220	370	4	21	19	24
DO	HIS	D	U	T	Y."

Captain Blackwood gives this description of what passed between himself and Nelson as to the making of the signal.

> I was walking with him on the poop when he said, 'I'll now amuse the fleet with a signal;' and he asked me 'if I did not think there was one thing yet wanting?' I answered that I thought the whole of the Fleet seemed very clearly to understand what they were about, and to vie with each other who should first go nearest the *Victory* or *Royal Sovereign*. These words were scarcely uttered when his last well-known signal was made: 'England expects every man will do his duty.' The shout with which it was received throughout the fleet was truly sublime. 'Now,' said Lord Nelson, 'I can do no more. We must trust to the Great Disposer of all Events, and the justice of our cause. I thank God for this great opportunity of doing my duty.'

As to the wording of the message, we have this from Flag-Lieutenant Pasco, the officer who superintended the hoisting of the flags on board the *Victory*.

> His Lordship came to me on the poop, and after ordering certain signals to be made, about a quarter to noon said, 'Mr. Pasco, I want to say to the fleet, "England confides that every man will do his duty."' He added, 'You must be quick, for I have one more to add, which is for "Close Action."' I replied, 'If your Lordship will permit me to substitute "expects" for "confides," the signal will sooner be completed, because the word "expects" is in the vocabulary, and "confides" must be spelt.'
>
> His Lordship replied in haste, and in seeming satisfaction, 'That will do, Pasco; make it directly.' As the last hoist was hauled down. Nelson turned to Captain Blackwood, who was stand-

ing by him, with, 'Now I can do no more. We must trust to the great Disposer of all events, and the justice of our cause. I thank God for this great opportunity of doing my duty.' When Lord Nelson's message had been answered by a few ships in the van, he ordered me to make the signal for 'Close Action' and keep it up. Accordingly I hoisted No. 16 at the top-gallant masthead, and there it remained until shot away.

"No. 16," it may be remarked by the way, was the very last signal that Nelson made to the fleet before the battle opened—"Engage more closely"—the ordinary signal for close action. It comprised two flags: the uppermost red, yellow, red, in three horizontal bars; the lower, a flag diagonally divided white and blue. That went up at the *Victory's* main-top-gallant masthead a little after twelve o'clock; after the enemy had begun firing.

There was, however, more than one alteration made in the wording of the historic message.

Lieutenant George Brown, who was helping Pasco with the signals on board the *Victory*, witnessed a short discussion that took place, and tells us about it.

> I was on the poop and quarter-deck whilst preparations for the fight were going on, and saw Lord N———, Captain Blackwood, and some other captains of the frigates, in earnest conversation together, and a slip of paper in the hand of the former (which Captain Blackwood had looked at), yet I have no recollection that I ever saw it pass through other hands till it was given to Pasco, who, after referring to the telegraph signal book, took it back to his Lordship, and it was then that, I believe, the substitution of the words took place. I think (though not sure), the substitution was 'expects' for the word 'confides,' the latter word not being in the telegraph book, and I think the word 'England' had been previously substituted for 'Nelson' for the same reason, at the suggestion of Captain Blackwood."

Was it Blackwood who offered the suggestion, or another officer? The credit of proposing the alteration has also been credited to Captain Hardy. This is what the son of an acquaintance of Captain Hardy (Mr. H. N. Purcell, of Fowey, in Cornwall), wrote a few years ago:

> Often have I heard my late father, together with his old friends and messmates, the late admirals Sir Henry Preston, Sir James

Scott, and others, speak of the celebrated signal given from the *Victory* at Trafalgar. They spoke of it (as I remember) as a well-known fact in naval circles that the signal, when ordered to be given by the admiral, ran thus: 'Nelson expects every man,' etc., but that the flag-captain (Lord Nelson's old friend, Captain Hardy), immediately made the happy suggestion which resulted in the glorious watchword being given instead: 'England expects that every man this day will do his duty.'

Surgeon Beatty, speaking for the officers and men on the main- and lower-decks of the *Victory*, has this to tell:

About half an hour before the enemy opened their fire, the memorable telegraphic signal was made that 'England expects every man will do his duty,' which was spread and received throughout the fleet with enthusiasm. It is impossible adequately to describe by any language the lively emotions excited in the crew of the *Victory* when this propitious communication was made known to them: confidence and resolution were strongly portrayed in the countenance of all, and the sentiment generally expressed to each other was that they would prove to their country that day how well British seamen could 'do their duty' when led to battle by their revered admiral.

How Nelson's message was received on board the ships of the fleet—in some of those, at least, that took note of it—is of itself an interesting story. A few, apparently, did not mark it at all, while others, too much occupied with their battle preparations, it may have been, merely noted the signal briefly in their logs and paid little further heed to it until after the battle.

Captain Blackwood, judging, it would seem, from the shouts he heard from the ships nearest the *Victory*, tells us that the admiral's message was greeted everywhere "with enthusiasm."

"It was received," says Southey, in his *Life of Nelson*, adopting Blackwood's account, "throughout the fleet with a shout of answering acclamation, made sublime by the spirit which it breathed and the feeling which it expressed."

Blackwood's situation, however, at that moment on board Nelson's flagship at the head of the weather line was by no means a good one for general observation. For one thing, some ships could not make out the signal owing to the lightness of the wind, which caused the flags to droop and prevented them from blowing out sufficiently to be read off. At the same time, also, owing to the wide spread of canvas in the *Victory* and the ships following her in line blocking out a full view, as well as to the wide extent over which the fleet extended, a number of the ships towards the rear could not "take in" the signal direct from the *Victory*. They only received the message after an interval, through the "repeating frigates," whose duty it was to pass the commander-in-chief's signals along the lines of ships.

Even then, too, certain of them paid so little regard to it that they did not even make reference to it in their logs. It so happened that just as the repeating frigates were passing the message along, the enemy began to fire, and this would naturally draw off everybody's attention. On board some of the ships, indeed, as it would appear, the men neither saw the signal nor heard a word about it till after the battle was over. Their captains, it may be, were too matter-of-fact to take in its significance, or they may not have thought it worthwhile to send anyone below to read it off the signal slate to the men between decks, then at quarters standing to the guns.

Rather curiously, too, scarcely any heed to it, beyond hoisting it to pass on to the farther end of the line, was paid on board the *Euryalus*, the frigate specially told off to repeat the *Victory's* signals—Blackwood's own ship. Midshipman Hercules Robinson of the *Euryalus*, commenting on Southey's paraphrase of Captain Blackwood's assertion about the signal that "the shout with which it was received throughout the fleet was truly sublime," makes this remark:

> Lord Nelson's 'England expects,' etc., was sublime, but, then, here is the historical lie—'It was received throughout the fleet with shouts of acclamation, and excited an unbounded enthusiasm!' Why, it was noted in the signal-book and in the log, and that was all about it in our ship till we heard of our alleged transports on our return to England.

Yet enough people in the fleet saw it and understood its real purport. Collingwood's biographer (the admiral's relative, Mr. G. L. Newnham Collingwood), who learned his facts at first-hand from officers of the *Royal Sovereign*, speaks of the manner in which Collingwood received the message.

> While they were running down, the well-known telegraphic signal was made—'England expects every man to do his duty.' When the admiral observed it first, he said that he wished Nelson would make no more signals, for they all understood what

they were to do; but when the purport of it was communicated to him, he expressed great delight and admiration, and made it known to the officers and ship's company.

Lieutenant John Barclay, of the *Britannia* (flagship of the Earl of Northesk, third in command at Trafalgar), says:

> At a ¼ before 12, answered signal from the *Victory*, 'England expects every man to do his duty,' which was joyfully welcomed by the ship's company.

Our friend Midshipman Badcock of the *Neptune*, third ship astern of the *Victory* at the moment the flags went up, quoting from his ship's log, says:

> At 11 answered the general telegraphic signal, 'England expects every man will do his duty.' Captain Fremantle inspected the different decks and made known the above signal, which was received with cheers.

Lieutenant Ellis of the *Ajax's* marines, who, with other officers, was told off to take the message round the ship, speaks thus of its reception below:

> I was desired to inform those on the main-deck of the admiral's signal. Upon acquainting one of the quartermasters of the order, he assembled the men with 'Avast there, lads, come and hear the admiral's words.' When the men were mustered, I delivered with becoming dignity the sentence, rather anticipating that the effect on the men would be to awe them by its grandeur. Jack, however, did not appreciate it, for there were murmurs from some, whilst others in an audible whisper, murmured, 'Do our duty! Of course we'll do our duty! I've always done mine, haven't you? Let us come alongside of 'em, and we'll soon show whether we'll do our duty.' Still, the men cheered vociferously—more, I believe, from love and admiration of their admiral and leader than from a full appreciation of this well-known signal."

Lieutenant Humphrey Senhouse, of the *Conqueror*, wrote this in a letter home a week after the battle:

> In the course of the morning our chief, in his short, energetic, and impressive style, telegraphed generally to the purpose:

'England expects this day that every man will do his duty.' The result, I trust, will fully prove that the stimulating consideration invigorated the mind of every individual, and that the first impulse which actuated the conduct of all was the welfare and glory of our country, our king, our chief, and ourselves.

Lieutenant Nicholas Harris Nicolas, of the Belleisles marines, also speaks of how Nelson's words appealed to the men in his ship:

> At half-past ten the *Victory* telegraphed, 'England expects every man will do his duty.' As this emphatic injunction was communicated through the decks, it was received with enthusiastic cheers, and each bosom glowed with ardour at this appeal to individual valour.

This is what appears in the log of the *Polyphemus*:

> At 12.15 the *Victory* made the general telegraphic signal, 'England expects that every man will do his duty,' which being told to the ship's company, was answered by three cheers, and returned by the *Dreadnought* on our starboard beam.

Midshipman Henry Walker, of the *Bellerophon*, describes how his shipmates received the message home, written on October 22, in a letter:

> A few minutes before firing commenced, Lord Nelson conveyed by telegraph the following sentence to the fleet: 'England expects that every man will do his duty.' This was received on board our ship with three cheers, and a general shout of 'No fear of that.'

Another midshipman of the same ship, writing home in a letter dated December 2, 1805, also says of the signal

> A few minutes before the action commenced Lord Nelson conveyed the following sentence by telegraph to the fleet: 'England expects every man will do his duty.' The loud and repeated cheering with which this was received was a convincing proof that such an injunction was needless.

According to a third officer in the *Bellerophon*, Captain Cooke went down below and exhorted his men on every deck, most earnestly entreating them to remember the words of their gallant admiral just communicated by signal: "England expects that every man will do

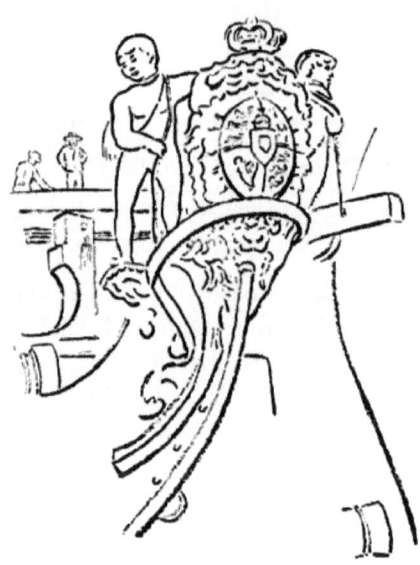

THE VICTORY'S FIGURE-HEAD AFTER TRAFALGAR
From a pencil sketch made in December, 1805, on
the *Victory's* return to England

FORE-TOP SAIL OF THE VICTORY RIDDLED WITH SHOT HOLES AS
RETURNED TO STORE AT CHATHAM DOCKYARD
AFTER TRAFALGAR

his duty." He was cheered on his return upward by the whole ship's company, who wrote on their guns in chalk, "*Bellerophon*! Death or glory!"

One of the marines of the *Prince*, in a letter home, also speaks of the general enthusiasm:

> You will easily judge what an effect this emphatic message, conveyed by telegraph to the fleet, from Lord Nelson, must have had on each individual: 'England expects that every man will do his duty.' How cheerfully Englishmen did do their duty the issue of the battle fully shows.

On Board the "Victory"

There were twenty-seven ships of the line on the British side at Trafalgar, and thirty-three on the enemy's side, under Admiral Villeneuve, the French officer who commanded the Franco-Spanish fleet that day. The British fleet advanced in two columns, one, of course, led by Nelson, and the other by Collingwood in his flagship the *Royal Sovereign*.

It was just about midday that the *Victory* began to come within long-range gunshot of the enemy, approaching at an angle to the long-drawn-out array of ships with which Villeneuve awaited Nelson's attack. Collingwood's column, in accordance with Nelson's plan of battle, began the fighting. Collingwood attacked, a very little after midday, at about the twelfth ship from the rear, dividing the enemy in two at that point, just astern of the Spanish second-in-command's flagship. Nelson's plan was for himself, in the *Victory*, to break through the enemy at about ten or eleven ships from the van, after Collingwood had opened the attack.

His design was to cut off the Franco-Spanish van squadron, and leave it to leeward, at the same time that he fell, with all his fleet of twenty-seven ships as they came up, on the enemy's centre and rear. He practically proposed to throw his whole force on to two-thirds of the enemy, twenty-seven to twenty-two, while the other third—the enemy's van ships—separated, and to leeward would be unable to work round against the wind and take part in the battle until too late, until after the others had been overpowered by weight of numbers.

As the *Victory*, sailing before the very light breeze, slowly forged ahead towards the great semicircle of ships that the enemy's array formed, she became a mark for a heavy and concentrated fire from most of the ships of the enemy's van and centre—all that could get her range. Collingwood had just broken through at his point of attack, and the Franco-Spanish rear-ships had enough to do facing him and his followers.

The first ship to fire at the *Victory* was the *Bucentaure*, Admiral Villeneuve's flagship, which at the outset led off with a trial shot at Nelson, when the *Victory* was about 800 yards off. The ball fell short. A second, fired three minutes later, struck the water close alongside the *Victory*. Then came a third shot, which went over the flagship between the masts. A fourth followed, and tore a gaping hole through one of the *Victory's* topsails. The enemy saw it, and there was a pause of ten or twelve seconds. Immediately afterwards, as if by signal, eight of the enemy's ships opened fire, blazing away at the British flagship with a continuous fire, which soon began to tell.

At six hundred yards off the *Victory's* mizzen topmast was shot away, and soon after that her steering-wheel was smashed. She had thenceforward to be steered on the main-deck below by means of relieving tackles. Her foremast was shot through, and her sails were torn to tatters. A cannon-ball struck down Mr. Scott, Nelson's official secretary, dead on the quarter-deck, and another smashed off a heavy splinter which passed close between Nelson and Hardy. Still, though severely knocked about in her hull and spars, and with some fifty of her men killed and wounded already, the *Victory* held her way in silence, not replying with a single gun, until she reached the enemy's line; steering to break through astern of the *Bucentaure*. Reaching the spot, she surged slowly past Villeneuve's flagship, pouring in a double-shotted broadside at such close quarters that the *Bucentaure's* ensign brushed against the *Victory's* rigging. That terrific discharge went far towards rendering the French flagship *hors de combat*. So the *Victory* went into action at Trafalgar.

Dr. Beatty says, speaking of what took place on board the *Victory:*

> At fifty minutes past eleven, the enemy opened their fire on the commander-in-chief. They showed great coolness in the commencement of the battle; for as the *Victory* approached their line, their ships lying immediately ahead of her and across her bows fired only one gun at a time, to ascertain whether she was yet within their range. This was frequently repeated by eight or nine of their ships, till at length a shot passed through the *Victory's* main top-gallant sail; the hole in which, being discovered by the enemy, they immediately opened their broadsides, sup-

porting an awful and tremendous fire.

In a very short time afterwards Mr. Scott, public secretary to the commander-in-chief, was killed by a cannon-shot while in conversation with Captain Hardy. Lord Nelson being then near them; Captain Adair, of the marines, with the assistance of a seaman, endeavoured to remove the body from His Lordship's sight: but he had already observed the fall of his secretary; and now said with anxiety, 'Is that poor Scott that is gone?' and on being answered in the affirmative by Captain Adair, he replied, 'Poor fellow?'

Lord Nelson and Captain Hardy walked the quarter-deck in conversation for some time after this, while the enemy kept up an incessant raking fire.

A double-headed shot struck one of the party of marines drawn up on the poop and killed eight of them; when his Lordship, perceiving this, ordered Captain Adair to disperse his men round the ship, that they might not suffer so much from being together.

In a few minutes afterwards a shot struck the fore-brace bits on the quarter-deck, and passed between Lord Nelson and Captain Hardy; a splinter from the bits bruising Captain Hardy's foot, and tearing the buckle from his shoe. They both instantly stopped, and were observed by the officers on deck to survey each other with inquiring looks, each supposing the other to be wounded. His Lordship then smiled, and said: 'This is too warm work, Hardy, to last long,' and declared that 'through all the battles he had been in, he had never witnessed more cool courage than was displayed by the *Victory's* crew on this occasion.'

The *Victory* by this time, having approached close to the enemy's van, had suffered very severely without firing a single gun: she had lost about twenty men killed, and had about thirty wounded. Her mizzen topmast, and all her studding-sails and their booms on both sides were shot away; the enemy's fire being chiefly directed at her rigging, with a view to disable her before she could close with them.

At four minutes past twelve o'clock, she opened her fire, from both sides of her decks, upon the enemy; when Captain Hardy represented to His Lordship, that 'it appeared impracticable to pass through the enemy's line without going on board some of their ships.'

Lord Nelson answered, 'I cannot help it: it does not signify which we run on board of; go on board which you please, take your choice.'

Hardy went straight ahead. He steered directly to force the passage close under the stern of the *Bucentaure*, and did so. The *Victory* drove through so near to the *Bucentaure* that her main yard-arm caught in the French flagship's after-rigging, her shrouds brushing against the French ensign as it hung down from its staff over the *Bucentaure's* taffrail, drooping from want of wind to blow it out. A hand, we are told, could have caught hold of the flag from the *Victory's* gangway. So close did the two ships pass that, as the *Victory* fired her first broadside, the fibres of shattered woodwork from the *Bucentaure's* stern spread over the *Victory* in a cloud of fine dust, that coated the clothes of Nelson and Hardy and all on the quarter-deck; while below, the smoke of the *Victory's* guns, fired practically in contact with the French ship's hull, came pouring back in-board, through the ports, rebuffed and beaten back, blinding and half stifling the men at quarters.

As she swept slowly by, first the port-carronade on the *Victory's* forecastle, crammed with a 68-pound shot and a keg of five hundred bullets, was fired right into Admiral Villeneuve's cabin windows, and then, gun by gun, as each bore, the *Victory's* whole port broadside followed, fifty-two guns all told—double-shotted some, treble-shotted the rest. How fearful was the havoc and devastation on board the hapless French flagship the officers of the *Bucentaure* told afterwards. Twenty of their guns were dismounted, they said, four hundred of their men—half the crew—were struck down, put *hors de combat,* or killed outright.

The *Victory* cleared the *Bucentaure*, receiving a warm fire from the French *Neptune* as she forged ahead, but paying no heed, she discharged her starboard broadside into another French ship, the *Redoutable*, alongside which she then ran. As she drove foul of the *Redoutable*, the *Victory's* starboard 68-pounder carronade was discharged with murderous effect along the crowded decks of the French seventy-four.

Resuming with Dr. Beatty, the narrative continues:—

> At twenty minutes past twelve, the tiller ropes being shot away, Mr. Atkinson, the master, was ordered below to get the helm put to port; which being done, the *Victory* was soon run on board the *Redoutable*, of seventy-four guns.
> On coming alongside, and nearly on board of her, that ship fired

her broadside into the *Victory*, and immediately let down her lower deck ports; which, as has been learnt, was done to prevent her from being boarded through them by the *Victory's* crew.

A few minutes after this, the *Téméraire* fell likewise on board of the *Redoutable*, on the side opposite to the *Victory*, having also an enemy's ship, said to be *La Fougeux*, on board of her on her other side; so that the extraordinary and unprecedented circumstance occurred here, of four ships of the line being on board of each other in the heat of the battle; forming as compact a tier as if they had been moored together, their heads lying all the same way. The *Téméraire*, as was just before mentioned, was between the *Redoutable* and *La Fougeux*.

The *Redoutable* commenced a heavy fire of musketry from the tops, which was continued for a considerable time with destructive effect to the *Victory's* crew; her great guns, however, being silent, it was supposed at different times that she had surrendered; and in consequence of this opinion, the *Victory* twice ceased firing upon her, by orders transmitted from the quarter-deck.

At this period, scarcely a person in the *Victory* escaped unhurt who was exposed to the enemy's musketry; but there were frequent huzzas and cheers heard from between the decks, in token of the surrender of different of the enemy's ships. An incessant fire was kept up from both sides of the *Victory*: her larboard guns played up the *Santissima Trinidada* and the *Bucentaure* and the starboard guns of the middle and lower-decks were depressed, and fired, with a diminished charge of powder, and three shot each, into the *Redoutable*. This mode of firing was adopted by Lieutenants Williams, King, Yule, and Browne, to obviate the danger of the *Téméraire's* suffering from the *Victory's* shot passing through the *Redoutable*, which must have been the case if the usual quantity of powder and the common elevation had been given to the guns.

A circumstance occurred in this situation which showed in a most striking manner the cool intrepidity of the officers and men stationed on the lower-deck of the *Victory*. When the guns on this deck were run out, their muzzles came into contact with the *Redoutable's* side; and, consequently, at every discharge there was reason to fear that the enemy would take fire, and both the *Victory* and the *Téméraire* be involved in her flames. Here there was seen the astonishing spectacle of the fireman of each gun standing ready with a bucket full of water, which as soon as his gun was discharged, he dashed into the enemy through the holes made in her side by the shot.

The *Victory*, all over the ship, everywhere on board, was shrouded in thick smoke, which hung in a dense, enveloping cloud over all. The breeze of the forenoon had fallen away and died down entirely. Below, the muzzles of some of the starboard guns were touching the *Redoutable's* side, and with every discharge the smoke came pouring back continuously in dense puffs through the ports, rolling heavily inboard, blurring out the weak gleam of light that the horn lanterns overhead gave, accumulating in the crammed space between decks like a thick fog until all was enveloped in opaque blackness. The men had to grope for their tackle and gear, and fight their guns blindfold.

On the port broadside, where they were firing at the *Santissima Trinidad* and other ships, they had to aim by ear, mechanically obeying orders passed down from above; now to train two points abaft the beam; now ahead; now a point aft, and so on—no one actually seeing what was being aimed at. In that manner they went on without pausing, firing as ordered, each man unmoved by what was happening round him, until either he was knocked down and had to be carried below to the cockpit, or a momentary pause in the firing gave him a chance of feeling his way to the nearest scuttle-butt to quench his parching thirst.

On the quarter-deck the smoke was but a little less dense. Dr. Scott, Nelson's chaplain, running up for fresh air and a moment's respite from the horrors of the cockpit, found everything on deck shrouded in a "pall of smoke and of dust, shattered out of the Spaniard (Frenchman) alongside, hanging so low that the figures of Nelson and Hardy walking up and down could hardly be seen through it."

Dr. Scott's duties, of course, confined him to the cockpit, which was crowded with wounded and dying men, "and such was the horror that filled his mind at this scene of suffering, that it haunted him like a shocking dream for years afterwards. He never talked of it. Indeed, the only record of a remark on the subject was one extorted from him by the inquiries of a friend, soon after his return home. The expression that escaped him at the moment was, 'it was like a butcher's shambles.'

"His natural tenderness of feeling," as we are told, "very much heightened by the shock on his nervous system, quite disqualified him for being a calm spectator of death and pain, as there exhibited in their most appalling shapes. But he suppressed his aversion as well as he could, and had for some time been engaged in helping and consoling those who were suffering around him, when a fine young lieutenant (Lieutenant Ram) was brought down desperately wounded. This officer was not aware of the extent of his injury until the surgeon's examination, but, on discovering it, he tore off with his own hand the ligatures that were being applied, and bled to death. Almost frenzied by the sight of this, Scott hurried wildly to the deck for relief, perfectly regardless of his own safety. He rushed up the companion ladder—now slippery with gore—the scene above was all noise, confusion, and smoke—but he had hardly time to breathe there, when Lord Nelson himself fell, and this event at once sobered his disordered mind. He followed his chief to the cockpit."

The *Victory's* marines were all the time keeping up a brisk exchange of musketry from behind the poop and quarter-deck bulwarks with the French soldiers in the *Redoutable's* tops. For reasons of his own, Nelson would not allow small-arm men in the tops of any of his ships. He disliked the practice, as he had often said. It was no better, he considered, than murder. It meant only the picking off of the most conspicuously dressed officers; a useless killing that could not affect the issue of the battle. More than that, there was a risk of fire. That, above everything, weighed with Nelson. Ever since the destruction of the *Alcide*, which he had witnessed with his own eyes in Hotham's battle off Genoa, ten years before, through a fire that broke out in her tops, and the catastrophe of *L'Orient* at the Nile, Nelson had had a horror of fire as the worst of all dangers that a ship was exposed to in battle. An accidental explosion in the tops might at any time, he said, result in grave disaster. Had Nelson lived through that day he would have had yet another reason to strengthen his opinion; he would have seen the destruction of one of the French ships at Trafalgar by a fire which broke out in her tops.

The *Victory's* marines had to make the best fight they could from on deck against the French soldiers and hand-grenade men in the *Redoutable's* top.

We take up the tale again as Dr. Beatty tells it:

> It was from this ship (the *Redoutable*) that Lord Nelson received his mortal wound. About fifteen minutes past one o'clock, which was in the heat of the engagement, he was walking in

the middle of the quarter-deck with Captain Hardy, and in the act of turning near the hatchway, with his face towards the stern of the *Victory*, when the fatal ball was fired from the enemy's mizzen top; which, from the situation of the two ships (lying on board of each other), was brought just abaft, and rather below, the *Victory's* main-yard, and, of course, not more than fifteen yards distant from that part of the deck where His Lordship stood. The ball struck the epaulette on his left shoulder and penetrated his chest. He fell with his face on the deck. Captain Hardy, who was on his right (the side farthest from the enemy) and (had) advanced some steps before his lordship, on turning round, saw the sergeant-major (Seeker) of the marines with two seamen raising him from the deck; where he had fallen on the same spot on which, a little before, his secretary had breathed his last, with whose blood His Lordship's clothes were much soiled.

Captain Hardy expressed a hope that he was not severely wounded, to which the gallant chief replied 'They have done for me at last, Hardy.'

'I hope not,' answered Captain Hardy.

'Yes,' replied his lordship; 'my backbone is shot through.'

Captain Hardy ordered the seamen to carry the admiral to the cockpit; and now two incidents occurred, strikingly characteristic of this great man, and strongly marking that energy and reflection which in his heroic mind rose superior even to the immediate consideration of his present awful condition. While the men were carrying him down the ladder from the middle-deck, his lordship observed that the tiller ropes were not yet replaced; and desired one of the midshipmen stationed there to go upon the quarter-deck and remind Captain Hardy of that circumstance, and request that new ones should be immediately rove. Having delivered this order, he took his handkerchief from his pocket and covered his face with it, that he might be conveyed to the cockpit at this crisis unnoticed by the crew.

The *Redoutable's* musketry fell on the *Victory* with intensified fierceness in the quarter of an hour after Nelson fell. It swept the upper-deck from end to end, and struck down so many men that the guns in the open had to be abandoned for the time, and the crews withdrawn to shelter below. On the poop and quarter-deck several officers and upwards of forty men were struck down, killed or wounded. So few people were indeed left about that a wild idea seized the captain of the *Redoutable* of actually carrying the *Victory* by a *coup de main*.

When the British three-decker first swung alongside them, the *Redoutable's* men—as has been said—shut down most of their ports on the side next the *Victory*, to prevent her men from clambering through and boarding. Through the ports that the French kept open at either end of the ship they had continued to fire with their guns, at the same time keeping up a fusillade of musketry into the open ports of the *Victory*, to hamper her men in the batteries. After that the *Victory* had ceased firing into the *Redoutable*. Nelson, as we have seen, thinking it possible from the slackness of the *Redoutable's* gun-fire that she was about to surrender, with the idea of preventing useless bloodshed, had personally sent down orders to cease firing. Misunderstanding the British cessation of fire, Captain Lucas replied by attempting to board "*pour en finir avec le Victory*," as he put it, in his report of his ship's doings to Napoleon.

He made one attempt before Nelson fell; but that had been brought to naught by a sweeping *mitraille* from the *Victory's* starboard sixty-eighty pounder carronade, which Boatswain Wilmot had swung round and discharged, crammed to the muzzle with round-shot and a keg of 500 musket bullets, right into the thick of the Frenchmen on deck at the critical moment, just as they were in the act of swarming up the hatchways. Incited to a second effort, a few minutes after Nelson had been taken below, by the sight of the havoc that his musketry and hand- grenades from the tops were causing. Captain Lucas once more called up his men. They hastened on deck, cutlass and boarding-pike in hand, and crowded along the gangways and into the nettings, shouting and yelling "*A l'abordage!*"

There was, though, before them more than they knew. To "rush" the *Victory*, to get across on to her deck, was impossible; owing to the deep recurve of the two ships' hulls, and the wide space of several feet that consequently separated the towering top-sides of the *Victory* from the bulwarks of the *Redoutable*. That brought the *Redoutable's* men up, balked at the outset. The next moment the *Victory's* nettings were lined from end to end with seamen and marines who had rushed up hastily, tumbling up the hatchways from below on the call "Repel boarders!"

Opening with a brisk fire of small arms on Captain Lucas' boarders, they gave their opponents more than the Frenchmen expected; but at the same time they lost heavily themselves, mostly from the French musketry in the tops and the hand-grenades, and from cannon-shot from the *Redoutable's* main-deck guns, fired with high-angle elevation slantwise up through the decks. Within three minutes Captain Adair of the *Victory's* marines and eighteen men had fallen dead, and a lieutenant and a midshipman, with eighteen men, been struck down wounded, many mortally. The lieutenant got his death-wound from a twenty-four pound ball that crashed up through the deck at his feet. The splinters from that one shot maimed five of the *Victory's* seamen nearby.

Then the *Téméraire* came on the scene and took the Frenchmen, so to speak, in rear. She fired her full broadside right among the enemy as they stood massed and packed together. All was over with the *Redoutable* after that, though her heroic little captain ("*Le petit Lucas*" was small, even for a Frenchman—only four feet ten inches in height) kept up the fight from his tops for some time longer. His topmen, indeed, in their frenzied eagerness, at one time set both the *Victory* and the *Téméraire* on fire with their hand-grenades, as well as their own ship. The *Victory's* men not only put their own fire out, but further lent a hand to the *Redoutable's* men themselves against the common danger, by flinging buckets of water from their gangway on to the burning forecastle of the *Redoutable*. Towards the end, indeed, after the *Redoutable* had practically ceased her opposition, but before the ship had actually surrendered, a couple of the *Victory's* midshipmen, with eight or ten men, dropped into a boat, and pulled round and clambered in at the stern ports of the *Redoutable*, to help to put out a fresh fire that had broken out in the after-part of the ship. They were, it is said, well received.

The *Victory* meanwhile also had to fire at intervals on her further broadside at others of the enemy's ships.

After the *Téméraire* had been made fast to the *Redoutable* there was little left for Nelson's flagship to do, except to boom herself clear and move away. She did so about two o'clock, leaving Captain Harvey to take possession of the prize. Except for exchanging a distant fire with the French van squadron as it doubled back and passed along outside the line in its effort to escape—the concussion from which tried the dying Nelson cruelly—there was nothing more for her beyond carrying out her general duties as commander-in-chief's flagship.

That service, of course, could in no circumstances be delegated. Shortly after the admiral fell, an officer (Lieutenant Hills) had been sent in a boat to inform Collingwood, as second in command, that

Nelson's Hardy:—
Captain Thomas Masterman Hardy shortly before he took command of the "Victory"

Silver pencil-case held in his mouth and used by Captain Hardy to note down signals at Trafalgar—
"showing marks of his teeth in moments of excitement"

Lord Nelson had been wounded; but Nelson's flag continued to fly at the fore throughout, and the fleet took their orders from the *Victory*. Captain Hardy, indeed, had practically the entire handling of the fleet at Trafalgar from half-past one o'clock to half-past four, and all that there was to do he did ably. The silver pencil-case which Hardy used to note down various signals which he ordered from time to time is treasured to this day by his descendants. He held it for most of the time between his teeth, and the pencil-case bears on it, in the words of the description appended to the relic when shown at the Naval Exhibition at Chelsea in 1891, "the marks of his teeth made in moments of excitement!"

On board the *Victory* there were on the morning of Trafalgar Day 830 officers and men all told, including Nelson and his suite. The quarter-deck officers, with Captain Hardy at their head, numbered 24; and there were also some 31 mates, midshipmen, and juniors. The heavy thirty-two-pounders on the lower-deck had 225 men to fight them, 15 men manning each gun. The same set of men had to man two guns; each gun's crew being responsible for the manning of the corresponding gun on the opposite side of the ship whenever it became necessary to fight both broadsides at once. Whenever that was the case the odd numbers in each gun-team remained at their original gun, the even numbers crossing the deck to man the gun on the opposite side. The long twenty-four-pounders, which were fought on both broadsides in the same manner, had 12 men to each.

These batteries were manned by guns' crews, numbering 180 in total. The twelve-pounders on the main-deck, and those on the quarter-deck and forecastle, were manned by 10 men each. A lieutenant and mate with 3 midshipmen and 9 men attended to the signals, being stationed on the poop, where also the marines had their post for musketry. In the *Victory's* three magazines 48 men and boys worked, together with 19 more stationed at the hatchways to pass cartridges, and the powder-boys on the different decks supplying the guns' crews—one boy to each gun. In the cockpit with the surgeon were 6 men; not a very large number, it would seem.

Besides these, there were the carpenter's gang, on the move all over the ship during battle to attend to shot-holes at the water-line, and other gangs variously employed attending to the rigging and in other duties.

There were men of many nationalities on board the *Victory*. The ship's books account for 663 officers and seamen on board, as mustered four days before the battle. The total does not include the marines and the boys. Some 441 of the 663 were Englishmen; 64 were Scotsmen, 63 Irishmen, and 18 Welshmen. There were on board 3 Shetlanders, 2 Channel Islanders, and 1 Manxman. No fewer than 71 of the *Victory's* Trafalgar crew were foreigners, from all over the world almost, the greater part of them men sent on board the *Victory* by press-gangs—*viz.*, 22 Americans, 7 Dutchmen, 6 Swedes, 3 Frenchmen, who thus found themselves fighting their own countrymen; 2 Danes, 3 Norwegians, 1 Russian, 3 Germans, 2 Swiss, 2 Portuguese, 4 Italians, 4 Maltese, 2 Asiatics from India, 1 African negro, and 9 coloured men from various islands in the West Indies.

Of the Englishmen, Kent had 27 representatives on board the *Victory* with Nelson at Trafalgar; Devonshire, 24; Hampshire, 20; Northumberland, Lancashire, and Yorkshire, 18 each; Durham, 17; Nelson's own county of Norfolk, 15; Hardy's, Dorset, 14. Twelve Suffolk men were at Trafalgar in the *Victory*; 9 from Essex; 7 from Lincolnshire, and the same number from Cornwall; 6 each from Oxfordshire and Herefordshire; 5 each from Wiltshire and Gloucestershire. Other counties, represented by four men or fewer on board, were Somerset, Berkshire, Bedford, Shropshire, Worcestershire, Cheshire, Surrey, Cambridge, Notts, Middlesex, Leicester, Staffordshire, Derby, Northampton, Cumberland, and Westmorland. London was represented by 115 men; Edinburgh by 11; Dublin by 14.

Men of all ages between 20 and 50 were in the *Victory's* crew, and boys from 10 years old, the age of little Johnny Doag, an Edinburgh boy, rated as a "first class boy," and probably the youngest person at Trafalgar in either fleet. There were four boys of 12 years old, and six of 13, on board the *Victory* at Trafalgar. The majority of the men on board were between 20 and 30 years of age; those over 40 were about 10 *per cent*, of the total. One "powder-monkey" on board the *Victory*, it may be added, was a woman, as came out later. She was married, and her husband was on board the ship as one of the Maltese seamen; but her sex was unknown to the rest of the crew, as she wore man's dress. She was alive in 1841, being then, we are told, "a sturdy woman of 70." The last survivor of the *Victory's* seamen at Trafalgar died at Dundee in November, 1876.

According to the *Victory's* official return after the battle, 54 men were killed, 25 dangerously wounded, 12 badly wounded, and 42 slightly wounded. Nelson is included in the number of the killed.

Under Fire with Collingwood and his "Tars of the Tyne"

I entered the admiral's cabin about daylight and found him up and dressing. He asked if I had seen the French fleet, and on my replying that I had not, he told me to look out at them, adding that in a very short time we should see a great deal more of them. I then observed a crowd of ships to leeward, but I could not help looking with still greater interest at the admiral, who during all this time was shaving himself with a composure that quite astonished me.

So Collingwood's body-servant, Smith, describes, speaking of that Monday morning. We are told by somebody else:

Admiral Collingwood dressed himself that morning with peculiar care, and soon after, meeting Lieutenant Clavell (his flag-lieutenant), advised him to pull off his boots. 'You had better,' said Collingwood, 'put on silk stockings as I have done, for if one should get a shot in the legs they would be so much more manageable for the surgeon.' He then proceeded to visit the decks, encouraged the men in the discharge of their duty, and, addressing the officers, said to them: 'Now, gentlemen, let us do something today which the world may talk of hereafter.'

As he was passing round the flagship's decks, Collingwood came across a group of men at the guns whom he knew personally. They were some of the "Old Dreadnoughts" who had served with Collingwood in his former flagship, and had been selected to accompany him into the *Royal Sovereign* just ten days before. They were north-countrymen, like the admiral, from Newcastle and Shields and the neighbourhood. "Today, my lads," exclaimed Collingwood, as he paused beside the men for a moment, "we must show those fellows what the Tars of the Tyne can do!"

Collingwood owed something that day to the shooting of his "Old Dreadnoughts." They were the men he himself had trained so assiduously during the two years that Collingwood flew his flag in the *Dreadnought* previous to October, 1805. Week in, week out, throughout all that time, whenever the weather allowed, Collingwood used to practise his men every day, we are told, "in firing at a mark, a cask with a flag on it, which had been hove overboard and allowed to drift until it was at a suitable distance to allow for aiming to begin." Gunnery was Collingwood's hobby on board ship, and his "Dreadnoughts" were taught their business under his eye, the admiral often taking charge personally of the firing, and going down between decks to "coach" the guns' crews himself. He made the *Dreadnought*, indeed, the best firing ship in the world of that time; unsurpassed alike in aiming straight and shooting quick.

Under Collingwood's tuition they were trained to fire three broadsides in ninety seconds—a wonderful gunnery feat as it was considered in those days and for long afterwards. By a curious coincidence our modern gunnery school of the Royal Navy goes by the name of the *Excellent*, from the name of the first ship on board which the establishment was housed, which man-of-war, it is a curious fact, was the same old *Excellent* which Collingwood had commanded as a captain and on board which he first inaugurated his gunnery system—the earliest essay of the kind ever attempted by any naval officer. There was, however, it must be added, no remembrance of Collingwood or his training system in the mind of the authorities when they first established the gunnery school on board the *Excellent*. They simply took the first available ship in the dockyard reserve at Portsmouth for their purpose, and that she happened to be Collingwood's old *Excellent* was a mere accident. The coincidence, however, is certainly interesting and curious.

Collingwood's *Dreadnought*, it may be added in passing, was in the fleet at Trafalgar, where those of Collingwood's former crew who remained on board and had not accompanied the admiral to the *Royal Sovereign* showed that they had not forgotten their instruction. One of those left in the ship mentions something of what they did.

> In fifteen minutes we dismasted our antagonist in the most gallant style, and then passed on to the *Prince of Asturias*, bearing the Spanish commander-in-chief's flag. She made from us with all sail, but not until we had raked her with three tremendous, well-directed broadsides.

It was in this way that Collingwood's *Royal Sovereign* came to lead into the battle as she did, nearly a mile in advance of the rest of the British fleet.

> Lieutenant Clavell observed that the *Victory* was setting her studding-sails, and with that spirit of honourable emulation which prevailed between the squadrons, and particularly between these two ships, pointed it out to Admiral Collingwood, and requested his permission to do the same. 'The ships of our

line,' replied the admiral, ' are not yet sufficiently up for us to do so now, but you may be getting ready.' The studding-sails and royal halliards were accordingly manned, and in about ten minutes the admiral, observing Lieutenant Clavell's eyes fixed on him with a look of expectation, gave him a nod, on which that officer went to Captain Rotherham and told him that the admiral desired him to make all sail. The order was given to rig out and hoist away, and in one instant the ship was under a crowd of sail, and went rapidly ahead. The admiral then directed the officers to see that all the men lay down on the decks and were kept quiet.

Another Northumbrian on board with Collingwood was Flag-Captain Edward Rotherham, the son of a Hexham doctor. This little story is told of him at Trafalgar. Just as they were getting under fire, somebody on the quarter-deck suggested to Captain Rotherham that he had better change the unusually big cocked-hat which he was wearing, for some less conspicuous head-gear, saying it would certainly make him a target for the marksmen, who, indeed, had begun firing from the enemy's tops. But the gallant Rotherham would have nothing to do with any idea of that sort. "Let me alone!" he bluntly replied, turning away from the officer who had made the suggestion, "let me alone; I've always fought in a cocked-hat, and I always will."

Captain Rotherham, according to one story, first went to sea on board a Newcastle collier. Finding his way into the Royal Navy, and in due course gaining quarter-deck rank, he was present at the "Glorious First of June" as first-lieutenant of the *Culloden*, one of Lord Howe's seventy-fours, in which capacity it fell to him to take possession of the French *Vengeur* on her surrender. All the world has heard the story of how the *Vengeur* went down at the end of the battle, her flag defiantly flying, her cannon firing, her crew massed on deck singing the *Marseillaise* and cheering "*Vive la Republique!*" That is the legend one may hear in France to this day, and as a notable picture in the Paris Salon a few years ago depicted.

As a fact, the *Vengeur* sank after the fighting was all over, a beaten and surrendered ship, while Renaudin, her captain, was hungrily devouring his dinner—the first food he had tasted since daybreak— "enjoying a hearty meal of pork chops" in the captain's cabin, as one of the *Culloden's* officers remarks, and while her crew were being taken off, as well as could be managed, by the *Culloden's* boats. Rotherham remained on the *Vengeur's* quarter-deck to the last, until just before the *Vengeur* went under water, standing in the midst of a crowd of frantic Frenchmen, clinging to his knees and imploring him to save them.

With every sail set and every reef shaken out, the magnificent *Royal Sovereign* dashed forward by herself, ahead of all the British fleet, sailing "like a frigate." At the bows, gleaming and resplendent in the brilliant sunshine of Trafalgar Monday, King George in effigy headed the British fleet to victory. The *Royal Sovereign's* figurehead was a gigantic full-length carving of King George III., represented, according to the taste of the time, in Roman costume, in the battle-day dress of a Roman Imperator, with sword at his side and red war-cloak on his shoulders, while two emblematic winged figures. Fortune and Fame, attended His Majesty on either side, blowing golden trumpets.

Drawing on herself as she advanced a hot fire from the enemy's ships in rear and centre, Collingwood's flagship swept forward without an instant's check until she reached the enemy's line, nearly at its centre, close astern of a towering Spanish three-decker, flying an admiral's flag, the *Santa Anna*. The nearest British ship to Collingwood at that moment was nearly a mile in rear. "The most remarkable incident of the battle, a feat unparalleled in naval history," is what the *Royal Sovereign's* daring advance has been called.

Nelson marked the impetuous dash forward of his old comrade's ship. "See," he exclaimed delightedly to Captain Hardy—"see how that noble fellow Collingwood carries his ship into action."

On the *Royal Sovereign's* quarter-deck at that very same moment, as it befell, Collingwood, on his side, was saying to his flag-captain, "Rotherham, what would not Nelson give to be here!"

Admiral Villeneuve, from the quarter-deck of the flagship *Bucentaure*, was intently watching Collingwood's advance. According to one French officer, the bold confidence of the move "positively appalled Villeneuve."

As the *Royal Sovereign* neared the enemy, the ship immediately astern of the *Santa Anna*, a French two-decker, the *Fougueux*, moved forward and closed up, so as to bar the passage through the line to the *Royal Sovereign*. Captain Rotherham marked this at once as he paced the deck by Collingwood's side, and drew the admiral's attention to it. Collingwood looked. "Steer straight for the Frenchman, and take his bowsprit"—that was all Collingwood said.

So they closed, and forging her way forward, regardless of the *Fougueux*, which gave back at the last moment and left the passage open, the *Royal Sovereign* broke the enemy's line, just shaving past the towering stern of the great Spanish flagship. As she did so Collingwood's men opened the battle, firing off their full broadside, each gun treble-shotted. The terrific discharge disabled, as it were at one blow, fourteen of the *Santa Anna's* guns, and struck down, dead or severely wounded, a terrible number of her crew. "*El rompio todos,*" were the words in which one of "the *Santa Anna's* officers described the devastation, when speaking to one of Collingwood's officers after the battle. As the men at the guns reloaded rapidly, the *Royal Sovereign* swung round, and then ranged alongside the giant Spaniard, to leeward of her, to fight the duel out with the muzzles of the guns almost touching.

A relative of Collingwood's, after the admiral's death, set himself to find out from those who fought on board the *Royal Sovereign* at Trafalgar as many details as possible of what took place in the ship. He describes the *Sovereign's* attack in these words:

> In passing the *Santa Anna*, the *Royal Sovereign* gave her a broadside and a half into her stern, tearing it down, and killing and wounding 400 of her men. Then, with her helm hard a-starboard, she ranged up alongside so closely that the lower yards of the two vessels were locked together. The Spanish admiral, having seen that it was the intention of the *Royal Sovereign* to engage to leeward, had collected all his strength on the starboard, and such was the weight of the *Santa Anna's* metal that her broadside made the *Sovereign* heel two strakes out of the water.

Collingwood was all the time calmly pacing up and down the poop, the most exposed place on board, absolutely cool and utterly indifferent to his personal danger.

> Her studding-sails and halliards were now shot away, and, as well as a top-gallant studding-sail, were hanging over the gangway hammocks. Admiral Collingwood called out to Lieutenant Clavell to come and help him to take it in, observing that they should want it again some other day. The two officers, accordingly, carefully rolled it up, and placed it in a boat.

That, by the way, was very much what Collingwood had done in the heat of the action at St. Vincent, when a broadside from a Spanish ship close by brought down one of the upper sails of the *Excellent* on the quarter-deck close by him. "Bless me, Mr. Peffers," was all Collingwood said as the mass of canvas and cordage fell crashing all round him, "why, they have quite ruined our new main-topsail!"

Very shortly after the Sovereigns had closed on the *Santa Anna*, four other enemies—two French ships, the *Fougueux* and the *Indomptable*, with two Spaniards, the *San Leandro* and the *San Justo*—took post nearby, to force the *Sovereign* off and disengage the *Santa Anna*, as they hoped. So incessant was the fierce crossfire that the four newcomers kept up on Collingwood that, as described by one of those on board the *Royal Sovereign*, "we could see their shots meeting and crashing in midair round us." One of the four, the *Fougueux*, also, as we are told, "at one time got so much on the quarter of the *Sovereign* that she almost touched."

In the British fleet elsewhere all could see the furious single-handed combat that Collingwood's Tars of the Tyne and their leader were so heroically maintaining.

> The English ships were pressing forward with the utmost speed in support, but doubtful at times of his fate, and rejoicing when, on the slackening of the *Santa Anna's* fire, they discovered his flag flying above the smoke.

Said one captain in Collingwood's division afterwards (Tyler, of the *Tonnant*) the *Royal Sovereign's* magnificent display "so arrested his attention that he felt for a few moments as if he himself had nothing to do but to look on and admire."

Throughout it all, for most of the time, Collingwood kept calmly "pacing up and down on the poop munching an apple," looking as tranquil and unperturbed as though he were walking in his own orchard at home at Morpeth.

Two eyewitnesses on board tell us, too, of Collingwood's cool demeanour and quiet composure under fire, while at the same time carrying on his duty. Remarks one,:

> The admiral directed Captain Vallack of the marines ... to take his men from off the poop, that they might not be unnecessarily exposed; but he remained there himself much longer. At length, descending to the quarter-deck, he visited the men there, enjoining them not to fire a shot in waste; looking himself along the guns to see that they were properly pointed, and commending the sailors, particularly a black man, who was afterwards killed, but who, while he stood beside him, fired ten times directly into the port-holes of the *Santa Anna*.

Smith, Collingwood's servant, tells us this:

> The admiral spoke to me about the middle of the action, and again for five minutes immediately after its close; and on neither occasion could I observe the slightest change from his ordinary manner. This, at the moment, made an impression on me which will never be effaced, for I wondered how a person whose mind was occupied by such a variety of most important concerns could, with the utmost ease and equanimity, inquire kindly after my welfare, and talk of common matters as if nothing of any consequence were taking place.

Collingwood and his men beat off the *Fougueux* by themselves before the nearest British ships, coming on astern of the *Royal Sovereign*, could get to them. The headmost of these arrived in due course, whereupon, a few minutes later, three of Collingwood's other assailants sheered off, and moved away elsewhere. The *Royal Sovereign*'s duel with the Spanish flagship, however, continued as fiercely as ever. It went on until the *Santa Anna's* colours came down in token of surrender. That, as it so happened, was just as a boat from the *Victory* arrived alongside with Captain's Hardy's first message to the effect "that Lord Nelson had been very severely wounded."

It would seem, from all accounts, that Collingwood's gallant fellows were disappointed at not finishing off the Spanish flagship before the nearest of the fleet joined them. Many on board, we are told, had expected their enemy to surrender at the outset, as the result of that first fearful broadside poured in as they broke the line. Captain Rotherham, in fact, we are told, within a very few minutes of the fight opening, "came up to the admiral, and, shaking him by the hand, said: 'I congratulate you, sir; she is slackening her fire. She must soon strike!'"

The Tars of the Tyne at the guns, it is on record also, fully anticipated that their ship would have the proud distinction of capturing an enemy's flagship in the midst of her own fleet before any of their consorts had got into action. The stubborn endurance of the Spaniards, and the encouragement given them by the four ships that came to the *Santa Anna's* aid, prevented the gallant Sovereigns from achieving the distinction they looked for. They had, though, this consolation, when in the end the *Santa Anna* did surrender. Wrote one of Collingwood's officers:

> No ship besides ourselves fired a shot at her, and you can have no conception how completely she was ruined.

Said Collingwood himself of the tremendous mauling his antagonist received: "Her side was almost entirely beat in."

The *Santa Anna* surrendered, but for the time being the conqueror in the titanic contest was reduced to little better case. For the moment Collingwood's flagship was almost as much *hors de combat*.

> The *Royal Sovereign* had been so much injured in her masts and yards by the ships that lay on her bow and quarter that she was unable to alter her position. Admiral Collingwood accordingly called the *Euryalus* to take her in tow and make the necessary signals.

Collingwood himself dispatched Captain Blackwood to escort the Spanish admiral to him, but that officer was stated to be at the point of death. Blackwood returned with, instead, the Spanish flag-captain. The Spaniard, as the story goes, on entering, asked one of our sailors the name of the ship.

When he was told that it was the *Royal Sovereign*, he replied, in broken English, while patting one of the guns with his hand, 'I think she should be called the *Royal Devil!*'

With the taking possession of the *Santa Anna*, the chief work of Collingwood's Tars of the Tyne at Trafalgar was over. The *Royal Sovereign*, to all intents, was as helpless as a hulk. Only her foremast remained standing; both main and mizzen masts, cut through by shot, had fallen as she sheered off from the *Santa Anna*. The *Sovereign* was towed away by Blackwood's frigate to seek for another antagonist elsewhere; but it was by then nearly three o'clock, and the enemy were broken up and scattered, their resistance everywhere on the point of collapsing. The most that the *Sovereign's* men after that had a chance of doing was to exchange broadsides every now and then with various enemies here and there, the *Euryalus* towing the ship's head round to enable the guns to be pointed. Towards the end she worked her way to join the crippled *Victory*, and formed one of the group of ships summoned by Hardy's signals to assist Nelson's flagship against the fresh French ships of the van squadron as they passed along the line in making their escape from Trafalgar.

Collingwood learned of Nelson's death about three quarters of an hour after it had taken place, just as the last shots of the battle were being fired. He was prepared for it. He himself describes how he was told the news.

> When my dear friend received his wound, he immediately sent

an officer to tell me of it, and give his love to me. Though the officer was directed to say the wound was not dangerous, I read in his countenance what I had to fear, and before the action was over Captain Hardy came to inform me of his death. I cannot tell you how deeply I was affected; my friendship for him was unlike anything I have left in the Navy—a brotherhood of more than thirty years.

In a letter Collingwood tells this of how the first news was given to him:

I asked the officer if his wound was dangerous. He hesitated, then said he hoped it was not; but I saw the fate of my friend in his eye, for his look told what his tongue could not utter.

That Collingwood himself was wounded at Trafalgar is perhaps not generally known. He said not a word about it in any of his letters at the time, nor would he allow his name to be entered in the list of wounded that was sent to England. It was only in reply to an anxious inquiry from his wife, who, some months afterwards, heard a rumour about it and wrote to ask, that Collingwood, nearly half a year after Trafalgar, first made mention of the matter. This is what he said in his letter to Lady Collingwood at the end of March, 1806:

Did I not tell you how my leg was hurt? It was by a splinter—a pretty severe blow. I had a good many thumps, one way or the other: one on the back, which, I think, was the wind of a great shot, for I never saw anything that did it. You know nearly all were killed or wounded on the quarter-deck or poop but myself, my captain, and secretary, Mr. Cosway.

Collingwood added this

The first inquiry of the Spaniards was about my wound, and exceedingly surprised they were when I made light of it, for when the captain of the *Santa Anna* was brought on board, it was bleeding and swelled and tied up with a handkerchief.

One of those killed quite close to Collingwood was the master of the flagship, Mr. William Chalmers, mortally wounded as he and the admiral were standing together on the quarter-deck, near the wheel. Described Collingwood:

He stood close to me when he received his death. A great shot almost divided his body. He laid his head upon my shoulder, and told me he was slain. I supported him till two men carried him off. He could say nothing to me but to bless me; but, as they carried him down, he wished he could but live to read the account of the action in a newspaper. He lay in the cockpit among the wounded until the *Santa Anna* struck, and, joining in the cheer which they gave her, expired with it on his lips.

Two letters from Collingwood's midshipmen, and a letter from a seaman from on board the *Royal Sovereign*, may be added. Says Midshipman George Castle:

> We led the van ran right down among them. This ship sails very well indeed; she was fifty-five minutes engaged with them before any other ship came to our assistance, and we were alongside of a great three-decker. I can assure you it was glorious work; I think you would have liked to have seen me thump it into her quarter. I'm stationed at the heaviest guns in the ship, and I stuck close to one gun and poured it into her; she was so close it was impossible to miss her. She behaved very rascally; for when she struck first to us, she went round our bows, and when right ahead of us, up with her ensign and raked us; but we soon brought our starboard guns to bear upon her.
> Crash went her masts, and then she was fairly sickened. She was a Spanish admiral's ship, but the admiral was killed, and after that we made an eighty-four strike to us. I looked once out of our stern ports; but I saw nothing but French and Spaniards round, firing at us in all directions. It was shocking to see the many brave seamen mangled so; some with their heads half shot away, others with their entrails mashed, lying panting on the deck. The greatest slaughter was on the quarter-deck and poop; we had seven ships on us at once. The *Belle Isle* was next to us in the action, and she kept off a great deal of fire from us . . . likewise the *Tonnant*. We began the engagement a quarter before twelve, and did not cease firing until three in the afternoon; but we had not ended entirely till sunset.
> I forgot to tell you our main and mizzen masts went overboard soon after the Spaniard struck to us; the admiral left us after the engagement, and went on board of the *Euryalus* frigate and took us in tow till next morning, when the *Neptune* took us, and he went to collect the ships—indeed, he is a fine old fellow—he is

a second Nelson. We have got 200 prisoners on board—French and Spaniards—they are droll-looking fellows; they say they took us for the Victory, and were determined to sink us, but I believe they found it hard work to sink a British man-of-war. The smoke was so thick in the action we could hardly make out the French from English. The *Belle Isle* (*sic*) fired into us till the admiral stopped her; we fired into the *Victory* once.

About the middle of the action a lieutenant came and said Lord Nelson was slightly wounded, but soon after the captain came and said he was dead; he said Lord Nelson was afraid we should go down. Indeed, she rolled so much after her masts were gone we could scarcely fight the lower-deck, the water was almost knee deep; however, it served to wash away the blood. We have 1 lieut., 1 do. marines, 2 midn., master and 40 men killed; 100 wounded, including Mr. Clavill, our 1st Lieut., Thompson, Kennicote, and another mid:—1 lieut, marines. The admiral, captain, and Mr. Cosway unhurt; we have not so many killed as the French, one of them had 400 killed. But the gale was worse than the action—it was dreadful; our foremast went overboard, and we broke our tow rope, and now we were left adrift entirely at the mercy of God.

The second letter has a pathetic interest attaching to it. It is an uncompleted letter to his parents, begun on the morning of the battle, by Midshipman John Aikenhead, who was killed in the action.

We have just piped to breakfast; thirty-five sail, besides smaller vessels, are now on our beam, about three miles off. Should I, my dear parents, fall in defence of my king, let that thought console you. I feel not the least dread on my spirits. Oh my parents, sisters, brothers, dear grandfather, grandmother, and aunt, believe me ever yours!

Accept, perhaps for the last time, your son's love; be assured I feel for my friends, should I die in this glorious action—glorious, no doubt, it will be. Every British heart pants for glory. Our old admiral (Admiral Collingwood) is quite young with the thoughts of it. If I survive, nothing will give me greater pleasure than embracing my dearest relations. Do not, in case I fall, grieve—it will be to no purpose. Many brave fellows will no doubt fall with me on both sides.

The letter added that the writer had made his will and put it in his desk. It gave also a statement of the property deposited in his chest, with ten pounds savings, added since the will was made. "Do not be surprised," says the lad in his letter, "to find £10 more—it is mine." The sailor's letter is in these words:

> *Honoured Father,*
> This comes to tell you I am alive and hearty except three fingers; but that's not much, it might have been my head. I told brother Tom I should like to see a greadly (*sic*) battle, and I have seen one, and we have peppered the combined rarely; and for the matter of that, they fought us pretty tightish for French and Spanish. Three of our mess are killed, and four more of us winged. But to tell you the truth of it, when the game began, I wished myself at Warnborough with my plough again; but when they had given us one duster, and I found myself snug and tight, I . . . set to in good earnest, and thought no more about being killed than if I were at Murrell Green Fair, and I was presently as busy and as black as a collier. How my fingers got knocked overboard I don't know, but off they are, and I never missed them till I wanted them. You see, by my writing, it was my left hand, so I can write to you and fight for my king yet. We have taken a rare parcel of ships, but the wind is so rough we cannot bring them home, else I should roll in money, so we are busy sinking 'em and blowing 'em up wholesale.
> Our dear Admiral Nelson is killed! so we have paid pretty sharply for licking 'em. I never sat (*sic*) eyes on him, for which I am both sorry and glad; for, to be sure, I should like to have seen him—but then, all the men in our ship who have seen him are such soft toads they have done nothing but blast their eyes, and cry, ever since he was killed. God bless you! chaps that fought like the devil sit down and cry like a wench. I am still in the *Royal Sovereign*, but the admiral has left her, for she is like a horse without a bridle; so he is in a frigate that he may be here and there and everywhere, for he's as 'cute as here and there one, and as bold as a lion, for all he can cry. I saw his tears with my own eyes, when the boat hailed and said my lord was dead. So no more at present from your dutiful son,   *Sam.*

This is the only description of Collingwood's personal appearance that there is; the only pen-portrait of the admiral that exists. It is from an officer of the *Royal George,* on meeting Collingwood for the first time in the year after Trafalgar:

> Being provided with a letter of recommendation to Lord Collingwood, the commander-in-chief, I took an early opportunity to wait upon His Lordship. . . . Lord Collingwood was between fifty and sixty, thin and spare in person, which was then slightly bent, and in height about five feet ten inches. His head was small, with a pale, smooth, round face, the features of which would pass without notice, were it not for the eyes, which were blue, clear, penetrating; and the mouth, the lips of which were thin and compressed, indicating firmness and decision of character. He wore his hair powdered, and tied in a queue, in the style of officers of his age at that time; and his clothes were squared and fashioned after the strictest rules of the good old sea-school. To his very ample coat, which had a stiff, stand-up collar, were appended broad and very long skirts; the deep flaps of his single-breasted waistcoat, descending far below his middle, covered a portion of his thighs; and blue knee-breeches with white stockings, and buckles to his shoes, completed his attire.
> On entering his presence, he took a rapid, searching survey of me from head to foot; then . . . in a quiet tone, amounting almost to gentleness, he put a few questions to me.

THE FIGHT OF THE "FIGHTING 'TÉMÉRAIRE'"

The "Fighting *Téméraire*" seconded the *Victory*—the term is a good "Old Navy" one—into action at Trafalgar. The "Fighting Téméraire," it should be said, was Turner's name, invented for his famous picture of the ship when he sent it to the Royal Academy of 1839. To the Jacks of the days after Trafalgar the ship was always the "Saucy *Téméraire*" in memory of the fine display that she made in the battle. Turner preferred to invent a sobriquet, although half an hour's looking round among the old "tops" of ships laid up in reserve, stacked away at Sheerness and Chatham dockyards, would have provided him with ample documentary evidence of the *Téméraire's* naval sobriquet. Numbers of these old "tops" were at that time to be seen lying about in the various dockyards, hacked over and scarred with carvings of fancy designs and would-be representations of men-of-war, the handiwork of men aloft on the lookout by way of whiling away the time, and, as a naval officer has recorded, no design was more common on them than rude representations of a ship in battle labelled "the Saucy *Téméraire*."

Nelson, on joining Collingwood, appointed the *Téméraire* leader of his own division in line of battle. Then, a little later, when he took that post for the *Victory*, he told off the *Téméraire* to be his "second," or chief supporter—the ship to follow into action immediately astern of the *Victory*. That was *Téméraire's* allotted post on the day of Trafalgar, a post that was, as it well might be, the envy of the fleet. As they were pressing forward into action, the suggestion was made that the *Téméraire* should go ahead of the *Victory*, so as, in some measure, to cover the flagship from the enemy's fire. "Oh yes," replied Nelson, with a significant smile, "let her go ahead if she can."

Captain Harvey promptly did his best to give Nelson a lead, with the result that the *Téméraire* gradually drew up on the *Victory's* quarter, as if about to pass the flagship. But Nelson intervened. He would not let himself be passed. Hailing the *Téméraire* with an "I'll thank you, Captain Harvey, to keep your station, which is astern of the *Victory*," spoken in a drawling voice with a Norfolk twang. Thus the admiral compelled her to drop back and follow the flagship through the enemy's line.

After the *Victory* had broken through the French Fleet and run foul of the *Redoutable*, the *Téméraire* passed through the same gap, exchanging broadsides with the French Neptune a little way off to starboard. Then she forged ahead slowly, until suddenly in the smoke Captain Harvey discovered the *Victory* and *Redoutable*, locked together, drifting down on him. Every effort was made to keep the *Téméraire* clear, but in vain, and the two ships collided in the end with the French seventy-four; the *Téméraire* on one side and the *Victory* on the other. This, of course, was after Nelson had fallen, just as the French captain made an attempt to board the *Victory*—which failed disastrously—thanks, in no small measure, to the *Téméraire*, whose port broadside, as she sheered alongside, was fired right in among the French boarding-parties as they stood massed and packed along the upper-deck, sweeping them down wholesale.

The three ships lay, locked fast together, "lying side by side as if in dock:" two three-deckers with a two-decker between them. So the *Téméraire's* great fight began.

The *Redoutable*, smaller ship though she was, proved herself a noble antagonist. With an incessant rain of bullets, she almost cleared the upper decks of the *Téméraire*, while her topmen flung down hand-grenades and fire-balls with such recklessness as to set the French ship herself alight. The fire so caused, indeed, spread across to the upper deck of the *Téméraire*. It was extinguished at the same moment that the pluck and presence of mind of the master-at-arms saved the magazine below from a fire-ball that rolled in almost among the powder-barrels.

Then, in the middle of the fight, a new antagonist, a French eighty-gun ship, the *Fougueux*, came on the scene, making for the *Téméraire*, attracted by the disabled appearance of the British ship, which seemed to offer an easy prize. Under the fire that the French *Neptune*, lying some two hundred yards off, had never ceased pouring into the *Téméraire*, spar after spar had come crashing down; the main-topmast and foreyard had collapsed over the side under the tangled wreck of the sails and rigging; while the foremast and bowsprit, badly shot through, seemed every moment about to follow them. The *Téméraire's* colours, too, had been shot away, and very few men were to be seen on her upper-decks. The *Fougueux's* captain decided to board the *Téméraire*, and so capture her out of hand. With rigging and upper-works crowded with boarders, he neared his chosen foe. But Captain Harvey had seen the newcomer's approach. He was ready for her.

The *Téméraire* had the triple row of twenty-four and thirty-two pounders on her starboard broadside double-shotted and ready for action; the captain of each gun standing expectant, trigger-lanyard strained tight in hand. Nearer and nearer the French ship swept down. She was two hundred yards off; then a hundred and fifty; one hundred; now only eighty! The captain of the *Fougueux*, if he lived through it, might well consider himself a made man!

The supreme moment came. Almost as the yard-arms touched, the *Téméraire's* starboard broadside went off in one tremendous salvo, like the discharge of a single giant gun. A terrific crash answered back, with yells and shrieks from all over the doomed *Fouigueux*. As the smoke drifted off, the *Téméraire's* men saw the enemy's rigging and upper-works swept bare. The next instant, with her whole side a mass of splinters, crushed in like an eggshell trampled underfoot, her rows of ports all smashed in and making one gaping cleft along the whole length of the hull, the hapless French ship drove blundering alongside the *Téméraire*.

As it had been with the *Redoutable*, the *Fougueux* was promptly lashed fast; and then, "Boarders away!" was the cry. A master's mate, a little middy, twenty seamen and six marines, followed close behind First-Lieutenant Kennedy (Thomas Fortescue Kennedy) as he sprang on to the *Fougueux's* deck—one of the seamen joining the boarding-party with a Union Jack rolled round his neck. "It'll come in handy," said the brave fellow as he followed his messmates: and it did. There was a sharp tussle on the upper-deck of the *Fougueux*, but the gallant twenty-nine were not to be denied. Slashing and stabbing their way, without one fresh man from the ship to reinforce them, in less than ten minutes they had brought down the *Fougueux's* tricolour, the "handy" Union Jack going up in its place.

Just about the same time the *Victory* broke clear from the row of four ships. She drifted away, leaving the *Redoutable* to be settled with by the *Téméraire*. It proved easy work. Scarcely had the British flagship moved off than the *Redoutable's* main and mizzen masts came down; and the main-mast, falling over the *Téméraire's* poop, formed a bridge across which a party of her officers and men, headed by the second-lieutenant, promptly boarded. The *Redoutable* was in no condition to face them. By that time more than five-sixths of her crew were lying dead or wounded. Her captain could only surrender at discretion. He did so; and was conducted on board the *Téméraire* to hand his sword to Captain Harvey.

The *Téméraire's* old enemy, the French *Neptune*, now began to look dangerous, but the approach of the British Leviathan caused the captain of the French ship to move away and withdraw. After that the *Téméraire* was left undisturbed to look after her prizes.

She had, indeed, done finely. Every man on board had done his duty, as Collingwood himself personally acknowledged to her captain the day after Trafalgar. In a letter to Captain Harvey, the admiral warmly eulogized the *Téméraire's* conduct.

> I congratulate you most sincerely on the noble and distinguished part that the *Téméraire* took in the battle; nothing could be finer. I have not words in which I can sufficiently express my admiration of it.

From one so temperate and measured in speech as Collingwood, this was the highest possible praise.

Captain Eliab Harvey, who commanded the "Fighting *Téméraire*" at Trafalgar, was an M.P. as well as a post-captain on active service. He sat as county member for Essex, his native county—one of the "Knights of the Shire," as the old term went. He was an "Old Westminster" boy, also, as was recalled on the occasion of the Trafalgar centenary celebration—one of the many distinguished naval officers who had their first training at the famous school. They number, in point of fact, more than those from all the other public schools in the kingdom put together.

Captain Harvey, in a letter to his wife immediately after the battle, describes the doings of his *Téméraire*.

Téméraire, on her Way to
Gibraltar, after the Action of the
21st October, 1805.

The first ship in action was the *Royal Sovereign*, with Vice-Admiral Collingwood's flag on board. I did not see any other ship engaged before Lord Nelson opened fire on the enemy, they having opened upon him, and from the *Santisima Trinidad* about 10 minutes, as well as from several other ships of theirs ahead of her. The *Téméraire* at this time almost touched the stern of the *Victory*, which station she had taken about a quarter of an hour previous to the enemy's having commenced their fire upon the *Victory*, in consequence of a signal made from the *Victory*. You are to understand from this statement that we bore down upon the enemy in two columns, the weather-column led by the commander-in-chief, the lee one by Vice-Admiral Collingwood, which occasioned my being astern instead of ahead of the *Victory*, but Lord Nelson had sent to me and given me leave to lead and break through the enemy's line about the 14th ship from the van; but afterwards made the signal referred to above. From this period for two hours we were so nearly engaged that I can give you no other account of this part of this most glorious day's work than what immediately concerned the *Victory* or myself.

We were engaged with the *Santisima Trinidad* and the other ships for perhaps 20 minutes or more, when for a minute or two I ceased my fire, fearing I might from the thickness of the smoke be firing into the *Victory*; but I soon saw the *Victory* close on board a French ship of two decks; and having the ship under command, notwithstanding we had suffered much in our masts and sails, etc., I placed the ship so as to give this *Redoutable* a most severe dressing by raking of her fore and aft; however, the *Victory* fell on board of her and she struck, and soon after they came on board the *Téméraire*, so that the Frenchman was exactly between the two ships, being upon my larboard side. Some time previous I had commenced upon another ship with my larboard (*sic*) guns, and very soon put her into so disabled a state that we fell on board of her also. I soon forced her to strike, and sent Lieutenant Kennedy, my first, with a party of men to secure this prize; and finding the *Victory* had got clear from the *Redoutable*, I sent my second-lieutenant to secure her and order both their ships to be securely lashed to the *Téméraire*.

When the smoke began to clear away I saw the *Royal Sovereign* nearly in the same place I had seen the *Santa Anna*. When for about half an hour or more I thought with us the battle was at an end, and we had but to secure the captured ships, and I had made a signal for a frigate to take us in tow, when, behold! I was informed some of the enemy's ships were coming up astern of us. They proved to be four French ships, apparently in good order, their intention to escape to the southward. When they were about three-quarters of a mile to windward they opened their guns upon *Téméraire* and her prizes, and for some time I could return no guns; but when those we could fight with were brought to bear upon the enemy, the gentlemen thought proper to haul to a more respectable distance, and thus towards evening with me ended this most glorious action, and perhaps never was a ship so circumstanced as mine to have for more than three hours two of the enemy's line-of-battle ships lashed to her, one upon each side, in one of, if not the most, decided actions ever fought.

There went into action on board the *Téméraire* at Trafalgar, according to the muster-book, as reported at the last muster on board, held the very day before the battle, on Sunday, October 20, 1805, 718 officers and men, including marines—only twenty men short of the ship's official complement of 738 men. According to the return on that Sunday morning, the numbers were these: Officers and men of all ratings, 550; volunteers and boys, 36; marines (officers and men), 130; supernumeraries, 2.

Of the sailors who manned the guns of the "Fighting *Téméraire*" at Trafalgar, Ireland contributed some two-fifths of the total ship's company—220 men out of 550. Scotland supplied the *Téméraire* with 53 men; Wales contributed 38 men all told. Of the Englishmen on board, one county by itself contributed practically a third—Devonshire. The Devonians in the "Fighting *Téméraire*" counted 52 men. From London came 30 men in all. Lancashire had as many representatives in the ship as all Wales—38, all except three hailing from Liverpool and Manchester. Somerset had 24; Cornwall, 20; Yorkshire, 13; Northumberland and Durham, 10 each.

From other English counties there came: Norfolk, 8 men; Hampshire, 7; Kent, 6; Cumberland and Gloucestershire, each 5; Essex, Dorset, Cheshire, each 4; Middlesex, 3; Derbyshire, Warwick, Sussex, Cambridge, Worcester and Suffolk, each 2; Oxfordshire, Buckinghamshire, Leicestershire, Surrey, Hereford and the "Isle of White" (*sic* in the muster-book), 1 man each. There were also 3 Manxmen on board, 2 Jerseymen, 1 Guernseyman, and 2 Newfoundlanders. There were 66 foreigners in the *Téméraire* at Trafalgar, according to the ship's books: 28 Americans, 9 Germans, 6 Swedes, 5 Portuguese, 3 Frenchmen, 3 Spaniards, 2 Dutchmen, 1 Russian, 1 Austrian, 1 African negro, the remainder of the foreigners hailing from various non-British West India Islands.

The "Belleisles" hold their Own at Bay

There are not many stories in our naval annals to equal that which tells of the fight the *Belleisle's* men made at Trafalgar, holding their own at bay amidst a host of foes, which girt them round with a ring of fire. So fiercely at times did the tempest of iron seem to beat on the men of this devoted ship that more than one British officer in the ships coming up astern hardly ventured to hope that they could stand up to it. More than one admitted anxiety lest, overwhelmed before help could get to her, the Belleisles might be overpowered.

From first to last the *Belleisle*—the second ship in Collingwood's line, and commanded by Captain William Hargood, a very old friend of Nelson's—did magnificently,

A few moments before they opened fire, we are told:

> The captain sent for the officers commanding at their several quarters. 'Gentlemen,' he said, 'I have only to say that I shall pass close under the stern of that ship: put in two round shot and then a grape, and give her that. Now go to your quarters and mind not to fire until each gun will bear with effect.' With this laconic instruction the gallant little man posted himself on the slide of the foremost carronade on the starboard side of the quarter-deck.

The Belleisles, as those in the ship called themselves in the usual naval way, began at the outset by calling forth Nelson's outspoken admiration. He was watching the ship as she went into action, and saw her break the enemy's line, as we are told by a midshipman on board the *Victory*, George Westphal:

> I had left my quarters to make a report to Quilliam, our first-

lieutenant, who was standing near Lord Nelson on the quarter-deck, watching the *Belleisle*. Every person thought she would have opened her fire long before she did, the enemy having been firing at her, and, indeed, having visibly damaged her spars some time previously. But the *Belleisle* still preserved her fire until she had brought both broadsides, as it appeared to us in the *Victory*, to bear on the ships on each side of her. She was within pistol-shot when her two broadsides were discharged simultaneously and with the precision of a volley of musketry; upon seeing which, Lord Nelson exclaimed, 'Nobly done, Hargood!'

What they went through on board the *Belleisle* is fully told by officers of the ship. Hardly a more vivid battle narrative, related as it is by eyewitnesses in their own words, is in existence. Describes one of the officers:

At a quarter before twelve, seven or eight of the enemy's ships opened their fire upon the *Royal Sovereign* and *Belleisle*, and as we were steering directly for them we could only remain passive, and perseveringly approach the post we were to occupy in this great battle. This was a trying moment. Captain Hargood had taken his station at the forepart of the quarter-deck, on the starboard side, occasionally standing on a carronade slide, whence he issued his orders for the men to lie down at their quarters, and with the utmost coolness directed the steering of the ship. The silence on board was almost awful. It was broken only by the firm voice of the captain, 'Steady!' or 'Starboard a little!' which was repeated by the master to the quartermaster at the helm, and occasionally by an officer calling to the now impatient men, 'Lie down there, you sir!'

A shriek soon followed—a cry of agony was produced by the next shot—and the loss of the head of a poor recruit was the effect of the succeeding; and, as we advanced, destruction rapidly increased. A severe contusion in the breast now prostrated our captain, but he soon resumed his station. My eyes were horror-struck at the bloody corpses round me, and my ears rang with the shrieks of the wounded and the moans of the dying. Of wounded and killed, we had more than fifty before we fired a shot; and our colours were three times shot away and rehoisted during the time.

Seeing that our men were falling fast, the first-lieutenant ventured to ask Captain Hargood if he had not better show his broadside to the enemy and fire, if only to cover the ship with smoke? The gallant man's reply was somewhat stern but emphatic: 'No; we are ordered to go through the line, and go she shall!'

This state of things had lasted about twenty minutes, and it required the tact of the more experienced officers to keep up the spirits of those round them, by repeating 'We shall soon begin our work,' when—as on another occasion the welcome order was given, 'Up, Guards, and at them!'—our energies were joyfully called into play by the command, 'Stand to your guns!' The master on that earnestly addressed the captain:

'Shall we go through, sir?'

'Go through by ——!' was the energetic reply.

'There's your ship, sir; place me close alongside of her!'

We were soon passing slowly through the line, and our fire was opened on a ship on each side; within less than pistol-shot.

The enemy's ship on our starboard side at once bore up and gallantly closed with us, running us on board on the beam. Her position, though, became so hot and uncomfortable that she was glad to drop astern, much disabled; not, however, till she had knocked away our main-topmast. This ship was the *Fougueux*, which soon afterwards fell on board the *Téméraire*. In the meantime another French ship, the *Achille*, had placed herself on our larboard quarter, where she remained with comparative impunity on account of our mizzen-mast having fallen in that direction and impeded our fire. Another ship of the line had also placed herself on our larboard bow and another on our starboard.

The firing was now tremendous, and at intervals the dispersion of the smoke gave us a sight of the colours of our adversaries.

For the men serving at the guns between-decks below, it was like this, as is told by someone else:

> At every moment the smoke accumulated more and more thickly, stagnating on board between-decks at times so densely as to blur over the nearest objects, and often blot out the men at the guns from those close at hand on each side. The guns had to be trained as it were mechanically by means of orders passed down from above, and on objects that the men fighting the guns hardly ever got a glimpse of. In these circumstances you frequently heard the order on the main and lower deck to

"Crippled but unconquered":
the rescue of the "Belleisle" at Trafalgar.

level the guns 'two points abaft the beam,' 'point-blank,' and so on. In fact, the men were as much in the dark as to external objects as if they had been blindfolded, and the only comfort to be derived from this serious inconvenience was that every man was so isolated from his neighbour that he was not put in mind of his danger by seeing his messmates go down all round. All that he knew was that he heard the crash of the shot smashing: through the rending timbers, and then followed at once the hoarse bellowings of the captains of the guns, as men were missed at their posts, calling out to the survivors, 'Close up there! close up!'

To take up again the former eyewitness's account:

About two o'clock the mainmast fell over the larboard side, and half an hour afterwards the foremast fell over the starboard bow. Thus was the *Belleisle* a total wreck, without the means of returning the fire of the enemy except from the very few guns still unencumbered by the wreck of the masts and rigging.

Says another officer:

When the mainmast fell, I was under the break of the poop, aiding in running out a carronade. A cry of 'Stand clear, there! here it comes!' made me look up, and at that instant the mainmast fell over the bulwarks just above me. This ponderous mass made the ship's whole frame shake; had it taken a central direction it would have gone through the poop, and added many to our list of sufferers.

Not for one instant, though, did the gallant fellows on board the *Belleisle* flinch.

Every exertion continued to be made for presenting the best resistance, and offering the greatest annoyance to the enemy. Guns were run out from the stern ports on each deck, and all that intelligence could suggest and discipline effect was done. Our loss, though, was by then becoming severe. The first and junior lieutenants had both been mortally wounded on the quarter-deck early in the action. About the same time the captain was knocked down and severely bruised by a splinter, but he refused to leave the deck.

That incident, according to one of those who witnessed the misadventure, had something of a humorous side.

The *sauve tête*, or splinter-netting, was cut away and knocked him down, and entangled him in the meshes. On getting clear, half stunned and excited by the blow, he called out: 'Let 'em come on; I'm d———d if I'll strike. No, never—to nobody whatever!' A most effective speech was this. It was heard on one deck, and repeated on others in the pauses of the firing, and the hearty guffaw with which it was received was more exhilarating than any amount of blank verse!

At half-past two our foremast was shot away close to the deck. In this unmanageable state we were but seldom capable of annoying our antagonists, while they had the power of choosing their distance, and every shot from them did considerable execution. We had suffered severely, and those on the poop were now ordered to assist at the quarter-deck guns, where we continued till the action ceased. Until half-past three we remained in this harassing position. The only means at all in our power of bringing our battery towards the enemy was to use the sweeps out of the gun-room ports. To these we had recourse, but without effect. Even in ships under perfect command they prove almost useless, and we lay a mere hulk, covered in wreck and rolling with the swell.

At this hour a two-decked ship was seen, apparently steering towards us. It can easily be imagined with what anxiety every eye turned towards this formidable object, which would either relieve us from our unwelcome neighbours or render our situation desperate. We had scarcely seen British colours since one o'clock—it was now half-past three—and it is impossible to express our emotion as an alteration of the stranger's course displayed the white ensign to our sight.

The *Swiftsure*, an English 74, came looming through the smoke, and passed our stern. Everyone eagerly looked towards our approaching friend, who came speedily on, and then, when within hail, manned the rigging, cheered, and boldly steered for the ship which had so long annoyed us.

Another British ship then came up to assist the *Belleisle*, who was thus finally rescued from her perilous situation.

Shortly afterwards the *Polyphemus* took the enemy's ship off our bows. Thus we were at length happily disengaged, after nearly four hours of a struggle, perhaps as severe as ever fell to the lot of a British man-of-war.

We are told this in a description of the dreadful scene on board that evening.

When, later, the officers came to make their report to the captain, the fatal result cast a gloom over the scene of our triumph. Our first-lieutenant had had an impression that he should not survive the contest. He was severely wounded in the thigh, and underwent amputation; but his prediction was realized, and he expired before the action ceased. The junior lieutenant was also mortally wounded on the quarter-deck. These gallant fellows were lying beside each other in the gun-room preparatory to their being committed to the deep, and here many met to take a last look at their departed friends, whose remains were soon followed by the promiscuous multitude, without distinction of either rank or station, to their wide ocean grave. In the act of launching a poor sailor over the poop he was discovered to breathe. He was, of course, saved, and after being a week in hospital the ball, which had entered at his temple, came out of his mouth.

From our extensive loss, thirty-four killed, and ninety-six wounded, our cockpit exhibited a scene of suffering and carnage which rarely occurs. I visited this abode of suffering with the natural impulse which led many others hither—namely, to ascertain the fate of a friend or companion. So many bodies in such a confined place and under such distressing circumstances would affect the most obdurate heart. Even the dangers of the battle did not seem more terrific than the spectacle before me. On a long table lay several, anxiously looking for their turn to receive the surgeon's care, yet dreading the fate which he might pronounce. One subject was undergoing amputation, and every part was heaped with sufferers; their piercing shrieks and expiring groans were echoed through the vault of misery.

What a contrast to the hilarity and enthusiastic mirth which reigned in this spot on the preceding evening! At all times the cockpit is the region of conviviality and good humour, for here it is that the happy midshipmen reside, and at whose board neither discord nor care interrupt social intercourse. But a few

Sir John Franklin—Signal-Midshipman on board the "Bill Ruff'n" at Trafalgar

short hours since, on these same benches, which were now covered with mutilated remains, sat these scions of their country's glory, who had hailed the coming hour of conflict with cheerful confidence, and each told his story to beguile the anxious moments, the younger ones eagerly listening to their experienced associates, and all uniting in the toast, 'May we meet again at this hour tomorrow!'

The Belleisles learned of Nelson's death about six o'clock that evening.

A boat with the lieutenant of the *Entreprenante* came on board, on his return from the *Victory*, to announce the death of the immortal Nelson. The melancholy tidings spread through the ship in an instant, and its paralysing effect was wonderful. Our captain had served under the illustrious chief for years, and had partaken in the anxious pursuit of the enemy across the Atlantic, with the same officers and crew. Lord Nelson is no more!' as repeated with such despondency and heartfelt sorrow that everyone seemed to mourn a parent. All exertion was suspended: the veteran sailor indulged in silent grief; and some eyes evinced that tenderness of heart is often concealed under the roughest exterior.

"'Billy Ruff'n'—Victory or Death!"

"No man can be a coward on board the *Bellerophon!*" So wrote one of the midshipmen of that most famous of hard-fighting ships of the Nelson time in a letter home on the night before Trafalgar. Another midshipman of the *Bellerophon*, writing a few days after the battle, says this:

Lord Nelson took the command of our fleet on the 29th of September, and though we had before that no doubt of success in the event of an action, yet the presence of such a man could not but inspire every individual in the fleet with additional confidence. Everyone felt himself more than a match for any enemy that there was any probability of being opposed to.

It was on board the "Billy Ruff'n" at Trafalgar that this took place: it was one of the finest feats of cool courage performed by anyone in the battle. The *Bellerophon* at that moment was in close fight with Napoleon's finest and newest seventy-four, *L'Aigle*—a man-of-war a third again bigger than herself. The two ships were in hot action side by side, at quarters so close that their sides were in contact, scraping and grinding together:—"We were fighting hand to hand at the ports," says one of the *Bellerophon's* midshipmen, "seizing each other's ramrods, etc., and several men were wounded by muskets fired from the enemy's ports into ours *à bout portant.*" The *Bellerophon's* colours at that moment also had just been shot down for the third time. Immediately on that was performed an exploit by one of the *Bellerophon's* men which nowadays would assuredly have gained him the V.C. Barely half a dozen men of the forty stationed on the poop when the battle opened, signalmen and marines, remained alive under the furious musketry fire that was blazed down on them by the French marksmen in the tops of *L'Aigle.*

One of the handful of survivors was a veteran sailor, a yeoman of signals—Christopher Beatty. "Well, well, that's too bad!" exclaimed the old sailor as he saw his ship's ensign shot away for the third time, "those fellows will say we've struck!" Beatty ran and quickly got hold of the largest Union Jack he could lay hands on in the flag-locker. Throwing it over his shoulder, the brave old fellow then began to clamber up the mizzen rigging to the masthead. Until that moment every man who had attempted to go aloft had been shot down by the soldiers in the French ship's tops. The Frenchmen blazed away at Beatty as soon as his figure showed above the bulwarks, but the veteran kept climbing higher quite calmly, paying no heed to the bullets that whizzed round his head.

He went on until he had got three-quarters of the way up the mast; several feet up. Then he stopped, spread out the flag as widely as his arms could stretch it across the shrouds, and, with the utmost deliberation, lashed it fast at each corner. After that Beatty slowly climbed down till he regained the deck. To the honour of the French marksmen it must be added that they, on their side, ceased firing at the brave fellow—one and all of them—after Beatty had begun to make fast the flag, and as soon as they realized what the old sailor was doing.

More than that, though. Had it been the present day yet another V.C. would have gone to the Bellerophons, to their first-lieutenant, Pryce Cumby (whose vivid and telling personal account of the battle forms the present section), for a no less real act of heroism. A modern naval officer who should pick up a live shell on board his ship in action and throw it into the sea would deserve and get the V.C. Just such an act as that won Gunner Harding the Victoria Cross at the bombardment of Alexandria in 1882; and also three V.C.'s were so won in the Crimean War.

Lieutenant Cumby did just that; and no official notice whatever was taken of it. He himself, it would seem, took the matter as, so to speak, all in the day's work—nothing more. He said nothing, apparently, about it at the time—nor did anyone else—only first mentioning the fact incidentally, as a casual remark by the way, in the private narrative of events at Trafalgar which he wrote for his son and family in after-years. In describing the reckless way in which the French flung down hand grenades broadcast all over the *Bellerophon's* upper-decks, and the murderous havoc they wrought, the modest officer simply remarks:

> One of them I took up myself from our gangway where the fuse was burning and threw it overboard.

Yet it was an act that required nerve and pluck, and was done at no small risk. Speaking of the havoc and destruction wrought by these deadly projectiles, just at that very moment indeed, and nearby where Lieutenant Cumby was, one of the *Bellerophon's* officers says:

> This explosion put upwards of twenty-five men *hors-de-combat*, many of them were dreadfully scorched. One of the sufferers in his agony, instead of going down to the surgeon, ran aft and threw himself out of one of the stern ports.

This is the splendid story of the *Bellerophon's* doings at Trafalgar, as told, from what he himself saw, by her gallant first-lieutenant:

> About a quarter before six I was roused from my slumbers by my messmate Overton, the master, who called out, 'Cumby, my boy, turn out; here they are all ready for you, three and thirty sail of the line close under our lee, and evidently disposed to await our attack.' You may readily conclude I did not remain long in a recumbent position, but springing out of bed hurried on my clothes, and kneeling down by the side of my cot put up a short but fervent prayer to the great God of battles for a glorious day to the arms of my country, 'committing myself individually to His all-wise disposal, and begging His gracious protection and favour for my dear wife and children, whatever His unerring wisdom might see fit to order for myself.' This was the substance and, as near as memory will serve me, the actual words of my petition.
> I was soon on deck, when the enemy's fleet was distinctly seen

to leeward, standing to the southward under easy sail, and forming in line on the starboard tack; at six o'clock the signal was made to form the order of sailing, and soon after to bear up and steer E.N.E. We made sail in our station, and at twenty minutes past six we answered the signal to prepare for battle, and soon afterwards to steer east; we then beat to quarters, and cleared ship for action.

After I had breakfasted as usual at eight o'clock with the captain in his cabin, he begged of me to wait a little as he had something to show me, when he produced, and requested me to peruse, Lord Nelson's private memorandum, addressed to the captains, relative to the conduct of the ships in action, which having read he inquired whether I perfectly understood the admiral's instructions. I replied that they were so distinct and explicit that it was quite impossible that they could be misunderstood. He then expressed his satisfaction, and said he wished me to be made acquainted with it, that in the event of his being 'bowl'd out' I might know how to conduct the ship agreeably to the admiral's wishes.

On this I observed that it was very possible that the same shot which disposed of him might have an equally tranquilizing effect on me, and under that idea I submitted to him the expediency of the master (as being the only officer who in such case would remain on the quarter-deck) being also apprised of the admiral's instructions, that he might be enabled to communicate them to the next officer, whoever he might be, that should succeed to the command of the ship. To this Captain Cooke immediately assented, and poor Overton the master was desired to read the memorandum, which he did. And here I may be permitted to remark *en passant* that, of the three officers who carried the knowledge of this private memorandum into the action, I was the only one who brought it out.

On going round the decks to see everything in its place and all in perfect order, before I reported to the captain the ship in readiness for action, the fifth, or junior, lieutenant (now Captain George Lawrence Saunders), who commanded the seven foremost guns on each side of the lower-deck, pointed out to me some of the guns at his quarters, where the zeal of the seamen had led them to chalk in large characters on their guns the words 'Victory or Death'—a very gratifying mark of the spirit with which they were going to their work.

At eleven o'clock, finding we should not be in action for an hour or more, we piped to dinner, which we had ordered to be in readiness for the ship's company at that hour, thinking that Englishmen would fight all the better for having a comfortable meal; and at the same time Captain Cooke joined us in partaking of some cold meat, &c., on the rudder head, all our bulk-heads, tables, &c., being necessarily taken down and carried below. I may here observe that all the enemy's fleet had changed their former position, having wore together, and were now forming their line on the larboard tack. The wind having shifted a few points to the southward of west, their rear ships were thrown far to windward of their centre and van, and the wind being light, they were, many of them, unable to gain their proper stations before the battle began.

A quarter past eleven Lord Nelson made the telegraphic signal, 'England expects that every man will do his duty,' which, you may believe, produced the most animating and inspiriting effect on the whole fleet; and at noon he made the last signal observed from the *Bellerophon* before the action began, which was to 'prepare to anchor after the close of the day.'

We were now rapidly closing with the enemy's line, and at ten minutes past noon the battle was begun by the *Royal Sovereign* opening her fire on the enemy, (who had for several minutes been firing on her); and at twenty minutes past twelve the *Royal Sovereign*, with the signal for close action flying, passed through the enemy's line under the stern of a Spanish three-decker bearing an admiral's flag and engaged her closely to leeward.

It had been Captain Cooke's original intention not to have a shot fired until we were in the act of passing through the enemy's line; but finding that we were losing men as we approached their ships from the effect of their fire, also suffering in our masts and rigging, he determined on opening our fire a few minutes sooner, from the double object of giving our men employment, and at the same time of rendering the ship a less ostensible mark to be shot at, by covering her with smoke.

At twenty minutes past twelve we opened our fire, and at half-past twelve we were engaged on both sides, passing through their line close under the stern of a Spanish seventy-four, into whom, from the lightness of the wind, being still farther lulled by the effect of the cannonade, we fired our carronades three times, and every long-gun on the larboard sides at least twice. Luckily for us, by this operation she had her hanging-magazine blown up, and was completely beaten, for, in hauling up to settle her business to leeward, we saw over the smoke the top-gallant sails of another ship close under our starboard bow, which proved to be the French seventy-four, *L'Aigle*, as the name on her stern showed us; and, although we hove back to avoid it, we could not sufficiently check our ship's way to prevent our running her on board with our starboard bow on her larboard quarter, our foreyard locking with her mainyard, which was squared.

By the captain's directions I went down to explain to the officers on the main and lower-decks the situation of the ship with respect to this new opponent, and to order them to direct their principal efforts against her. Having so done, as I was returning along the main deck, I met my poor messmate Overton, the master, carried by two men, with his leg dreadfully shattered; and before I reached the quarter-deck ladder, having stopped to give some directions by the way, I was met by a quartermaster, who came to inform me that the captain was very badly wounded and, as he believed, dead.

I went immediately on the quarter-deck and assumed the command of the ship—this would be about a quarter past one o'clock—when I found we were still engaged with *L'Aigle*, on whom we kept up a brisk fire, and also on our old opponent on our larboard bow, the *Monarca*, who by this time was nearly silenced, though her colours were still flying; at the same time we were receiving the fire of two other of the enemy's ships, one nearly astern of the other on the larboard quarter. Our quarter-deck, poop, and forecastle were at this time almost cleared by musketry from troops on board *L'Aigle*, her poop and gangway completely commanding those decks, and the troops on board appearing very numerous.

At this moment I ordered all the remaining men down from the poop, and, calling the boarders, had them mustered under the half-deck, and held them in readiness to repel any attempt that might be made by the enemy to board us; their position rendering it quite impracticable for us to board them in the face of such a fire of musketry so advantageously situated.

But whatever advantage they had over us on these upper-decks was greatly overbalanced by the superiority of our fire on the lower and main decks, *L'Aigle* soon ceasing entirely to fire on us from her lower-deck, the ports of which were lowered down, whilst the fire from ours was vigorously maintained, the ports having, by my orders, been hauled up close against the side when we first fell on board her, to prevent their being torn from their hinges when the ships came in contact. While thus closely engaged and rubbing sides with *L'Aigle*, she threw many hand grenades on board us, both on our forecastle and gangway and in at the ports. Some of these exploded and dreadfully scorched several of our men; one of them I took up myself from our gangway where the fuse was burning, and threw it overboard.

One of these grenades had been thrown in at a lower-deck port and in its explosion had blown off the scuttle of the gunner's storeroom, setting fire to the storeroom and forcing open the door into the magazine passage; most providentially, this door was so placed with respect to that opening from the passage into the magazine that the same blast which blew open the storeroom door shut-to the door of the magazine; otherwise we must all in both ships inevitably have been blown up together. The gunner, who was in the storeroom at the time, went quietly up to Lieutenant Saunders on the lower-deck, and acquainted him that the storeroom was on fire, requested a few hands with water to extinguish it; these being instantly granted he returned with them and put the fire out without its having been known to any person on board, except to those employed in its extinction.

At forty minutes past one *L'Aigle* hoisted her jib and dropped clear of us, under a tremendous raking fire from us as she paid off: our ship at this time was totally unmanageable, the main and mizzen topmasts hanging over the side, the jib-boom spanker-boom and gaff shot away, and not a brace or bowline serviceable. We observed that *L'Aigle* was engaged by the *Defiance*, and soon after two o'clock she struck. On the smoke clearing, we observed that several of the enemy's ships had struck their colours, and amongst them our first opponent, the *Monarca*, of whom we took possession.

We were now without any opponent within reach of our guns,

and our fire consequently ceasing, I had a message from the surgeon stating that the cockpit was so crowded with wounded men that it was quite impossible for him to attempt some operations which were highly requisite, and begging I would allow him to bring some subjects up into the captain's cabin for amputation if the fire was not likely to be renewed for a quarter of an hour. I gave him the requested permission, with an understanding that he must be prepared to go down again if any of the enemy's van who had not been engaged should approach us.

It had been my unvarying rule from the commencement of the action to avoid speaking to any of my messmates and friends who might be wounded, not wishing to trust my private feelings at a time when all my energies were called for in the discharge of my public duty; and on this ground I had passed Overton, as I have already related, without exchanging a word. But now my much-esteemed messmate. Captain Wemyss of the marines came up the quarter-deck ladder wounded, just at the moment I approached it, and not being able to avoid speaking to him without apparent unkindness, I said: 'Wemyss, my good fellow, I'm sorry you've been wounded, but I trust you will do well;' to which he replied with the utmost cheerfulness, ''Tis only a mere scratch, and I shall have to apologize to you by and by for having left the deck on so trifling an occasion.' He was then entering the cabin to have his arm amputated!

At four o'clock, observing that five ships of the enemy's van under a French rear-admiral had tacked in succession and were making off to windward, I ordered the cabin again to be cleared, and at ten minutes past four we opened our fire upon those five ships, the stern-most of which (a Spanish two-decker) was cut off and struck to the *Minotaur*. The other four ships escaped. At seven minutes after five the firing ceased; we counted nineteen of the enemy's line-of-battle ships who had struck, one of which (the *Achille*, seventy-four) took fire and blew up. At half-past five we took possession of the Spanish seventy-four, *Bahama*, ten sail of the enemy's line, six frigates, and two brigs making off to leeward towards Cadiz.

At half-past seven we observed that the *Euryalus*, to which ship we knew Vice-Admiral Collingwood had shifted his flag, carried the lights of the commander-in-chief, and that there were no lights on board the *Victory*; from which we were left to draw the melancholy inference that our gallant, our beloved chief, the incomparable Nelson, had fallen. But so unwilling were we to believe what we could scarcely bring ourselves to doubt, that I actually went on board the *Euryalus* the next morning and breakfasted with Admiral Collingwood, from whom I received orders, without being once told, or even asking the question, whether Lord Nelson was slain.

I cannot and must not, omit to record the spirited and gallant conduct of a young midshipman named Pearson, of about fourteen years of age; 'tis so creditable to our profession and to our country. This youngster, the son of a clergyman in the west of England, who held, I believe, the living of Queen Camel, had joined *Bellerophon*, as his first ship, just before we left England in the preceding May. He was stationed on the quarter-deck, and when he saw Captain Cooke fall he ran to his assistance, but ere he reached his captain he was himself brought down by a splinter in the thigh. As I was coming up to take command of the ship, I met on the quarter-deck ladder, little Pearson in the arms of a quartermaster, who was carrying him to the surgeon in the cockpit. I here made an exception to my general rule of silence on such occasions and said, 'Pearson, my boy, I'm sorry you've been hit; but never mind—you and I'll talk over this day's work fifty years hence, depend upon it.' He smiled, and I passed on.

Three days afterwards ten sail of the enemy's line came out of Cadiz in good condition, and made a demonstration of attacking some of our crippled ships and prizes, who had been driven near Cadiz in the gale. When the signal was made to prepare for battle, and our drums had beat to quarters for the purpose, the first person that caught my eye on the quarter-deck was little Pearson, dragging with difficulty one leg after the other. I said to him, 'Pearson, you had better go below; wounded as you are, you will be better there.'

He answered, 'I had rather stay at my quarters. Sir, if you please!'

On which I replied, 'You had much better go down; someone will be running against you and do you further mischief.'

To this he exclaimed, the tears standing in his eyes, 'I hope, Sir, you will not order me below; I should be very sorry to be below at a time like this.'

I instantly said, 'Indeed, I will not order you down, and if you live you'll be a second Nelson.' Poor fellow! he did live to be made a lieutenant some years after, and then died of fever.

In justice to the memory of my gallant friend and captain, Cooke, I must also add that more zeal, judgement, and gallantry could not have been displayed than marked his conduct from the moment we saw the enemy till the close of his honourable and valuable life. At eleven minutes past one o'clock he received a musket ball in his chest and fell. To the seamen who went to raise him, he merely said, 'Let me lie a minute,' and immediately breathed his last.

On the evening of the following day, I had the painful duty of reading the funeral service over his body and that of my valued friend Overton, as they were committed to the deep amid the heartfelt regrets and unbought tears of their surviving shipmates. A similar sense of justice to the officers and crew of the *Bellerophon* compels me to record, as a proof of their steadiness and discipline, that in the course of the action the ship was three times on fire without its ever having come to my knowledge (except in one instance where I put it out myself), until it came out in the course of conversation long after the action was over. Our loss in the *Bellerophon* was 26 killed and 126 wounded out of 540 at the commencement of the action.

So the first-lieutenant tells the tale of what passed under his own eyes. This, as others saw that happen, is how his captain fell.

The *Bellerophon's* gallant captain, John Cooke, fell early in the fight, not long after his ship's duel with *L'Aigle* had begun. It was, as Lieutenant Cumby has just told, just after the master of the *Bellerophon*, Mr. Overton, had gone down, mortally wounded, as he stood by the wheel. A devoted "Nelsonian" for years, Captain Cooke had never before had the honour of actually serving under Nelson's immediate command, but he had often been heard to say that it was "the dearest wish of his life that he might one day take part in a battle under Nelson's leadership." He was killed at Trafalgar—shot dead by a musket bullet in the breast—almost at the same time that Nelson fell on board the *Victory*.

A little while earlier Lieutenant Cumby, while walking with the captain on the quarter-deck, had suggested that he should dispense with the glittering bullion epaulettes that he wore as likely to mark him out conspicuously to the enemy. Could he not take them off and do without them, suggested the first-lieutenant; they made him such a target for the French sharp-shooters in the tops. "It's too late to take them off," was the reply, in a quiet tone. "I see my situation; I can only die like a man!"

A minute or two later Captain Cooke sent the first-lieutenant below to have the guns on the main-deck elevated so as to fire high, and burst up and shatter *L'Aigle's* upper decks; and before Lieutenant Cumby was able to return to the quarter-deck, his brave chief had fallen.

Describing Captain Cooke's fate, an eyewitness says this:

> He had discharged his pistols very frequently at the enemy, who as often attempted to board, and he had killed a French officer on his own quarter-deck. He was in the act of reloading his pistols (and upon the very same plank where Captain Pasley lost his leg on the 1st of June), when he received two musket balls in his breast. He immediately fell, and upon the quartermaster's going up and asking him if he should take him down below, his answer was: '*No, let me lie quietly one minute. Tell Lieutenant Cumby never to strike!*'

Captain Cooke has his memorial tablet in St. Paul's, on the walls of the crypt close by Nelson's tomb, set up there by order of Parliament. The marble slab bears this inscription:

> Erected at the public expense to the memory of
> Captain John Cooke,
> Who was killed commanding the *Bellerophon*,
> in the Battle of Trafalgar.
> In the forty-fourth year of his age,
> and the thirtieth of his service.

And of another of the brave Bellerophons on that day, Sir John Franklin, the heroic central figure of British Arctic exploration in after times, was one of the officers in the "Billy Ruff'n" at Trafalgar. He was the signal-midshipman, in charge of the ship's signalmen, in which capacity young Franklin, then a lad of nineteen, took in Nelson's message to the fleet, and wrote it down on his signal slate for the captain. Trafalgar was Midshipman Franklin's second battle under Nelson. Copenhagen was his first.

He went through Trafalgar without a wound, being one out of the lucky four or five stationed on the poop—out of forty there—who escaped unwounded. But even then it left its mark on him. "After Trafalgar," says one of his relatives, "he was always a little deaf." To the end of his life Sir John Franklin bore about with him that reminder of the terrific experience he went through.

One of Franklin's brother mids., in a letter home after the battle, gives this glimpse of how the "Billy Ruff'ns" did their duty.

> At 12.23, we opened out fire; at 12.30 broke the line astern a Spanish 2-decker, fighting both sides in passing through. At 12.36, whilst hauling up, fell on board *L'Aigle*, a French 80-gun ship, our foreyard locking with her main-yard. The action soon after became general. *L'Aigle* was the best manned ship in the combined fleet, and was full of picked grenadiers, who annoyed us most dreadfully with musketry. The *Bellerophon* was equally well manned, and had she been fairly alongside her opponent, would soon have carried her; and even in the disadvantageous situation in which we were placed, we very soon drove them from the lower deck; and though we could only bring our foremost guns to bear upon her whilst we received her whole broadside and the fire of four other ships, we had nearly silenced her fire when she dropped astern of us.
>
> After we had thus got clear of our principal opponent, who did not return a single gun whilst we raked her, and two others of them had been engaged by the *Dreadnought* and *Colossus*, we were now only opposed to two Spanish seventy-fours, one of which, the *Monarca*, shortly afterwards struck, and was at 3 o'clock taken possession of by our second-lieutenant, myself, and 8 men. The remaining one, the *Bahama*, struck to us in about half an hour afterwards, and was taken possession of by our fourth- lieutenant. There was very little firing after this, except from five French ships making off to windward, which fired on both the *Bellerophon* and the *Monarca*. One of them was taken by the *Minotaur*, and at 7 minutes after 5 the firing ceased.

Another of the midshipmen mentions:

> Two actual attempts were made by the crew of *L'Aigle* to board us, while the French captain was seen and heard vociferating '*À l'abordage!*' On one of these occasions five of the enemy got upon our starboard sprit-sail yard-arm, and were making their way to

the bowsprit when a seaman named McFarlane let go the sprit-sail brace (a rope supporting that end of the yard), which suddenly canting with their weight, they all fell into the water.

The same writer adds these other details:

> Our main topmast being shot away, the sail, in falling between the ships (*L'Aigle* and *Bellerophon*), had been hooked, or held, by something in our main chains, and consequently hung like a curtain before the muzzles of our guns. It was soon in a blaze, but sail trimmers were immediately sent to clear the sail, etc., which dropped into the water. Soon after this, the first-lieutenant (Captain Cumby), being now in command, walked round the decks to encourage the men and stimulate their exertions at the guns, observing that 'we had nothing else to trust to, as the ship aloft had become an unmanageable wreck.'

Finally we have a word as to the manner in which the "Billy Ruff'ns" bore themselves at Trafalgar. Observes one of the officers:

> I must say I was astonished at the coolness and undaunted bravery displayed by our gallant and veteran crew, when surrounded by five enemy's ships, and for a length of time unassisted by any of ours.

First-Lieutenant Cumby, for his part, wrote to Collingwood, in his official statement to the admiral after the battle:

> In consequence of the death of Captain Cooke, I feel it my duty to represent to you the highly-spirited conduct of every officer, man and boy on board the *Bellerophon* in the action of the 21st instant. The gallantry with which the ship was placed in action by our much regretted captain, and the animated support I received from every individual on board after his fall, left nothing to me but the honour of having succeeded by seniority of commission to the command of such men.

How the captain of the "Mars" met his fate

The crew of another ship of Collingwood's line, the *Mars*, shared with the Bellerophons the sad distinction of losing their captain at Trafalgar. A remarkably fine officer, and one of the noblest-hearted of men was he, also a gallant Scot—George Duff, a Banffshire man, and nearly related to the family of the old Earls of Fife. He had been a sailor from his boyhood. When quite a child young Duff had showed an invincible inclination to go to sea, in spite of family opposition. Indeed, it is said that when only nine he stowed himself away on board a merchant ship.

His parents after that ceased to oppose his desire to enter the navy, with the result that, before he was sixteen, young Duff had seen service as a midshipman in no fewer than thirteen actions. Three of them were battles under Rodney, as inspiring a chief to learn his business under as a young officer could well have. Midshipman Duff was with Rodney, for one fight, in the midnight battle off Cape St. Vincent, so daringly carried out close to the reefs of a perilous coast in the midst of a fierce January storm, which brought about the first relief of Gibraltar during the great siege. He was with Rodney again, as a newly-made lieutenant, on that tremendous battle-day in the West Indies—the "Glorious Twelfth of April," 1782—when the pride of the French Navy at its best, under the leadership of the famous De Grasse, went down in irretrievable ruin within sight of the mountain peaks of Dominica.

A brave and popular captain, although a strict officer and firm disciplinarian. Captain Duff was one of the few officers who succeeded in maintaining good order on board ship during the dark period of the Spithead and Nore mutinies. He had partly to thank for that, on one occasion, his powerful physique, which enabled him once to quell a mutiny at one stroke, by personally seizing the ringleader, collaring and dragging him out from among the rest of the excited and insubordinate crew, and then holding him out at arm's length over the bulwarks until the wretched would-be mutineer cried out for mercy and forgiveness.

How Captain Duff fell at Trafalgar in the heat of the battle, and a glimpse of the distinguished part that his ship, the *Mars*, took on that day, is told us by one of his officers:

> Captain Duff knowing that his ship sailed ill, ordered every stitch of canvas to be set, and while bearing down upon the enemy went through his ship to see that everything was in readiness for action. He spoke to his officers and men in every part of the ship, and, among other directions for their conduct, strictly enjoined them not to waste their fire, as he would undertake to lay them close enough to the enemy. The *Mars*, notwithstanding every exertion, was passed by the *Royal Sovereign*, bearing the flag of Vice-Admiral Collingwood, then the *Bel-*

leisle shot ahead, and they were in action a few minutes before the *Mars*, each ship breaking through at a different part of the enemy's line.

The wind, which had been light, then became more uncertain, and prevented the rest of the ships from closing immediately with the enemy, so that the few who were first engaged were in a manner surrounded, and had for some time to maintain a most severe conflict. There was a French ship on each side of the *Mars*, and a Spanish ship, a first-rate, on the bow, and a fourth ship also within range of shot. The ship on the starboard quarter, the *Fongueux*, was soon disabled, and it was thought she had struck, but her colours had only been shot away, as she had never ceased to fire.

The captain of marines, on the poop, seeing that the *Fongueux* in dropping to leeward was getting into a position that would enable her to rake the *Mars*, and that she was preparing to do so, came down to the quarter-deck to inform Captain Duff. The want of wind, though, rendered it impossible to alter the position of the *Mars*, nor could it with safety be attempted, having regard to the enemy's other ships.

On being spoken to by the captain of marines, Captain Duff asked him, 'Do you think our guns would bear on her?' He answered, 'I think not, but I cannot see for smoke.' 'Then,' replied the captain, 'we must point our guns on the ships on which they bear. I shall go and look, but the men below may see better, as there will be less smoke there.' Captain Duff on that went to the end of the quarter-deck to look over the side. He then told his *aide-de-camp*, Mr. Arbuthnot, to go below and order the guns to be pointed more aft, meaning against the *Fougueux*. The midshipman had scarcely turned to go with these orders when the *Fougueux* raked the *Mars* with a broadside. It struck down the gallant commander. A cannon-ball killed Captain Duff and two seamen who were immediately behind him. His body fell on the gangway, where it lay covered with a spare colour, a Union Jack, until after the action.

About the same time as the gallant Duff fell in the *Mars*, being one hour and five minutes after the commencement of the action. Captain Cooke, the companion of his youth, was killed in the *Bellerophon*, and their commander-in-chief, the illustrious Lord Nelson, was mortally wounded on board the *Victory*.

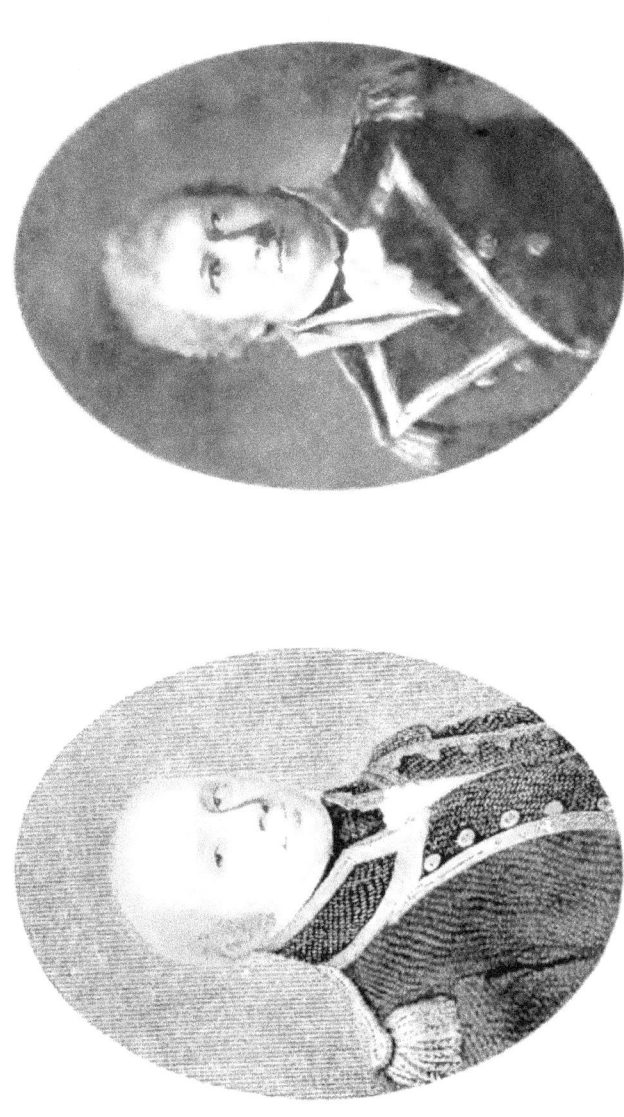

The two captains who fell at Trafalgar:
Captain John Cooke of the "Bellerophon" and Captain George Duff of the "Mars"

The *Mars* continued engaged during the whole of the action, frequently with fresh ships, but suffered from none so severely as she had done from the *Fougueux*, which continued to drift to leeward, until she was engaged by other of our ships, and finally captured by the *Téméraire*.

When the battle had ceased, and it was generally known in the *Mars* that their gallant captain was killed, there was scarcely a dry eye among the crew. Everyone felt that he had lost his friend and benefactor, and they all exclaimed, 'We never shall have again such a commander!'

In all, ninety-eight officers and men were killed or wounded on board the *Mars* at Trafalgar.

Captain Duff, from all accounts, was one of the best of men in his private life, a gentleman and true-hearted Christian in the fullest sense of the word. As evidence of his happy domestic relations there exists this letter, which was written by the captain to his wife in the early hours of that morning just before they cleared for action on board. It was found in the captain's desk, on the dead officer's personal belongings being gone through:

> Monday Morning, October 21, 1805.
>
> My dear Sophia,
>
> I have just time to tell you that we are going into action with the Combined Fleet. I hope and trust in God that we shall all behave as becomes us, and that I may yet have the happiness of taking my beloved wife and children in my arms. Norwich is quite well and happy. I have, however, ordered him off the quarter-deck.
>
> Yours ever, and most truly,
>
> George Duff.

Norwich Duff was the captain's son, a young midshipman, a boy twelve years old. To his lot it fell to break the terrible news of his father's death to the mother at home in Scotland. This is the letter that he wrote:

> My dear Mamma,
>
> You cannot possibly imagine how unwilling I am to begin this melancholy letter. However, as you must unavoidably hear of the fate of dear Papa, I write you these few lines to request you to bear it as patiently as you can. He died like a hero, having

gallantly led his ship into action, and his memory will ever be dear to his king, his country, and his friends. It was about fifteen minutes past twelve in the afternoon of the 21st of October when the engagement began, and it was not finished till five. Many a brave hero sacrificed his life upon that occasion to his king and his country. You will hear that Lord Viscount Nelson was wounded in the commencement of the engagement, and only survived long enough to learn that the victory was ours. 'Then,' said that brave hero, 'I die happy, since I die victorious,' and in a few minutes he expired.

We are now all on board the *Euryalus*, with the Hon. Captain Blackwood, and, in compliance with the wish of Admiral Collingwood, are now on our way to England that we may have an opportunity of more readily knowing your wishes respecting our future conduct. Captain Blackwood has indeed been very polite and kind to me, and has requested Mr. Dalrymple to let my uncle know that on account of his acquaintance with my Papa he will feel very happy in keeping me on board his ship.

My dear Mama, I have again to request you to endeavour to make yourself as happy and easy as possible. It has been the will of Heaven, and it is our duty to submit.

Believe me your obedient and affectionate,

N. Duff.

Like Captain Cooke of the *Bellerophon*, Captain Duff has his memorial tablet in the crypt of St. Paul's beside Nelson's tomb, similarly erected by Parliament as a mark of national gratitude. Portraits of the two dead captains of Trafalgar have also been placed in our British Naval National Gallery, the Painted Hall of Greenwich Hospital.

Captains Duff and Cooke, it may be added by the way, were intimate friends of long standing; they had known each other all through their service. Both of them had been lieutenants in battle with Rodney on his great day,—Duff in the *Montagu*, Cooke in the *Duke*. Captain Duff, in fact, wrote this of his friend Cooke, a few weeks before Trafalgar, in one of his letters to his wife:

> A ship from England has been in sight all day; I take her to be the *Bellerophon*, our old friend Cooke, and I hope to have some letters by him from you. He is one of my oldest friends in the service, and was, till the other day, captain of the guardship at

Plymouth; but he was no sooner appointed to the *Bellerophon* than he was ordered for foreign service. If we go to the Mediterranean, I shall be very glad to have so good and old a friend of the party.

THE "CONQUERORS" MAKE GOOD THEIR NAME

The *Conqueror*, a fine seventy-four, was in Nelson's line, one of the ships in the weather division, and raced the *Leviathan* for fifth place as the fleet neared the enemy. Then the *Leviathan*, pressing forward in response to a verbal order from Nelson brought by Captain Blackwood, to pass ahead of the *Victory*, drew a little in advance. That was just as the first shots went off.

The famous Lord Exmouth's younger brother, Israel Pellew, one of the finest sailors that Cornwall ever sent to sea, captained the *Conqueror* that day. Thanks to Captain Pellew's foresight, not a single man was wounded on board as they advanced, although shots were flying thickly all about them, and ships nearby lost heavily. As the enemy began to fire, every man was ordered to lie down on the deck beside his gun until the word was given to commence action. More than that, Captain Pellew, on making out that the French ships were full of soldiers and had marksmen in their tops, ordered his marines below, with every other man who could be spared from on deck. Those who had to remain he told to place themselves where they would best be screened from the enemy's bullets.

He sent most of the marines to the lower deck to reinforce the sailors stationed at the big 32-pounders there, a measure that proved of marked advantage. The *Conqueror* was thus easily able to man her guns on both sides and fight every gun she carried. She soon found occasion to do so as her part in the battle took shape.

A smart, well-drilled set of fellows were the Conquerors, the ship's crew sturdy Cornish lads largely, and not a few of them got through their captain's reputation as an exceptionally smart officer. A fine gunnery officer was Israel Pellew, and personally a dead shot behind cannon-sights. Every Cornishman had heard of how, in one memorable frigate fight—that of the *Nymphe* and the *Cleopatra* twelve years before—his straight eye had enabled him to knock away the enemy's steering-wheel, and win the battle. His men in the *Conqueror* had been given constant practice with their guns, and well knew how to shoot fast and to shoot straight.

This is how they watched the opening of the battle from the quarter-deck; as the *Conqueror* followed Nelson's lead, coming on some twenty minutes or so behind the *Victory*, each point being noted down as marked:

At 12.45 *Victory* commenced action.
At 1.00 *Victory's* mizzen-topmast shot away in close action.
At 1.20 *Tonnant* lost her fore-topmast. Observed a Spanish three-decker with a flag at the fore with her mizzen-mast gone by the board, and the *Téméraire's* main and mizzen-topmasts gone; and the *Royal Sovereign's* main and mizzen-topmasts gone. A French two-decker's main and mizzen-topmasts shot away.

So the opening entries read. But their own turn had come before that.

At 1.30 *Conqueror* commenced action with the *Bucentaure* of 80 guns.

At that moment the *Victory* was fighting the *Redoutable* at a short distance to the right. Farther off, the *Téméraire* had just broken through the enemy. On the port bow, a little to the left, were the *Britannia*, *Neptune*, and the *Leviathan*. All were more or less intermingled with the enemy, while the smoke of their firing drifted thickly and heavily in the calm air all round them.

It was not difficult to distinguish the enemy's ships. Their hulls, and often their colours, were obscured by the smoke; but thanks to Nelson's forethought, there was ever at hand a ready means of distinguishing friend from foe—the practical result of Nelson's order that the hoops on the masts of all the British ships should be whitewashed, coloured a yellowish-white, like timber colour, the same colour as the masts. That made it plain shooting, for the French and Spanish ships had black hoops on their masts. All our men had to do was to look out for black hoops as a ship loomed up ahead through the smoke, and on seeing them fire away without hesitation.

Their first antagonist was soon reached. It was the *Bucentaure*, which at the moment that the *Conqueror* came up was a little ahead of where the *Victory* lay grappled alongside of the French *Redoutable*. The *Bucentaure* had already been hard hit, and, as has been told, had suffered severely from the opening broadside the *Victory* dealt her as Nelson broke the line. She had also been roughly handled by the *Britannia* and *Neptune*, besides undergoing a sharp attack from the *Leviathan*. But she could still hit back hard. Though she had lost between 100 and 200 men already, there were over 600 on board to fight the ship. Also they were a picked crew, the pick of the French fleet, for—if unsuspected by the British as yet—the *Bucentaure* was the French flagship, and had on board Admiral Villeneuve, the commander-in-chief of the combined Franco-Spanish *armada*. By some chance the *Bucentaure* had no admiral's flag flying, apparently by accident. The halyards, as the story goes, had got entangled, and Admiral Villeneuve's flag of command in consequence was not run up.

At once the *Conqueror's* guns opened.

A cannonading commenced at so short a distance that every shot flew winged with death and destruction.

So one of the *Conqueror's* lieutenants describes. He goes on:

> Our men, who from constant practice had gained great quickness in the use of their guns, aimed with deliberate precision, as if they had only been firing at a mark, and tore their opponent to pieces. In ten minutes the *Bucentaure's* main and mizzen masts went by the board; twenty minutes after, her foremasts shared a similar fate; at half-past two she struck to the *Conqueror*.

Less than half an hour's firing from the *Conqueror*, indeed, decided the *Bucentatire's* fate. The fall of the main and mizzen masts placed Admiral Villeneuve at the mercy of Captain Pellew and his men. As again our officer in the *Conqueror* tells:

> Though the French ship did not immediately surrender, she was reduced to complete helplessness, for the masts falling on the side engaged, the main-topsail covered her guns. Her people attempted to cut away the wreck, but they were swept into the water, and the wreck itself was soon cleared by the *Conqueror's* shot.

Even after the French colours had come down, though, in the confusion on board the *Bucentaure*, they continued firing from some of their guns. A midshipman named Hicks who was stationed throughout on the *Conqueror*s quarter-deck as captain's *aide-de-camp* describes:

> After her colours were hauled down, two guns from her starboard quarter began to play on us. Sir Israel Pellew, thinking that they were disposed to renew the fight, ordered the guns which would bear on her foremast to knock it away; and the mast was cut away successfully in a few minutes. The officers of

the French ship waving their handkerchiefs in sign of surrender, we sent a cutter and took possession of the *Bucentaure*.

Captain Pellew sent off an officer to take possession of the prize immediately the tricolour came down. Unaware of what ship it was, and being unable to spare his first-lieutenant, he sent off on the duty the nearest officer at hand on the quarter-deck at the moment, the captain of marines, Captain James Atcherley. Atcherley went in the cutter, pulled by a couple of seamen and taking with him a corporal and two marines. He was pulled alongside the *Bucentaure*, and clambered on board the French two-decker. He, to that moment, had not the smallest idea of what was waiting for him.

As he reached the *Bucentaure's* upper-deck and his red coat showed itself on the quarter-deck of the French flagship, to Atcherley's utter astonishment four French officers of rank stepped forward to meet him, all bowing and presenting their swords. The leader was a tall, thin, swarthy-complexioned, sad-faced man of about forty-two, in a French admiral's gold-embroidered uniform. It was Admiral Villeneuve himself. The second, a stout, broad, fat-faced, short man, followed the admiral: Captain Magendie, in command of the *Bucentaure*. The third officer was Villeneuve's chief of the staff, Rear-Admiral Prigny; the fourth, a soldier in the uniform and blue ostrich plumes of a brigadier of the Grand Army, General de Contamine, the military chief over the four thousand troops (three regiments of infantry) on board the French fleet at Trafalgar.

"To whom," asked Admiral Villeneuve in good English, "have I the honour of surrendering?"

"To Captain Pellew of the *Conqueror*."

"It is a satisfaction to me that it is to one so fortunate as Sir Edward Pellew I have lowered my flag," said the admiral then, with a mournful smile.

"It is his brother, sir," answered back Captain Atcherley.

"His brother!" ejaculated Villeneuve, with a gesture of surprise. "What! are there two of them? *Hélas!*"

"*Fortune de la guerre*," was all that Captain Magendie said, with a shrug of his shoulders and making a grimace, as he became a captive to the British Navy for the third time in his life. Prigny and De Contamine said nothing, staring in front of them with fixed faces and glumly presenting their swords.

Captain Atcherley, quite taken aback at the rank of the officers facing him, was nonplussed for a moment. He could only suggest that the swords of officers of such high rank had better be given up later to someone of superior position to himself—to Captain Pellew, his captain.

He then went below to secure the magazines, passing, we are told, amid an awful scene.

> The dead, thrown back as they fell, lay along the middle of the decks in heaps, and shot passing through these had frightfully mangled the bodies. More than four hundred had been killed and wounded, of whom an extraordinary proportion had lost their heads. A raking shot, which entered on the lower-deck, had glanced along the beams and through the thickest of the people; and a French officer declared that this shot alone had killed or disabled nearly forty men.

Atcherley locked up the magazines fore and aft, and put the keys in his pocket, posting his marines as sentries. Then, returning on deck, he conducted Villeneuve, Magendie, and Flag-Captain Prigny down the ship's side into his little boat, which rowed off to regain the *Conqueror*. That ship, however, had meanwhile ranged ahead to engage another enemy, and as her whereabouts could not readily be discovered in the smoke, the prisoners were temporarily rowed on board the nearest British ship, which happened to be the *Mars*. There Admiral Villeneuve's sword was formally accepted by Lieutenant Hennah, the first-lieutenant, in charge of the ship in consequence of Captain Duff's death, who sent it after the battle to Collingwood.

But the French flagship was not the *Conqueror's* only antagonist. While fighting the *Bucentaure* on her port broadside she had had at the same time to keep up a sharp cannonade with some of her starboard guns on the great Spanish four-decker, the *Santissima Trinidad*, first brought to action by the *Neptune*. As soon as Captain Atcherley's boat rowed off, the *Conqueror* moved on ahead to assist the *Neptune* in dealing with the great Spaniard. Barely twenty minutes sufficed to settle with the Trinidad.

> Captain Pellew, with his accustomed coolness and discrimination, took up a position on the Spaniard's quarter within pistol-shot.

After ten minutes close action:

> At 2.25, the four-decker's main and mizzen masts went by the board.

At 2.32, shot her foremast away.
At 2.35, she struck to the *Neptune* and *Conqueror*.

So the ship's log outlines the story.

One of the *Conqueror's* officers, differing from the log account, says that the Trinidad's three masts came down together with one crash, and describes the fall as seen with his own eyes. The *Santissima Trinidad:*

> .... gave a deep roll with the swell to leeward, then back to windward; and in her return every mast went by the board, leaving an unmanageable hulk on the water. Her immense topsails had every reef out, her royals were sheeted home but lowered, and the falling of the mass of the square sails and rigging, plunging into the water at the very muzzles of our guns, was one of the most magnificent sights I ever beheld. Immediately after this a Spaniard showed an English Union on the lee gangway in token of submission.

Again the *Conqueror* passed on; now to attempt a blow at the ships of the French van. The battle smoke clearing off somewhat, showed the van ships of the enemy coming down directly towards the *Conqueror*. Captain Pellew and his brave fellows, however, were ready for them.

> After a short time to breathe, we endeavoured to close with them as well as the shattered state of our rigging would permit, every running rope being shot away but one of the main-topsail braces.

But the newcomers had little fight in them after all. They kept away, and although at one moment they looked threatening, made no serious effort to press home an attack. To use again the words of one of the ship's officers—

> The *Conqueror* received a heavy fire from them, and as they prepared to board. Captain Pellew ordered the boarders to be called.

The French officer in command, however—Rear-Admiral Dumanoir—had already changed his mind. He saw that his commander-in-chief had surrendered, and preferred not to compromise his own squadron. On seeing that other British ships were nearing the *Conqueror*, he kept off, at nearly two hundred yards distance, firing at Captain Pellew from there, and then he moved away. Notes the *Conqueror's* log:

Five of the enemy's ships bore down on us and commenced a heavy fire. Three of our ships coming to our assistance, the enemy passed our starboard quarter.

Yet some mischief was done on board. Brief as the exchange of fire was, it cost the lives of two of the *Conqueror's* officers. One of them. Lieutenant St. George, the second-lieutenant, was passing his friend Lloyd, the third-lieutenant, on the quarter-deck, when Lloyd good-humouredly tapped him on the shoulder and congratulated him on his prospects of promotion to commander. Lieutenant St. George took a step forward, and was in the act of turning towards the other with a smile on his face, when a bullet from one of the French ships struck Lloyd dead on the spot, the same ball striking the second-lieutenant down, inflicting fatal injuries.

> Lieutenant Lloyd was struck in the mouth, the bullet passing through the back of his head. So little was his countenance changed at the moment that an officer who just then reached the quarter-deck with a party of boarders, and ran to assist him, thought he had only been stunned by the wind of a shot. Lieutenant St. George was shot through the neck. He had gone into action with a strong impression that he should fall; and that morning, when his brother officers proposed to him to take some refreshment in the ward-room, with the half-serious, half-jocular remark that it might be the last time, he replied that he felt that it would indeed be so. Just after the deaths of these officers Captain Pellew reeled and fell, stunned by the wind of a shot. He recovered immediately, but it was found afterwards that he had received permanent injury.

As full of fight as ever, the gallant Conquerors then turned once more to help a friend. The *Leviathan* was seen to be engaged with two enemies at once, a Spanish and a French two-decker. The *Conqueror* moved down promptly and opened a fire on the Frenchman, which drove that enemy off. The two British ships cheered each other as the *Conqueror* came up,:

> ....for the crews were well acquainted, their stations in the sailing order of the fleet being next each other. The *Leviathan*, left now with a single opponent, quickly overpowered, boarded, and carried her, the people cheering from the poop as they tore down her colours, 'Huzza, *Conqueror*, she's ours!'

The French ship was *L'Intrépide,* which had got separated from the rest of the van squadron. Turning away from the Leviathan, she exchanged a cannonade with the *Conqueror,* and then sheered off, to be closely engaged at once by the *Africa,* and immediately afterwards by the *Orion.* While fighting the *Orion* her main and mizzen masts were both shot away, on which *L'Intrépide* surrendered. One of the officers of the *Conqueror* describes her end.

> We engaged at too great a distance to do any material execution on either part; our shattered state prevented our closing nearer. The distant cannonade continued until the *Africa*, a perfect ship, dashed in between us with several others, directing their fire against the deserted ship. Her captain surrendered after one of the most gallant defences I ever witnessed. The Frenchman's name was Infernet, a member of the Legion of Honour, and it deserves to be recorded in the memory of those who admire true heroism. The *Intrépide* was the last ship that struck her colours: about half-past five.

The narrative of the *Conqueror's* day at Trafalgar may be closed with these anecdotes from the ship of incidents on board during the battle. Two will serve to show the chivalrous spirit that inspired Nelson's officers at Trafalgar. One concerns the gallant captain of the *Conqueror* himself, and refers to an incident towards the close of the battle.

> The remains of the most splendid and powerful fleet ever drawn up in a line of battle were now making their escape to Cadiz, and the *Conqueror* hauled across the course of one of them which had only her foresail. Her captain stood upon the poop, holding the lower corner of a small French jack, while he pinned the upper with his sword to the stump of the mizzenmast. She fired two or three guns, probably to provoke a return, which might spare the discredit of a tame surrender. The *Conqueror's* broadside was ready; but Captain Pellew exclaimed: 'Don't hurt the brave fellow; fire a single shot across his bow!' Her captain immediately lowered his sword, thus dropping the colours, and, taking off his hat, bowed his surrender.

The second story has to do with another officer in the *Conqueror* at Trafalgar, Lieutenant Toole. It also refers to an incident as the battle was drawing to its end.

> On the stump of the main-mast of one of the enemy's ships

which she (the *Conqueror*) had engaged and dismasted, a man was seen most fearlessly occupied in placing the tricoloured flag. Lieutenant Toole had three times raised a musket to his shoulder and levelled it; but a compassionate feeling forbade him to execute his threat, and the gallant fellow was suffered to live, to share the fate of his soon after captured companions.

Two other stories relate to lower-deck incidents on board.

A seaman of the *Conqueror*, on losing a leg and having the stump amputated, calmly told the purser, who was assisting the surgeon in the cockpit, while the maimed limb was being bound up:

> Ah, Mr. Beattie, I shall live now half as cheap as before; one pair of stockings will serve me twice as long.

Another of the *Conqueror's* wounded men:

> ....while waiting to be taken below, was seen to amuse himself by picking up French grape-shot which were falling all round him and sticking in the planks of the deck, collecting them and pitching marbles with them.

This is a dog story also from the ship:

A Sardinian pointer belonging to an officer of the *Conqueror* was by misadventure, while the ship was being cleared for action, thrown out of one of the main-deck ports. The poor beast, however, did not fall into the sea. After the battle the dog was found, in a dazed and half stupefied condition, "lodged on the ridge of the swinging-boom on the side engaged." It had continued there unharmed all through the battle, with gun-muzzles belching out their fiery discharges close to it on each side and above, and French cannon-balls smashing into the ship's sides all round—a terrifying experience indeed for the unfortunate dog. The ship's company of the *Conqueror*, we are told, "ever afterwards took so strong an affection to the dog that when, later, they turned over to the *Barham* they took him with them." The dog, it is stated, was alive in 1820, fifteen years after Trafalgar.

As a special memorial of Nelson and Trafalgar the *Conqueror*, as long as she lasted, bore for her figurehead a carved effigy of Nelson, heroic size. In the battle the ship had had her original figurehead shot away, and immediately on their return to England the crew, we are told:

> .... applied for permission through their first-lieutenant,

Mr. Couch (like Captain Pellew, a gallant Cornishman), who warmly seconded their request, to have the mutilated figure replaced with one of their lamented admiral. Accordingly, after their return to England, a figure of Nelson, remarkable for the correct likeness and superior workmanship, which the crew ornamented at their own expense, was placed at the bows of the *Conqueror*.

WHAT THE CAPTAIN OF THE "ORION" SAW AND DID

This is what Captain Codrington of the *Orion* (afterwards famous as Admiral Sir Edward Codrington, the victor at Navarino) saw and did at Trafalgar. The *Orion* was the ninth ship from Nelson's van, and her officers and men had ample time and exceptional opportunities for observing events at the outset, while pressing forward to join in the fray. The story is told here in the captain's own words, as related in letters that Codrington wrote home in his first spare moments during the week after the battle:

> At eleven o'clock, when first steering down for them, I gave the ship's company their dinner, and ate the leg of a turkey myself, which was prepared beforehand, so that we were all strong, fresh, hearty, and in high spirits.
>
> I suppose no man ever before saw such a sight so clearly as I did, or rather as we did, for I called all my Lieutenants up to see it. After passing *Santa Anna*, dismasted, and her opponent, the *Royal Sovereign*, little better, on our larboard side, besides three of our ships and some of those of the enemy all lumped together on our starboard bow, we passed close to the *Victory*, *L'Indomptable* (French), *Téméraire*, and *Bucentaure* (French), all abreast or aboard each other, each firing her broadside and boarding the other at the same time.
>
> Passing down, as the *Orion* did, through the whole group of those whose fortune it was to be placed foremost in the attack, and who were then all engaged with their various opponents, without firing a single shot to impede my view, although the ship next astern, as well as all those ahead of us, were firing broadside after broadside, I had an opportunity of seeing more of what was doing than perhaps any other captain in the whole fleet, and so grand and so tremendous was the scene before me, that the impression will be ever fresh on my mind.
>
> We all scrambled into battle as soon as we could, and I believe

have done our best in imitation of the noble example before us. I was in the middle of the battle before I fired a gun, not liking to waste our fire, and my men behaved as coolly as possible.

The shot from both friends and foes were flying about us like hailstones, and yet did us hardly any damage whatever, and, to the honour of the *Orion's* crew, they did not attempt to break my orders to reserve their fire till I could put the ship where I wished. The occasional request from —— to fire, who was very anxious to be doing, was the only interruption I met with. All the rest were as cool as if they were used to such scenes, and Croft (the first-lieutenant) all astonishment at the sight and all attention to my orders. I still persevered in my reserve in spite of the firing all around us, until I saw an unfortunate Frenchman, the *Swiftsure*, not closely occupied, and going close under his stern we poured him in such a dose as carried away his three masts and made him strike his colours. Having repeatedly pointed out to my men the waste of shot from other ships, I had now a fine opportunity of convincing them of the benefit of cool reserve.

Singling out an opponent in the thick of the fighting however, Codrington found no easy business.

In my next attempt to close with a French two-decker which annoyed the *Victory*, my second ahead (*Ajax*) cut me out, and I could only fire at a little distance. I then made for Admiral Gravina in the *Prince of Asturias*, but the *Dreadnought* again cut me out here, and yet, like the *Ajax*, did not close and make a finish of it. I had, therefore, to undergo what always alarms me, a distant cannonade, for a considerable time, and what mischief we met with was from that said *Prince of Asturias*, with whom we had three of these distant salutes in the course of the action between the fleets, and who escaped for want of being more closely attacked.

This, was our *finale*, and, I believe, the *finale* of the whole affair. Seeing *Leviathan* make a fine and well-judged attack on a Spanish seventy-four, *St. Augustin* (in the van of the enemy where there were eight or nine others, French and Spanish untouched, which ought to have come to her support), I made sail to assist her. *L'Intrépide*, however, was the only one which wore and came to action gallantly, keeping up a very good fire on both *Leviathan* and the Spaniard, of whom she was taking possession.

After several fruitless attempts to pass by one or two of our ships, who kept up a distant cannonade on her, I managed first to back all sail so as to get under *Ajax's* stern, then to make all sail so as to pass close across *Leviathan's* head, who hailed me and said he hoped, laughing, that I should 'make a better fist of it' (if not elegant, still very cheering to me to meet so much confidence and good opinion); and then to bear down sufficiently to get our starboard guns to bear on *L'Intrépide's* starboard quarter, and then to turn gradually round from thence under his stern, pass his broadside, and bring to on his larboard bow. He had said he would not strike until his masts and rudder were shot away, and this we did for him in so handsome a way that he had no time to do us much injury.

We got up what studding sails were left, began on his starboard quarter, and in turning round from thence to his lee bow (almost calm), we carried away his tiller and his three masts, and took possession. He had fought bravely with several others, and was determined to fight to the last extremity, as he did. When I first made for him, I thought we should have had their whole van also upon about four of us, but *Dieu merci* they only fired on us at a distance.

Each ship engaged must have fought with a dozen enemies, and those headmost in the line had much the greater part of the action. It was all confusion when *Ajax* and *Orion* got down, and Croft was afraid I should find no ship to engage closely, as I had promised my men; but there was still enough for us to keep up a cannonade for five hours, as I expected, and for which I had prepared myself by not wasting our fire. This reserve did well for me, for our fire on *L'Intrépide* within shot of their whole van was the best directed and best kept up I ever saw.

I do not mean to say *Orion* did more than others; and I should be guilty of hypocrisy if I gave you the impression. Those who were in action first had most to do, and doing their best, did best; and the great difficulties they had to contend with, and their proportionate sufferings, entitle them to a greater share of honour; but this I will say for *Orion*, that she took all the fighting she could get coolly and deliberately, always reserving her firing to produce decision, and never risking the firing into, but cautiously assisting, her own friends. Ten minutes before I thought myself near enough to fire a gun into a ship I was approaching, was I obliged to desire a ship on *Orion's* quarter not to fire into us in her eagerness to fire at the distant enemy. But, however, it was all well done, errors excepted, and I hope we shall have no abuse about want of good conduct.

In the week of stormy weather that immediately followed the battle, the *Orion* was very nearly wrecked. She was only enabled to save herself by a sudden glimpse of the stars, which gave those on board the opportunity of realizing their whereabouts just in time. For a succession of days they had seen neither sun, moon, nor stars, when suddenly a small break in the sky to the north-west revealed a few stars and heralded a momentary shift of the wind from south-west to north-west, which just enabled the ship to claw off and work her way clear of a dangerous reef close at hand to leeward. Singularly enough those stars, as the captain himself notes, were the three forming the belt of the constellation of Orion, and never was good omen more welcome than were those stars to the nearly worn-out crew of the storm-beaten ship.

With the men of the "Revenge"

The *Revenge* was among the ships that followed Collingwood into action. Captain Robert Moorsom, a highly talented officer and artillery expert, commanded on board. Like Codrington of the *Orion*, Captain Moorsom bore down until close to the enemy without firing a shot. The sailor of the *Revenge* we have had to do with earlier tells the story:

> It fell to our lot to cut off the five sternmost ships, and while we were running down to them, of course we were favoured with several shots, and some of our men were wounded. Many of the men thought it hard the firing should be all on one side, and became impatient to return the compliment; but our captain had given orders not to fire until we had got close in with them, so that all our shot might tell. Indeed, these were his words:
>
> 'We shall want all our shot when we get close in; never mind their firing. When I fire a carronade from the quarter-deck, that will be the signal for you to begin, and I know you will do your duty as Englishmen!'

In a few minutes the gun was fired, and our ship bore in and broke the line; but we paid dear for our temerity, as those ships we had thrown into disorder turned round and made an attempt to board.

A Spanish three-decker ran her bowsprit over our poop, with a number of her crew on it and in her fore-rigging. Two or three hundred men were ready to follow, but they caught a Tartar; for their design was discovered, and our marines, with their small-arms and the carronades on the poop, loaded with canister shot, swept them off so fast that they were glad to sheer off. While this was going on aft, we were engaged with a two-deck French ship on our starboard side, and on our larboard bow another, so that many of their shots must have struck their own ships and done severe execution.

After being engaged about an hour two other ships fortunately came up and received some of the fire intended for us. We were now enabled to get at some of the shot-holes between wind and water and plug them up. This is a duty performed by the carpenter and his crew. We were unable to work the ship, our yards, sails, and masts being disabled, and the braces completely shot away. In this condition we lay by the side of the enemy, firing away, and now and then we received a good raking from them, passing under our stern. It was a busy time for us, for we had not only to endeavour to repair our damage, but to keep to our duty. The most destructive shot to us appeared to be the thirty-two pounds double-headed. Two of these deafeners we observed to be sticking in our main-mast, which, miraculously and fortunately for us, was not carried away.

Often during the battle we could not see for the smoke whether we were firing at a friend or foe, and as to hearing orders, the noise of the guns so completely made us deaf that we were obliged to look only to the motions that were made!

In this manner we continued the battle until nearly five o'clock, when it ceased.

Orders were now given to fetch the dead bodies from the cockpit and throw them overboard. These were the bodies of the men who were taken down to the doctor during the battle badly wounded, and who, by the time the engagement was ended, were dead. Some of them, perhaps, could not have recovered, but others might had timely assistance been rendered. But it was impossible, for the rule is, as order is requisite, that every person shall be dressed in rotation as they are brought down wounded, and in many instances some have bled to death.

The next call was 'all hands to splice the mainbrace,' which was the giving out of a gill of rum to each man, and indeed they much needed it, for they had not ate or drank from breakfast time.

MIDSHIPMAN JACK SPRATT OF THE "DEFIANCE"

The splendid deed of daring at Trafalgar by which Midshipman Jack Spratt of the *Defiance* won his lieutenant's commission, took place while the *Defiance* was fighting *L'Aigle*, on the French ship, already badly hammered, drawing off from alongside the *Bellerophon*. This is the story as told by one of the heroic fellow's shipmates.

> After the *Defiance* and *L'Aigle* (74) had been for some time hotly engaged, and the fire of the French ship, within pistol shot of her opponent, had slackened. Captain Durham, in the hope that a breeze—it being at the time a dead calm—would spring up, prepared to board his enemy. Mr. Spratt, who had been selected to lead the men in the desperate service that awaited them, volunteered, as all the boats had been disabled, to board the enemy by swimming. His offer being accepted, he instantly, with his sword in his teeth and his battle-axe in his belt, dashed into the sea, calling at the same time upon the others to follow. The order, however, in the general din, was not heard; at any rate it was not heeded.
>
> Undaunted, though alone, Spratt on reaching the French ship, contrived by the means of the rudder chains, to enter the stern gun-room port, and thence to fight his way through all the decks until he reached the poop. Here, he was charged by three grenadiers with fixed bayonets, but, springing with dexterity past them, by the assistance of the signal halyards he got upon an arm-chest, and before they could repeat the operation, disabled two of them. Seizing the third one, he threw him from the poop down on to the quarter-deck, where he fell and broke his neck. He dragged Spratt with him, but the British officer escaped injury.
>
> By this time a boarding party from the *Defiance*, who had been at first repulsed, were making a second, and successful, attempt to carry the enemy's ship. Midshipman Spratt joined in the desperate hand-to-hand conflict which raged on the quarter-deck,

and had the happiness of saving the life of a French officer from the fury of his assailants. Scarcely had he discharged this act of humanity, when an endeavour was made by a French grenadier to run him through with his bayonet. The thrust was parried, whereupon the Frenchman presented his musket at Spratt's breast, and fired. Although the midshipman succeeded in striking the muzzle down with his cutlass, the charge passed through his right leg a little below the knee, shattering both bones. Spratt immediately backed in between two of the quarter-deck guns to prevent being cut down from behind, in which position he continued to defend himself against his old tormentor and two others, until, at length, relieved by some of his party.

As soon as the *L'Aigle's* colours had been struck, Spratt swung himself by one of the boat-tackle falls across the *Defiance*, and landing on a lower-deck port lid, which happened to be up, was carried to the cockpit.

A few days afterwards, Mr. Burnett, surgeon on board the *Defiance*, came to Captain Durham and asked for a written order to cut off Mr. Spratt's leg, saying that it could not be cured, and that he refused to submit to the operation. The captain replied that he could not give such an order, but that he would see Mr. Spratt, which he managed to do in spite of his own wounds. Upon the captain remonstrating with him, Spratt held out the other leg (certainly a very good one) and exclaimed, 'Never! If I lose my leg, where shall I find a match for this?' He was a high-spirited young Irishman, and one of the handsomest men in the Navy. He was safely landed at Gibraltar, where he remained sixteen weeks in hospital.

Jack Spratt, we are told, lived for many years after Trafalgar on a pension as a retired commander, being resident in Devonshire, in a little west-country town, where he used to ride about on a little Dartmoor pony. "Captain Spratt," one who knew him relates also, "had a useless leg, yet he was a splendid swimmer, and when nearly sixty years old, swam a fourteen-mile race for a wager with a French gentleman and won it."

This incidental note in connexion with the *Defiance* at Trafalgar may be added by the way. It is from a letter that an officer of the *Defiance* wrote on December 16, 1805, to the *Hampshire Telegraph* in reply to a paragraph in a London newspaper that: "Captain Blackwood of the *Euryalus* had delivered to the Lords of the Admiralty the jack, etc., of the French ship *L'Aigle*:"

> I beg to inform you that *L'Aigle* struck to the *Defiance*; that Lieutenant Simons most gallantly boarded her, hauled down her colours, which he brought, partly lashed round his body, into this ship, and then returned to *L'Aigle* in aid of the boarders, and was unfortunately shot on her poop. . . . The ensign, jack, and pennant of *L'Aigle* were sent to the Lords of the Admiralty by Captain Durham.

On board Nelson's Nile prize, the "Tonnant"

One of the hardest fighters of our Trafalgar fleet was originally a French ship, and one of Nelson's prizes from the Nile. She fought her former friends under her old French name which had been specially retained for her on the roll of the Royal Navy—the *Tonnant*.

"We went down in no order, but every man to take his bird," is the way in which one of the officers of the *Tonnant* puts it in describing how the battle opened. He then goes on:

> At 11.30 the signal was made, 'England expects every individual will do his duty.' At 12 the enemy's ships opened a most tremendous fire on the *Royal Sovereign*, which she returned in a style that did honour to old England; then on the *Belleisle*, then on the *Tonnant*—the *Mars* seconded us. At this moment Lord Nelson's line began. From smoke, guns, etc., from this moment all became confusion.
>
> They cut us up a good deal, until we got our broadside to bear on a Spanish ship in breaking the line, when we gave her such a murdering broadside that she did not return a gun for some minutes. The French *Algisuras* (Admiral Magor)[1] was the ship astern of the ship we had saluted. She filled her main topsail and shot up to rake us. We put our helm up and tumbled on board of her and fought it out. The fire from both ships was tremendous; one or the other must give way.
>
> At this critical time a Spanish and a French ship crossed our bow. Being stationed on the forecastle and seeing the situation we were in, I went aft to inform Captain Tyler, when I found he had been carried below wounded. The first-lieutenant became captain—he said he had sent for the officers to consult what

---

1. *Algéçiras*—Rear-Admiral Magon.

was best to be done, and at that moment the second-lieutenant came up. We three agreed to keep the boarders aft, and turn-to on those gentlemen on the bow. They kept up a very heavy fire on us for some time, we accommodating them with as good as they sent.

Then came on as desperate a ship to ship set-to as any even on that day, as another of the *Tonnant's* officers narrates the tale:

A French ship of eighty guns, with an admiral's flag, came up and poured a raking broadside into our stern, which killed or wounded forty petty officers and men, nearly cut the rudder in two, and shattered the whole of the stern, with the quarter galleries. She then, in the most gallant manner, locked her bowsprit in our starboard main shrouds and attempted to board us with the greater part of her officers and ship's company. She had riflemen in her tops who did great execution. Our poop was soon cleared, and our gallant captain shot through the left thigh, and obliged to be carried below.

During this time we were not idle. We gave it to her most gloriously with the starboard and main-deckers, and turned the forecastle guns, loaded with grape, on the gentlemen who wished to give us so fraternal a hug. The marines kept up a warm destructive fire on the boarders. Only one man made good his footing on our quarter-deck, when he was pinned through the calf of his right leg by one of the crew with his half-pike, whilst another was going to cut him down, which I prevented, and desired him to be taken to the cockpit. Our severe contest with the French admiral lasted more than half an hour, our sides grinding so much against each other that we were obliged to fire the lower-deck guns without running them out.

At length both ships caught fire before the chess-trees, and our firemen, with all the coolness and courage so inherent in British seamen, got the engine and played on both ships, finally extinguishing the flames, although two of them were severely wounded in doing so. At length we had the satisfaction of seeing her three lower masts go by the board, ripping the partners up in their fall, as they had been shot through the lower-deck, and carrying with them all their sharpshooters to look sharper in the next world, for, as all our boats were shot through, we could not save one of them in this. The crew were then ordered, with the second-lieutenant, to board her. They cheered, and in a short time carried her. They found the gallant French admiral Magon killed at the foot of the poop ladder, and the captain dangerously wounded.

Out of eight lieutenants, five were killed, with three hundred petty officers and men, and about one hundred wounded. We left the second-lieutenant and sixty men in charge of her, and took some of the prisoners on board, when she swung clear of us. We had pummelled her so handsomely that fourteen of her lower-deck guns were dismounted, and her larboard bow exhibited a mass of splinters.

During this time we were hard at it on the Spanish ship. When at last down came her colours, I hailed a Spanish officer and asked him if he had struck. When he said 'Yes,' I came aft and informed the first-lieutenant. He ordered me to board her. We had no boat but what was shot, but he told me I must try, so I went away in the jolly-boat with two men, but had not got above a quarter of the way when the boat swamped. I cannot swim, but the two men who were with me could, one a black man and the other a quartermaster; he was the last man in her, when a shot struck her and knocked her quarter off, and she was turned bottom up. Macnamara, the black man, staid by me on one side, and Maclay, the quartermaster, on the other, until I got hold of the jolly-boat's fall, that was hanging overboard. I got my leg between the fall, and as the ship lifted by the sea so was I, and as she descended, I was ducked. I found myself weak, and thought I was not long for this world. Macnamara swam to the ship and got a rope and to me again, and made it fast under my arms, when I swung off, and was hauled into the stern port.

One of the other officers mentions:

> Having no boat that would float four of the seamen jumped overboard to rescue those who could not swim, and they all regained the ship. Mr. C, the lieutenant, was nearly drowned, and had it not been for a black man, who took him on his back, he must have sunk.

There was certainly no lack of fine fellows on board the *Tonnant*. Here is a glance, incidentally, at some of them, again from an officer's letter home soon after the battle:

We had hoisted our colours before the action in different places; at the ensign staff, peak, and in the fore and main-topmast shrouds, so that if one was shot away the others might be flying. A number of our fleet had done the same, and several of the enemy had followed our example. The French admiral's ship, who so gallantly attempted to board us, had his hoisted in three places. One of our men, Fitzgerald, ran up his rigging and cut away one of them and placed it round his waist, and had nearly after this daring exploit reached his ship, when a rifleman shot him and he fell between the two ships and was no more seen.

The principal signalman, whose name was White, and captain of one of the guns on the poop, had his right great-toe nearly severed from his foot. He deliberately took his knife and cut it away. He was desired to go below to the doctor. 'No, sir,' was his reply, 'I am not the fellow to go below for such a scratch as that! I wish to give the beggars' (meaning the enemy) 'a few more hard pills before I have done with them!' Saying this he bound his foot up in his neck-handkerchief and served out double allowance, until his carronade was dismounted by the carriage of it being shattered to pieces; he then hopped to another gun, where he amused himself at the Frenchmen's expense until the action ceased.

Again, we have this incident:

> During the latter part of the action the captain, who was lying on a cot in the purser's cabin, sent for me. On entering the cockpit, I found fourteen men awaiting amputation of either an arm or a leg. A marine who had sailed with me in a former ship, was standing up as I passed, with his left arm hanging down. 'What's the matter, Connelly?' said I to him. 'Not much, sir,' replied he; 'I am only winged above my elbow, and I am waiting my turn to be lopped.' His arm was dreadfully shattered by a grape-shot.

We are also told, by another of the *Tonnant's* lieutenants:

> One of the men, whose name was Smith, after his leg was taken off, heard the cheering on deck in consequence of another of the enemy striking her colours, and cheered also. The exertion he made burst the blood-vessels, and before they could be taken up he died. In the cockpit, which was half below the water-line

and very dark, the amputations were done by the surgeon, with his two assistants holding tallow candles for the doctor to see by. Helping him were the purser and a petty officer's wife, a very big woman, who, as fast as the unfortunate wounded were operated on, lifted them off the table bodily in her arms and bore them off as if they were children to their temporary berths out of the way elsewhere.

5

The Man Who Hoisted Nelson's Signal at Trafalgar

The finding in a state of abject destitution, forty-one years after Trafalgar, of the man who with his own hands hoisted Nelson's signal on board the *Victory* is a pathetic little story. The discovery was quite accidental, and through a medical man, then living in South London, the son of the surgeon of another Trafalgar man-of-war, the *Tonnant*. The doctor, as he himself relates, had a practice in the then fairly well-to-do neighbourhood of Upper Stamford Street, Blackfriars, when one day in the winter of 1846 something prompted him to take notice of "an old and broken-down man who made a scanty livelihood by crying watercress and red herrings through the streets."

He had often seen the old fellow on his round, and had observed that he "appeared to be a quick, sharp-witted old man, and had a great reputation for sagacity among the lower class of neighbours." Becoming interested in him, the doctor, in due course, was led to have inquiries made as to the man's antecedents, during which a surprising fact came out. Relates the doctor:

> We discovered that he was an old sailor named John Roome, and that he had served with Nelson at Trafalgar—in fact, that he had been a signalman on board the *Victory*.

That led to further inquiries being made, with the result that one day the old man was called indoors by the doctor and questioned, with a view of seeing if anything could be done to better his position.

> I at length took the opportunity of calling the man in, and seating him before me, asked him: 'Who was the signal-officer on

board the *Victory* at Trafalgar?'
He replied, 'Mr. Pasco, sir.'
'Did you serve under him?'
'Yes.'
'Who, then, hoisted the signal, "England expects every man to do his duty?"'
'I did.'
I had felt somewhat prepared for this answer; still, as it was uttered I could scarcely refrain from a demonstration of reverence towards the old embarrassed signalman, who sat uneasily before me.

A number of additional questions on minor points were satisfactorily answered, and Roome's identity as the *Victory's* Trafalgar signalman was proved beyond doubt.

Old Roome was then sixty-eight years of age—a Londoner, born in Battersea. He had been a barge-hand in his youth, until taken by the press-gang in the spring of 1803, when he was sent on board the *Victory*, then fitting at Chatham for Nelson's flag. His intelligence and smartness as a lad got him noticed by Captain Hardy, and though only rated "L.M.," a "landman," he was put on the signal staff. After Trafalgar, unfortunately, he deserted, and the letter "R" (Run) against his name in the ship's books debarred him from pension and Greenwich Hospital. His case was, however, brought to the notice of Captain Pasco (Nelson's signal-lieutenant at Trafalgar), then holding the post of captain of the *Victory*, and he took up the cause of "my old shipmate," as Pasco spoke of Roome; in the end so successfully, that he was able to get Roome admitted to Greenwich Hospital as an in-pensioner.

The Admiralty, it would appear, made a special exception in Roome's case, as having been the man who hoisted Nelson's signal at Trafalgar. They consented to allow that Roome had technically purged his offence by having previously surrendered to be "whitewashed," as the old man himself put it, under the Naval Deserters' Amnesty Act of 1813.

At Greenwich old Roome lived for thirteen years in comfort, making a "good thing," we are told, out of the tips given him by old naval officers and their friends. He died in December, 1860, in the same month that saw the launch of the *Warrior*, the first ironclad ever built for the British Navy.

It would seem though that Roome's discovery and arrival at Greenwich Hospital was not received very cordially by the old pensioners there. He turned out, on intimate acquaintance, to be a querulous and cantankerous old fellow, and soon became personally unpopular for that reason. His presence at Greenwich was, however, still more unpopular for another reason. It spoiled a nice little game that had been going on there for years, seriously affecting a very profitable little business that some of the Greenwich pensioners had long carried on, particularly with country visitors to the hospital, who were always asking to be shown "the man who hoisted Nelson's signal," and of course the pensioners, as we are told, were always ready to oblige.

At that time "Greenwich Canary" was the name locally for pensioners in disgrace for being drunk on the previous Sunday, and they had to wear during the following week the "punishment dress" of a yellow coat with red sleeves in place of the ordinary long dark blue uniform coat. One of these "Canaries"—and there were always half a dozen or so about—was, it is on record, as a regular thing palmed off on the visitors as "the very man you want." Largesse—coppers, shillings, half-crowns—sometimes quite an appreciable sum, was the result, the "Canary" in due course sharing profits with his friends. To explain the presence of more than one "Canary" about the grounds, and to improve the occasion, also drawing more shillings, it was generally added that the peculiar garb of the old reprobates seen walking within the hospital precincts was "worn as a special Admiralty privilege exclusively enjoyed by men who had fought on board the *Victory* at Trafalgar."

We are told furthermore that occasionally two or three "Canaries" would be showing the people round at the same time, each passing himself off on his own little party of sightseers as the one and only existing Trafalgar signalman. The news in the papers of Roome's discovery and admission to Greenwich made the trick impossible for the future, and the pensioners did not fail to let Roome know that his presence was by no means welcome.

There is in existence, it may be mentioned incidentally, a very curious and interesting relic of the *Victory* in connexion with Nelson's message. The relic is a snuff-box, which purports to have been "made from the block by which Roome hoisted the signal." The snuff-box was originally made, it is stated, for Captain Ben Hallowell (captain of the *Swiftsure* at the Battle of the Nile, who presented Nelson with the coffin made from part of the French flagship's main-mast, in which the hero now rests in his tomb in St. Paul's). Hallowell, in October, 1805, commanded one of the ships in Nelson's fleet, but shortly before Trafalgar his ship was detached to Gibraltar to fill up water-casks, and so was not in the battle. He was, though, at Gibraltar when the shattered *Victory*, with Nelson's body on board, was towed in.

If a theory held at Portsmouth nowadays is correct, that, owing to the necessity of haste, the hoists of the signal were made simultaneously from masthead and yards, Captain Hardy gave his old friend a spurious memento. The snuff-box was presented by Captain Hallowell in after-years to Mr. Richard Nesbit, an officer who had served with him, in whose family it has remained, as originally inscribed, ever since.

The avenger of Nelson: Captain John Pollard, R.N.
A Mid. of the "Victory" at Trafalgar

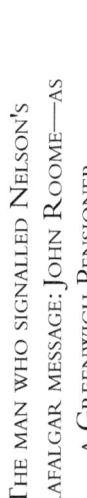

The man who signalled Nelson's Trafalgar message: John Roome—as a Greenwich Pensioner.

6

The Avenger of Nelson

It was about two o'clock in the afternoon, half an hour after Nelson had been carried below to the cockpit. By that time only a handful of officers and men were left alive on the *Victory's* upper-decks. Over a hundred had fallen, wounded or killed outright; shot dead by musket bullets, or gashed to death by the iron splinters from bursting hand-grenades—small bomb-shells of about the size of a cricket-ball, filled with powder, and thrown by hand, to explode by means of a time-fuse. The tops of the *Redoutable* were filled with soldiers, trained marksmen, who were armed with muskets and provided with baskets of hand-grenades. Nelson, as has been said, condemned that kind of fighting as murder. It could have no influence on the issue of the battle, he ever maintained, and he refused to countenance shooting from the tops on board any of his ships.

From eight to twelve men fought in each of the tops of the French ships, which were platforms, roughly in the shape of a half-moon, about half-way up the masts, and provided for spreading the upper rigging.

On board the *Redoutable*, for the eighteen months that the ship had been in commission, her commander. Captain Lucas, as he himself has related, had paid special attention to that kind of fighting. Day after day, for eighteen months before Trafalgar, he had drilled some of his men aloft at that work, employing special musketry instructors to teach them how to judge distances, allow for the rolling of the ship at sea, and take aim at dummies—targets meant to represent people walking on the decks of a ship alongside. Others of the *Redoutable's* crew had been taught how to fling pasteboard, or wooden, balls, weighted to the usual weight of hand-grenades, and as the men got expert they had practised on shore with real iron grenades and live fuses, exactly as in battle at sea. So indeed. Captain Lucas himself states in a document he drew up. One can understand how the *Victory's* officers on deck and Nelson himself had the odds against them at Trafalgar if they were to escape death and wounds from such missiles.

It fell to the British midshipman who personally saw to the hoisting of Nelson's message, "England expects that every man will do his duty," to avenge Nelson's death. He was a lad of nineteen, John Pollard his name, the *Victory's* senior midshipman. Midshipman Pollard was on deck from the early morning, stationed on the poop, until the battle closed, an hour before sunset.

As they were nearing the enemy, just after the *Victory* had hoisted her colours, a French cannon-ball, smashing through the poop bulwarks, scattered heavy splinters of jagged oak all round. One of the splinters gave Midshipman Pollard an ugly wound on his right arm, but, tying up the wound on the spot, he went on with his work; and then attended Lieutenant Pasco, with the signal-slate in hand, according to which the flags were made up for each hoist of Nelson's historic signal. He was the first of those on the poop to be wounded that day.

Then Midshipman Pollard had another narrow escape. When the *Victory* collided with the *Redoutable* after breaking through the French line, one of the bullets of the first volleys fired down on the Victory's deck from the *Redoutable's* three tops smashed the telescope Pollard held in his hand, shattering the metal tube. A few minutes afterwards a bullet hit him on the thigh. It smashed to pieces the watch he was wearing in his fob-pocket, but was fortunately stopped by that, and Midshipman Pollard escaped unharmed, although the thump was a severe one.

Fast and furious fell the bullets all round him now. Within half an hour practically all near him on the poop and quarter-deck had been shot down, dead or wounded. At one time, towards two o'clock, after Nelson had fallen and been taken below, only Captain Hardy, Signal-Lieutenant Pasco, and Midshipman Pollard stood alive on the upper-decks. Every now and again Pollard had to step down the ladder from the poop to the quarter-deck to report to Captain Hardy what other ships were doing in different quarters of the battle.

Nelson was gone, but his admiral's flag of command, according to the custom of the British Navy ever since the days of Blake, still flew at the masthead of his ship, and all the captains in other ships looked to the *Victory* for orders. An officer had gone off in a boat to give Collingwood the news of Nelson's fall and request him, if possible, to come on board the *Victory* and take charge of the fleet from there; but the *Royal Sovereign* was at that moment a considerable distance off, and the boat had to thread its way through the enemy. No answer from Collingwood had as yet come back, and meanwhile the responsibility rested with Captain Hardy to act, as the commander-in-chief's *locum tenens*, and make whatever signals the situation might require. Midshipman Pollard had to keep in close touch with Captain Hardy all through, and make constant reports to him, as Hardy paced up and down the quarter-deck.

Just before two o'clock something attracted Midshipman Pollard's attention to the Frenchmen in the mizzen-top of the *Redoutable*, which was about eighteen or twenty feet above the *Victory's* poop as the two ships lay together. He could make out through the fog of smoke that hung low over the two ships, three or four figures in the top who kept bobbing up to fire down on to the *Victory's* decks from behind a strip of canvas three feet high, banded like a tricoloured flag, blue, white, and red, and then crouching down to load for the next shot behind their screen.

Pollard picked up the musket of a dead marine, lying on the poop nearby, and fired back at them. He kept on firing as rapidly as he could, being assisted by a quartermaster of signals, an old sailor named King, who helped by handing him cartridges from a couple of barrels that stood on the poop for the use of the marines who had been posted there. The marines had mostly been killed or carried below wounded, after which the few survivors had been ordered elsewhere, to a less exposed place. Pollard had not long begun firing when a brother midshipman, named Francis Collingwood, came up from the quarter-deck to him. He pointed out the Frenchmen to Collingwood, who took up a musket and had a shot at them; after which Collingwood had to go back to his duty on the quarter-deck.

Midshipman Pollard went on firing, and a sharp duel was carried on between the single British midshipman on one side, standing in the open, and the Frenchmen, sheltering behind their screen or dodging round the mast, on the other. The plucky British lad, though, stuck coolly to his task, well backed up by King, who also got hold of some empty muskets lying about, and, loading them as he got the chance, handed them, one after the other, to the midshipman to fire. For some time the affair went on, not a French bullet touching Pollard; but one by one the enemy on the top got fewer. Apparently the Frenchmen had become too excited to take steady aim as Pollard's deadly bullets struck down first one and then another.

In the end only one Frenchman was left alive. He kept dodging to fire, now over the edge of the screen, now from behind the mast. Almost his last shot killed poor King. It struck the quartermaster between the eyes, dropping him dead on deck as he was in the act of handing a fresh packet of cartridges to the midshipman. Midshipman Pollard took swift vengeance for that a moment later, as the Frenchman made an attempt to escape from the top by clambering down the rigging to the deck, before Pollard could reload. He was, however, not quick enough. The British midshipman got his gun to his shoulder and snapped a shot at the man as he was slipping out of the top. The Frenchman dropped out of the shrouds to the deck like a stone. No more bullets came from the top of the *Redoutable* after that, and within a short time the *Victory* broke away from alongside and boomed herself clear, leaving the *Redoutable*, as has been told, to surrender to the "Fighting *Téméraire*."

Midshipman John Pollard, years afterwards, when a retired captain, wrote down a concise account of how he slew the slayer of Nelson; induced to do so apparently by hearing that the credit of the act was being publicly attributed to his brother-midshipman Collingwood, who had died some time previously. That officer, by the way, was Midshipman Edward Francis Collingwood, but although he bore the same name as Nelson's great companion-in-arms, he was in no way related to the admiral.

Midshipman Collingwood, it may be remarked in passing, was only one of a number of Trafalgar veterans to whom the avenging of Nelson was credited. Not long before Pollard wrote his personal account there had died an old cobbler of Islington who for many years past had boasted that it was he who had "killed the man who killed Nelson," getting, in consequence, as we are told, "many tips given him and many a glass of beer." The man had, in fact, in his young days been a marine, and he had also been at Trafalgar, but beyond that his story was a made-up yarn.

This is the real "Avenger of Nelson's" account, as set forth in his own words:

> I was on the poop of the *Victory* from the time the men were beat to quarters before the action until late in evening. I was the first struck, as a splinter hit my right arm; and I was the only officer left alive of all who had been originally stationed on the poop. It is true my old friend Collingwood (who has now been

dead for some years) came on the poop after I had for some time discovered the men in the top of the *Redoutable*; they were in a crouching position, and rose breast-high to fire. I pointed them out to Collingwood as I made my aim; he took up a musket, and fired once, and then left the poop, I concluded, to return to the quarter-deck, which was his station during the battle. I remained firing at the top until not a man was to be seen; the last one I discovered coming down the mizzen rigging, and from my fire he fell also.

King, a quartermaster, was killed while in the act of handing me a parcel of ball-cartridge long after Collingwood had left the poop. I remained till after the action was over, and assisted in superintending the rigging off the jury-mast. Then I was ushered into the ward-room, where Sir Thomas Hardy and other officers were assembled, and was complimented by them on ' avenging Lord Nelson's death,' which fact afterwards appeared in the *Gazette*. I did not go on board the *Redoutable* with Mr. Collingwood at all, therefore could not have discovered the man 'lying in the mizzen-top, with one ball in his head, and another in his breast.' At the time of the action I was nineteen years of age.

Two ingenious French literary men, C. O. Barbaroux, son of the celebrated Girondin, and A. T. Lardier, fabricated a story some twenty years after Trafalgar to the effect that the man who shot Nelson came through Trafalgar safely, and was specially rewarded by Napoleon for what he had done. The collaborators brought out their work of imagination in 1826, as a book which purported to be the personal memoirs of a certain Robert Guillemard[1], a sergeant of the Grand Army. The Trafalgar episode, as related in the book, certainly makes interesting reading—"an admixture of a lie," so Bacon tells us, "doth always add pleasure."

"Sergeant Robert Guillemard" is made to declare himself the man who shot Nelson from the mizzen-top of the *Redoutable*. He describes in these words how he did it:

> All our top-men had been killed, when two sailors and four soldiers (of whom I was one) were ordered to occupy their posts in the tops. When we were going aloft the balls and grape-shot

---

1. *Sergeant Guillemard: the Man Who Shot Nelson?* by Robert Guillemard also published by Leonaur.

showered around us, struck the yards and masts, knocked large splinters out of them, and cut the rigging in pieces. One of my companions was wounded beside me, and fell from a height of thirty feet upon the deck, where he broke his neck.

On the poop of the English vessel was an officer covered with orders, and with only one arm. From what I had heard of Nelson, I had no doubt that it was he. He was surrounded by several officers, to whom he seemed to be giving orders. At the moment I first perceived him, several of his sailors were wounded beside him by the fire of the *Redoutable*. As I had received no orders to go down, and saw myself forgotten in the tops, I thought it my duty to fire on the poop of the English vessel, which I saw quite exposed and close to me. I could even have taken aim at the men I saw, but I fired at hazard among the groups nearest, of sailors and officers.

All at once I saw great confusion on board the *Victory*; the men crowded round the officer whom I had taken for Nelson. He had just fallen, and was being taken below, covered with a cloak. The agitation shown at this moment left me no doubt that I had judged rightly, and that it was really the English admiral. An instant afterwards the *Victory* ceased from firing; the deck was abandoned by all those who occupied it; and I presumed the consternation produced by the admiral's fall was the cause of this sudden change. I hurried below to inform the captain of what I had seen of the enemy's situation. He believed me the more readily as the slackening of the enemy's fire indicated that an event of the highest importance occupied the attention of the English ship's crew, and prevented them from continuing the action.

7

How England Heard the News of Nelson's Death

The battle was fought on Monday, October 21. The first authentic news of it, and of Nelson's death, only reached London on Wednesday, November 6, at one o'clock in the morning.

Collingwood sent off his first Trafalgar dispatch on Sunday, October 27, as soon as the lulling of the storm after the battle allowed of the delivery of the casualty reports and returns from the scattered ships of the fleet. Six days had gone by since the battle, but it was the first opportunity he had had of getting his dispatch off. At half-past twelve on that day the *Pickle*, an eight-gun schooner, Lieutenant Lapenotière in command, left the fleet for England, carrying Collingwood's "public letter." Collingwood, according to the tradition in the Lapenotière family, chose that particular man—so junior an officer as a Lieutenant—to carry the Trafalgar dispatch home in virtue of a promise he had once made to Lieutenant Lapenotière. The story runs:

> When a young man he had been a passenger on board a ship which also conveyed Lord Collingwood. An order was given on deck to the man at the wheel, and he saw that if obeyed the ship would be on the rocks. He instantly gave another order and saved the ship. Lord Collingwood thanked him and said: 'If ever I have the opportunity I will do you a service.' After the action at Trafalgar he sent for him and reminded him of his promise, adding: 'Now take these dispatches to England; you will receive; £500 and your commander's commission. Now I have kept my word.'

The Lapenotière family, it may be mentioned, originally settled in

England at the revolution of 1688, and both the father and grandfather of the commander of the *Pickle* had served in the Royal Navy. The name is to be found in Navy lists of William III and Queen Anne.

The *Pickle's* voyage home was a rough one—a hard beat against a head wind for most of the way. It took nine days. Off Cape Finisterre they had to heave four of their eight guns overboard to keep the ship afloat, and throughout the day of November 1 all hands were at the pumps, or employed in baling water out of the little vessel. To the southwest of the Scilly Isles, on November 2, they ran into a dead calm, and had to use their sweeps—long oars—to keep the *Pickle's* head in the right direction. Then bad weather and squalls came on again. In that slow manner was the news of Trafalgar brought to England.

Two British vessels only were spoken on the voyage—the *Nautilus* ("Notlis" is how the *Pickle's* log spells the name) off the Tagus, and the *Superb*, Captain Keats, a short distance to southward of the Land's End. The *Nautilus* turned back, and ran into Lisbon with the news. Keats and his Superbs—fervent Nelsonians to a man—were on their way to join Nelson's fleet, hoping against hope to be in time for the expected battle off Cadiz. Deep groans throughout the ship, we are told, and openly shed tears by many, greeted Lieutenant Lapenotière's announcement of Nelson's death, which dire news the *Pickle's* commander went on board the *Superb* to impart personally to Captain Keats.

The Lizard lights were sighted ahead at two in the morning on the 4th. The Manacles were on the beam between seven and eight o'clock. At a quarter to ten, off Pendennis Castle, the *Pickle* shortened sail and hove-to. A boat was at once lowered, and Lieutenant Lapenotière went on shore with his dispatches to post off at once for London.

Beyond the bare fact of the victory and Nelson's death, little was told at Falmouth. Lapenotière was off within half an hour of landing, and as soon as he stepped ashore his boat pulled back to the *Pickle*, which, before two o'clock, was under all sail for Plymouth Sound. There was no semaphore telegraph in 1805 farther west than Portsmouth, so that it was impossible to send on the news to London by that means. They had begun setting up stations along the South Coast between Portsmouth and Plymouth, but the line was not yet in working order.

Lieutenant Lapenotière was on his way by noon, taking the post road by Truro, Liskeard, Tavistock, across Dartmoor, by Postbridge to Chagford and Exeter; and thence along the coach road by Honiton, Axminster, Crewkerne, Yeovil, Sherborne, Salisbury, Andover, Basingstoke, to London. He changed horses nineteen times along the 266 miles of his route. So the Trafalgar dispatches travelled to London. None met by the way could imagine that the ordinary-looking post-chaise passing along, with a quiet-mannered naval lieutenant seated inside, was bearing the most moving news perhaps that had ever reached the shores of England. The roads were fair travelling—no rain had fallen in the south of England since October 30—and excellent time was kept. The post-chaise drew up at the gates of the Admiralty at one o'clock in the morning of November 6.

As it did so, by an extraordinary coincidence, a second messenger arrived with the news. Another post-chaise raced up; it brought another naval officer, bearing the same intelligence. He was Captain Sykes of the *Nautilus*, which the *Pickle* had fallen in with off the Tagus, when Lieutenant Lapenotière had told Sykes of what had taken place. The *Nautilus*, after going into Lisbon with the news, had been hastened off thence to England by the English ambassador. She was a faster ship than the *Pickle*, and had better weather on the route she steered. Landing at Plymouth, Captain Sykes posted to London, and his conveyance arrived at the Admiralty exactly at the moment that Lapenotière's chaise was pulling up.

Of the dramatic scene that followed within doors at the Admiralty, and how the news was broken to the first lord in his bedroom, we have an eyewitness's account from a high official at the Admiralty, Mr. Marsden, first secretary to the board.

> Admiral Collingwood's important dispatches were delivered to me about one o'clock a.m., November 6, when I was in the act of withdrawing from the board room to my private apartments.

Mr. Marsden was informed that an officer had arrived with important dispatches, and the officer was shown up at once.

One can imagine the scene. A large, lofty, old-fashioned room, decorated with frieze-work and tall Ionic pilasters at the sides; the curtains drawn closely, and everything very still—the dead of the night; the fire burning low, or flickering fitfully out; dim shadows in the background on either hand, beyond the gleam of light cast by tall wax-candles on a long table in the centre of the room, piled with tied-up documents. An elderly gentleman *en déshabille*, somewhat of the prim civilian official type, the sole occupant of the room, has just risen wearily from his chair by the table, and turns away with a sigh of relief as he casts round his last glance for the night at the bundles of returns he has for hours been laboriously perusing, to take up his chamber candlestick and shuffle off at last to bed.

Suddenly there is a sharp knock. The door opens abruptly, and the night-porter announces an arrival, and then he ushers in a naval officer in uniform, travel-worn, and showing traces of fatigue, but with an air of suppressed emotion in every feature of his countenance. A moment's pause, and immediately the officer, without word or preface or personal introduction, in a very grave tone accosts the wondering secretary:

> In accosting me the officer used these impressive words: 'Sir, we have gained a great victory, but we have lost Lord Nelson!' The effect thus produced it is not to my purpose to describe; nor had I time to indulge in reflections, who was at that moment the only person informed of one of the greatest events recorded in our history, and which it was my duty to make known with the utmost promptitude.

The first lord of the Admiralty, Lord Barham, had to be informed at once, and Mr. Marsden, leaving Lapenotière to himself, and sending for refreshments for him, set out a few moments later, candle in hand, to find the first lord's bedroom in the big building.

> The first lord had retired to rest, as had his domestics, and it was not until after some research that I could discover the room in which he slept. Drawing aside his curtains with a candle in my hand, I woke the old peer from a sound slumber, and to the credit of his nerves, be it mentioned, he showed no symptom of alarm or surprise, but calmly asked, 'What news, Mr. Marsden?' We then discussed in a few words what was to be done, and I sat up the remainder of the night with such of the clerks as I could collect, in order to make the necessary communications at an early hour to the king, Prince of Wales, Duke of York, the ministers and other members of the cabinet, and to the lord mayor, who communicated the intelligence to the shipping interest at Lloyd's Coffee House. A notice for a royal salute was also necessary.

Says Sir John Barrow, the second secretary, who learned the news on arriving at the Admiralty next morning:

> Never can I forget the shock I received on opening the boardroom door the morning after the arrival of the dispatches, when Mr. Marsden called out: 'Glorious news! The most glorious vic-

tory our brave Navy has ever achieved—but Nelson is dead!' The vivid recollection of my interview with this incomparable man, and the idea that I was probably the last person he had taken leave of in London, left an impression of gloom on my mind that required some time to remove.

The news was sent off to Windsor Castle immediately, and reached there at seven in the morning.

> The king was so affected by it that some minutes elapsed before he could give utterance to his feelings. The queen called the princesses around her to read the dispatches, while the whole royal group shed tears to the memory of Lord Nelson.

In his reply to Mr. Marsden, on behalf of His Majesty, Colonel Sir Herbert Taylor, the king's private secretary, wrote as follows:

> However His Majesty rejoices at the signal success of his gallant fleet, he has not heard without expressions of very deep regret of the death of its valuable and distinguished commander, although a life so replete with glory, and marked by a rapid succession of such meritorious services and exertions, could not have ended more gloriously.

Colonel Taylor added this on his own account:

> I have not, upon any occasion, seen His Majesty more affected.

It is to George III also that history owes the naming of the victory. The private secretary, in a postscript, announced the royal choice with these words:

> The king is of opinion that the battle should be styled that of Trafalgar.

The *London Gazette Extraordinary* was out before breakfast-time, and the newspapers and the park and tower guns, and the church bells, announced the news to all London before nine o'clock. Its effect was astounding—literally stunning. Never was a great triumph received with so little manifestation of outward rejoicing. Immediately after the first rumours got about, between five and six o'clock in the morning, the doors of the newspaper offices were besieged with crowds, all wanting to know one thing. It was not about the victory. The one thing people asked about was this: If it was really true about Lord Nelson? That—Nelson's death—was the uppermost thought in everybody's mind. The victory was, of course, a tremendous one—the greatest ever heard of—but Nelson, "Our Nel," as all sailors called him, was gone!

Says Lord Malmesbury:

> The first impression was not joy, for Nelson fell. . . . Not one individual who felt joy at the victory so well timed and complete, but first had an instinctive feeling of sorrow . . . the sorrow of affection and gratitude for what had been done for us.

Mr. Pitt, the prime minister, told Lord Malmesbury that evening how the news had affected him, as Lord Malmesbury himself has related.

> On the receipt of the news of the memorable battle of Trafalgar (some day in November, 1805), I happened to dine with Pitt, and it was naturally the engrossing subject of our conversation. I shall never forget the eloquent manner in which he described his conflicting feelings when roused in the night to read Collingwood's dispatches. Pitt observed that he had been called up at various hours through his eventful life by the arrival of news of various hues, but that, whether good or bad, he could always lay his head on his pillow and sink into a sound sleep again. On this occasion, however, the great event announced brought with it so much to weep over, as well as to rejoice at, that he could not calm his thoughts, but at length got up, though it was three in the morning.

Lady Elizabeth Hervey, writing to her son in America, speaks of the "mingled pride and consternation" with which the news was everywhere received. "The illuminations began but were discontinued, the people being unable to rejoice." Writing on November 29, she says it would have been useless to write when the news first arrived.

> Nothing that I could have said would have conveyed to you any idea of the impression made on the public by the loss of their favourite hero. . . . As we came away (from the Admiralty) there was a vast rush of people, but all silent, or a murmur of respect and sorrow; some of the common people saying, 'It is bad news if Nelson is killed;' yet they knew that twenty ships were taken. A man at the turnpike gate said to Sir Ellis who was going through, 'Sir, have you heard the bad news? We have taken twenty ships from the enemy, but Lord Nelson is killed!'

A country gentleman in Hertfordshire says this:

> Not a peasant have I met since the disastrous story has been told, that has not, with a warmth which I scarce conceived them capable of, inquired the truth of the disastrous event, and on receiving the painful confirmation have hung their heads and mourned the fallen flower of English manhood.

Lady Castlereagh wrote from Ireland, on the news reaching her:

> Never was there, indeed, an event so mournfully and so triumphantly important to England as the Battle of Trafalgar. The sentiment of lamenting the individual, more than the rejoicing in the victory, shows the humanity and affection of the people of England; but their good sense on reflection will dwell only on the conquest, because no death at a future moment could have been more glorious, and might have been less so. The public would never have sent him on another expedition; his health was not equal to another effort, and he might have yielded to the more natural but less imposing efforts of more worldly honours. Whereas he now begins his immortal career, having nothing to achieve on earth, and bequeathing to the English fleet a legacy which they alone are able to improve. Had I been his wife or his mother, I would rather have wept him dead than see him languish on a less splendid day. In such a death there is no sting, and in such a grave everlasting victory.

Throughout the country the celebrations were marked by the same note of personal grief at the loss of the nation's darling hero. At Norwich, the county town of Nelson's own home county, the corporation went into mourning for a week. At Chester the cathedral bells rang merry peals of rejoicing for the victory; alternating with deep, solemn tolling for Nelson. Three of the great bells pealed out together exultantly—the fourth tolled throughout a slow and solemn note.

In many towns, we are told, the bells were muffled and rang dumb peals only. All over the country, when the mayors of the towns read out the *Gazette* announcing the victory, instead of huzzas and shouts, there was gloom and tears and silence, everyone saying, "Poor Nelson! Had he only lived!"

Even children in the schoolroom realized Nelson's death as a sort of personal loss. Said Lady Wenlock, who died in 1869:

> I well remember the Battle of Trafalgar, I was seven years old

then, but I knew the names of all the ships and captains. My sister was then mistress of my father's house, and I was sent for down to her. She was not up, and the newspaper was lying on the bed. 'Oh, my dear,' she said, 'my father has sent me up the newspaper, and we have taken twenty ships of the line; but—Nelson is dead!' Child as I was, I burst into tears; one had been taught to think that nothing could go on without him!

Countess Brownlow (who died in 1872), a daughter of the second Earl of Mount Edgcumbe, relates in her *Reminiscences of a Septuagenarian*, that in 1805, when she was in the schoolroom at lessons, the news of Trafalgar and of Nelson's death was brought in, and that she "dropped to the ground in horror at the news, although I had never seen Nelson."

An old Christ's Hospital "boy," who died at the age of 103, was at school at the time. When the news arrived, he used to relate:

We let up fireworks for the victory, and then drank a little glass of sherry for Lord Nelson in solemn silence.

Celebrations in honour of the victory were held during the following week at the various ports and garrisons and military stations, and gun salutes and *feux de joie* were fired. At every place, according to the newspapers, the officers appeared on parade in full mourning and the regiments had their colours and band instruments "draped in crape ribbon."

On Sir Richard Strachan's squadron reaching Plymouth with its prizes (the four French ships captured off Cape Finisterre while escaping after Trafalgar), in the week after the arrival of Collingwood's dispatch, we are also told:

The seamen coming ashore on leave, each wore a knot of love-crape ribbon fastened above his left elbow.

As to how the news was received by the fleet elsewhere:

We are told this from an officer of the frigate *Immortalité*, belonging to one of the squadrons watching the French coast near Boulogne:

It was during this cruise that we first heard of the mighty victory of Trafalgar . . . and I can well remember how much the pride and exultation, which we should otherwise have felt at our country's success, were saddened and subdued by the irreparable loss of her favourite hero. Instead of shouts and songs of triumph and gratulation, the subject was mentioned in broken whispers, and all seemed to feel, not only that some great national calamity had befallen the land, but as if each individual had lost a friend and leader, with whom it would have been the happiness of his life to serve and follow.

An officer on the East Indies station says in a letter that when the news reached his ship a number of his men, who had once served with Nelson, "simply broke down on hearing of his death, and were useless for duty for some days."

In the West Indies, where the British islands had been saved from Villeneuve's raid by Nelson during the previous summer, sorrow for his death completely overshadowed the rejoicings for the victory. At Kingston, in Jamaica, a huge funeral pyre was erected, forty-seven feet in height and forty-seven each way, the number of feet corresponding with the years of Nelson's age. At six in the evening on the day appointed for the official commemoration of the victory of Trafalgar, the Jamaica militia marched to the spot and formed up in a hollow square round the pyre, which, at a given signal, was set alight at forty-seven points at once. Forty-seven minute-guns were fired at the same time by a battery of the Royal Artillery, all the militiamen firing a volley of musketry between each shot, and forty-seven discharges of rockets were sent up.

How England paid the last honours to the remains of the dead Nelson on his final home-coming all the world knows:

Such honours Ilium to her hero paid,
And peaceful slept the mighty Hector's shade.

www.ingramcontent.com/pod-product-compliance
Lightning Source LLC
Chambersburg PA
CBHW031619160426
43196CB00006B/192